# EXPLORING THE
# NORTH OF IRELAND

# EXPLORING THE NORTH OF IRELAND

Paddy Dillon

Photographs by the author

**A WARD LOCK BOOK**

First published in the UK 1996
by Ward Lock
Wellington House
125 Strand
LONDON
WC2R 0BB

A Cassell Imprint

Distributed in the United States
by Sterling Publishing Co., Inc.
387 Park Avenue South, New York, NY 10016-8810

A British Library Cataloguing in Publication Data block for this book may
be obtained from the British Library

The maps in this book were prepared from out-of-copyright
Ordnance Survey material

ISBN 0 7063 7471 1
Typeset by Business Color Print, Welshpool, Powys, Wales
Printed and bound in Slovenia

# Contents

# Preface

Welcome to walking in Ireland – and in particular to walking in the ancient and historic Province of Ulster. The purpose of this book is to guide your steps around a selection of classic walks across the Province, as well as to reveal a few lesser-known areas for you to enjoy. In addition, there are notes explaining how you can shorten or extend the majority of these walks, while the final route takes up the challenge of the immense long-distance trail known as the Ulster Way.

At least some portion of each of Ulster's nine historic counties is included in this collection of routes. You will not be disappointed as you marvel at the varied scenery of the Causeway Coast Path, or climb on to lofty Slieve Donard in the Mountains of Mourne. You will be captivated by the sight of Slieve League's rugged cliffs plunging into the Atlantic, or delighted to discover the sprawling moorlands of the Sperrin Mountains. Parts of the Fermanagh Lakelands also offer interesting walking, and even the Border areas are now becoming popular, with a growing influx of curious travellers looking for inspiration and information.

The walks have been chosen to inspire you through their sheer variety – including mountains, moorlands and national parks. The information is as detailed as you will need, provided that you supplement this book with maps, a compass, and the skills to use them all together. There are also lists of further contacts, so that you can smooth your travelling arrangements. How you travel is largely up to you, but all the walks start from a parking place, and many of them are easily accessed using public transport. Choose routes which are suited to your own ability, so that you can enjoy these walks both safely and comfortably.

*The final approach to the summit of Slieve League, which is a broad plateau (Route 16).*

## Acknowledgements

There are many people throughout Ireland, and particularly in the Province of Ulster, to whom I owe a debt of thanks for their help and advice over the years. Wilfrid Capper springs immediately to mind as a person who has spent over half a century helping to protect and preserve the Ulster countryside, and he was the foremost campaigner for the establishment of the Ulster Way. Frank Greally had the vision to launch *Walking World Ireland* , a magazine dedicated to covering walks in all parts of Ireland. Rosemary Evans and others in the Northern Ireland Tourist Board have helped to produce and promote information booklets and brochures for walkers, while Ross Millar and others of the Environment Service are continually striving to protect the countryside and help to develop access to it. Veronica McCann and the Wee Binnian Walking Club have provided me with entertainment and splendid walks, and their annual Walking Festival is recommended.

Help and assistance has been gratefully received from representatives of the Ordnance Survey of Northern Ireland, Down District Council, Newry and Mourne District Council, Moyle District Council, Donegal County Council, Glenveagh National Park, Mourne Farm Country Holidays, Omagh Rural Forum, Lakeland Country Breaks in Fermanagh, and many small community associations striving to improve access and facilities.

Accommodation providers have often gone out of their way to welcome me and help me with extra services, while local visitor centres and information points have provided me with an abundance of extra facts. You are benefitting from their enthusiasm and expertise as you follow the routes in this book, and I apologize for not being able to mention everyone involved.

# Using the Book

To avoid running into any confusion over terms, the following fact should be appreciated at the outset: Ulster and Northern Ireland are not the same place. Ulster is comprised of nine counties: Antrim, Armagh, Cavan, Derry, Donegal, Down, Fermanagh, Monaghan and Tyrone. Northern Ireland is comprised of six of these: Antrim, Armagh, Derry, Down, Fermanagh and Tyrone. Walking provides great exercise and is a great social leveller; the Border was never an obstacle to walking, and there are at least two cross-Border walking clubs in operation. If the truth now be told, the Border is very much an asset when it comes to applying for cross-Border funding, and some of that funding is being used to develop access and facilities for walkers.

## Arrangement

The layout of this book is basically quite simple. There are 31 walking routes which are arranged roughly in a clockwise direction around Ulster. Starting with routes around Belfast, the reader is taken to the Mountains of Mourne, across the Border areas, into Fermanagh and then through Donegal, returning via the Sperrins to end in Antrim. Many of the walks which are described are in areas visited by the enormous Ulster Way, which itself features as the final route. This long-distance trail visits eight of Ulster's nine counties – and you can easily access the ninth with a short diversion! Not everyone is capable of walking the whole of the Ulster Way, but fortunately many of the routes offered as one-day walks cover the most scenic parts of the trail. Most of the walks are high level, climbing hills and mountains and crossing moorland terrain, but there are also a few low-level routes along coasts and rivers. In total, they cover over 500km (300 miles), with the Ulster Way adding more than another 900km (560 miles) for long-distance walkers. The cumulative ascent over the 31 routes is around 19,000m (62,000ft), with the Ulster Way adding around another 15,250m (50,000ft) – around twice the height of Everest!

*A lonely standing stone reached before the cliffs of the Sallagh Braes.*

## Summary tables

The relevant statistics for each walk are provided in a summary table at the start of the description of the route. The information provided includes:

- time to allow for the walk
- starting and finishing locations, with details of maps, available car parking and public transport
- an overview of the route and features of interest
- details on the state of footpaths
- distance covered
- total height gained
- principal heights scaled

## Alternative routes

For each walk, details of alternative routes are provided. These are divided into 'escapes', which allow you to shorten the route for whatever reason, and 'extensions', which provide fit walkers with the option of a longer route.

## Abbreviations

The minimum of abbreviations has been used, and only to avoid constant repetition. These are listed below.

| | |
|---|---|
| N | north |
| NNE | north north-east |
| NE | north-east |
| ENE | east north-east |
| E | east |
| ESE | east south-east |
| SE | south-east |
| SSE | south south-east |
| S | south |
| SSW | south south-west |
| SW | south-west |
| WSW | west south-west |
| W | west |
| WNW | west north-west |
| NW | north-west |
| NNW | north north-west |

| | |
|---|---|
| m | metre(s) |
| ft | foot/feet |
| km | kilometre(s) |
| GR | grid reference |
| OSNI | Ordnance Survey of Northern Ireland |
| OSI | Ordnance Survey of Ireland |

## Photographs

Walkers who like to take photographs are very much at the mercy of the weather in Ireland. Clouds roll in from the Atlantic and cover the whole country, bringing rain and mist on the high ground. Persevere; it often clears wonderfully in between times, and the air can be crystal clear after frequent rain-washing, so that colours are especially vibrant. Ireland has a reputation for being '40 shades of green', which is unfortunate for anyone wanting contrasting colours, but sometimes you get a blue sky, shadowed crags, autumnal trees – and someone obligingly wearing a startlingly red jacket posing in the right place! The photographs in this guidebook illustrate the changeable nature of the weather and the varied terrain which is crossed on the walks.

## Maps

The outline map provided for each walk is marked with the following information:

- start and finish locations
- line of the route, with directional arrows
- relevant place names and features

Relief cross-sections give the rise and fall along each route from the start location. These indicate where the climbs appear and how steep they are.

The standard scale of mapping which is available across the Province of Ulster is 1:50,000, although there are a couple of useful maps at 1:25,000 scale. The maps you should use are quoted in the summary table relating to each of the walks.

There are two publishers of maps: the Ordnance Survey of Northern Ireland, based in Belfast, and the Ordnance Survey of Ireland, based in Dublin. The two bodies produce maps at the same scale showing basically the same sort of information, but in different styles. Walkers who are used to following maps will have no difficulty with these, but anyone new to map reading should proceed cautiously. Despite the maps in Ulster being produced by two bodies, they are numbered as part of an all-Ireland series, so that the maps you will be using along with this guidebook appear as sheets numbered in the range 1 to 29.

The Ordnance Survey Holiday Map of Ireland – North is produced at a scale of 1:250,000 and is therefore a useful travelling map and good for overall planning. This small-scale map also shows the entire course of the Ulster Way.

## Place names

The place names throughout this guidebook are taken from Ordnance Survey maps, unless there is a very strong case to be made for spelling to be at variance. The chapter headings are fairly arbitrary, and may not appear as such on the maps, but within the body of each route description the recorded map place names are used. Bear in mind that local people may use different spellings and pronunciations, or may even be accustomed to using wildly different names which simply aren't on your map – and there is always the possibility that they have never heard of the map names.

Place names are half the fun of exploring an area, and those which come from a Gaelic root are often highly descriptive. However, it is important to remember that although they may have been accurately descriptive 2,000 years ago, they may not be so apt today!

## Heights

There are two methods used to indicate heights in the text. One is to give the full figure for the height of a mountain or hill, taken from the map. These are displayed in both metres and feet. Anyone converting one to another, or vice versa, will find that the values often do not match exactly. This is because the newer metric maps are drawn from a different Ordnance Datum than the previous imperial maps: the older maps were drawn from a low-water Ordnance Datum, while the newer maps are based upon a mean sea-level Ordnance Datum. The practical upshot of this is that the metric heights may appear 'shorter' than the imperial values given, if you try to convert them. However, the metric heights are given as they are taken from metric maps – and these are the ones you should be using. The imperial values are taken from the older maps and their height information is presented unchanged.

The other way of expressing heights is to give them in a rounded-up form – eg 100m (300ft) – which, while not being an exact conversion, is near enough for the purposes of presenting approximate values.

## Transport

While the car is undoubtedly the most convenient way of accessing these walks, there may not always be large car parks available. The provision of car parks is indicated in the introduction to each walk, and the routes are often structured to take advantage of these; however, in some areas there may only be small parking spaces capable of holding one, two or three cars. If these prove to be full, you will need to park elsewhere.

Some of the routes are fairly well served by public transport. Rail transport is not particularly useful, but some bus services are quite good.

For instance, all three walks around Belfast are best done as linear walks and the public transport to either end is frequent. In and around Belfast, Citybus services are the ones to use. Outside Belfast, and throughout Northern Ireland, Ulsterbus services are useful. In the Republic of Ireland, Bus Eireann provides occasional useful services, while in northern Donegal the Lough Swilly Buses offer a good selection of local bus services.

## Accommodation

Almost any Tourist Information Office can handle enquiries about local accommodation. The larger offices can book you into accommodation on an all-Ireland basis, so you do not necessarily have to contact the Northern Ireland Tourist Board and Bord Failte. In the peak summer season, advance booking is recommended and some areas have been known to run out of accommodation. If you book through a Tourist Information Office or a travel agency, then you will almost certainly be booked into 'approved' accommodation which meets certain standards. If you simply travel in hope and sort out accommodation, then you may have to settle for 'unapproved' addresses, where you may be unable to check facilities or standards.

The range of accommodation varies from campsites to hostels, self-catering, bed & breakfast, guest houses and hotels. Some places are particularly good for walkers and you should make a habit of searching them out in all the best walking areas. Both the Northern Ireland Tourist Board and Bord Failte produce general accommodation guides, and there are also specific groupings of accommodation providers who produce their own listings. There is even a list for the Ulster Way, available from the Northern Ireland Tourist Board.

## Safety

Safety is largely a matter of common sense. If you are going walking, then you need to wear appropriate walking gear, which means warm or cool clothes, depending on the weather, and comfortable boots, with waterproofs readily available. You will need to carry a rucksack containing your food and drink for the day, plus a little extra to cope with unexpected emergencies; a small, comprehensive first aid kit and the knowlege to use it; and possibly a change of clothing – do bear in mind that the weather can change rapidly and unexpectedly at all times of year. Your map and compass should be easily accessible, and you must have the necessary skills to use them effectively.

Safety is about being ready for any eventuality by being aware of what can go wrong and making sure that it doesn't have the chance to do so. However, accidents can happen and people may become lost, injured, or caught out in darkness. When things go badly wrong and you are alone, then you are in trouble, especially as many of the walks in this book are in remote and unfrequented countryside. If you have more than one companion, then some can stay with you and others can go for help. There are Mountain Rescue Teams ready to help, and no matter what side of the Border you are on, you alert them by getting to a telephone, dialling 999 and asking for Mountain Rescue. The actual call-out may be co-ordinated by the police – the RUC in Northern Ireland and the Gardai in the Republic. Decisions will be based on the information you can supply, so make sure you can give details of any injury or illness, the timing of the accident, any first aid given, the map reference of the spot and any distinctive land features there. Once you have made contact, do as you are told and leave the rest to the experts. Better still – do your very best to avoid getting into difficulty in the first place. Aim to enjoy the walks in safety.

# Route 1: THE BELFAST HILLS

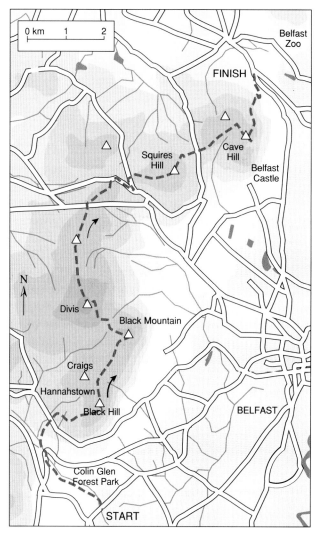

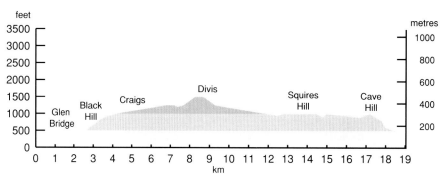

# 1

# AROUND BELFAST

## Route 1: The Belfast Hills

**TIME ALLOWANCE**   8 hours.

**STARTING LOCATION**
Colin Glen Forest Park Centre.
OSNI Discoverer 15: GR 285705.
Small car park at the Forest Park Centre.
Frequent Citybus services to Colin Glen.

**FINISHING LOCATION**
Belfast Zoo, Antrim Road.
OSNI Discoverer 15: GR 325813.
Large car park at Belfast Zoo.
Frequent Citybus services on the Antrim Road.

**OVERVIEW/INTEREST**
Passes through Colin Glen Forest Park.
Crosses open moorlands and hills.
Features McArt's Fort, Cave Hill Country Park and
   Hazelwood National Nature Reserve.
Includes part of the Ulster Way.

**FOOTPATHS**
Low-level paths and tracks are clear.
There are few trodden paths on the hills.
Cave Hill has plenty of paths.

**STATISTICS**
**WALKING DISTANCE**   20km (12½ miles)
**TOTAL HEIGHT GAINED**   710m (2,330ft)
**PRINCIPAL HEIGHTS**
Black Hill   360m (1,180ft)
Black Mountain   390m (1,280ft)
Divis   478m (1,568ft)
Squires Hill   374m (1,227ft)
Cave Hill   368m (1,207ft)

### The way to Black Mountain          *Allow 3 hours*

The Colin Glen Forest Park Centre is located on Stewartstown Road in West Belfast. The Centre is a large building with its own car park surrounded by a security fence. If you park a car here you must be sure to return for it before the gates are locked, so check the closing times with the staff. However, a car is hardly necessary in this instance as both ends of this walk are well served by frequent Citybus services: use the Twinbrook services to reach the Forest Park Centre.

The Centre is worth a visit as it contains plenty of interesting information about Colin Glen Forest Park. The park has grown from a series of cross-community environmental projects, and within living memory the glen has had its trees clear-felled and has been used as a landfill site. Fortunately, the varied tree cover is re-establishing itself and the landfill site has been landscaped. The surfacing of paths and the construction of bridges across the Colin River has resulted in the glen becoming a valuable amenity and green space with easy access from all the surrounding housing estates. Some older residents in the area still refer to the place as McCance's Glen, after a family who once operated a mill which drew power from the mountain stream.

Start the walk by leaving the Forest Park Centre car park, and follow a path into the wooded glen beyond. Before long, you will notice a red footbridge on the right which spans the Colin River. Do not cross this bridge, as it leads you out on to the Suffolk Road, but continue following the

13

well-wooded pathway upstream. Later, you will find the Gamekeeper's Bridge. You can cross this if you wish, or stay on the same side of the river for a while longer. The same applies when you reach the Weir Bridge, as there are again paths on both sides of the river. At the next bridge, a curious structure called the Tri Bridge (where three paths meet on the bridge itself), you must be sure to walk on the eastern side of the Colin River. The path will lead you further upstream to pass beneath the high, old stone arch of the Glen Bridge, which carries a main road over Colin Glen.

At the Glen Bridge you enter a more maturely wooded part of Colin Glen, which is managed by the National Trust. The paths and bridges in the upper part of the glen are not as well maintained as those in the lower part. After passing under the Glen Bridge, the path climbs a short way and you should then turn left to continue upstream. The path stays above the river for a while, then descends to cross a wooden bridge. Almost immediately, you have to cross back over the river using only what appears to be two tree trunks. In fact, these are the remains of a collapsed footbridge. You could get very wet here when the river is running high! This is no great obstacle, however, as you could detour back across the earlier footbridge and find an alternative route.

Once across the Colin River, steps lead up a steep, wooded slope and you should turn left at the top. Further on, you will find a clear, gravel path leading away to the right from the top edge of the wood: look out for it shortly after crossing a small footbridge over an inflowing stream. The gravel path leads up to a disused basalt quarry. Pass the quarry and keep to the right to follow the path up to a busy road at Hannahstown. Cross straight over this, the B38, and start walking up the narrow road opposite which is signposted as private. Although vehicles are barred from using it, walkers can follow it up to a tall transmitter mast on the slopes of Black Hill. Keep to the left of the mast, then climb uphill and cross a low fence to reach the sparsely heathered summit of Black Hill. There is a

*Cave Hill rises above Belfast Castle in the Cave Hill Country Park.*

trig point at 360m (1,180ft). The view overlooks Belfast and the Lagan Valley, as well as stretching to the distant Mountains of Mourne.

Leave the summit of Black Hill and walk roughly northwards beneath an electricity transmission line and cross a heathery gap to reach the minor hump of Craigs. The broad moorland crest runs roughly north-east towards Black Mountain and features squelchy ground. A slight diversion down a gentle slope leads to a trig point overlooking the urban sprawl of Belfast, although the true summit of Black Mountain stands at 390m (1,280ft). You will find a short but clear track leading to another tall transmitter mast which sits on a broad moorland gap behind the crest of Black Mountain.

## The way to Flush Road          *Allow 2 hours*

Keep to the right of the transmitter mast and start climbing uphill. Cross over a gravel track, but turn right to follow a narrow tarmac road up the slopes of Divis. This road climbs steadily, then it turns sharply left on the final run up to an army installation on the summit of the hill. Twin masts stand behind a security fence of coiled barbed wire, next to a strange pyramidal structure, so you will not be able to visit the 478m (1,568ft) summit of Divis. You cannot sample the whole of the view at once, but by walking around the summit of Divis in clear weather, you should be able to spot:

| | |
|---|---|
| NNE | Squires Hill |
| NE | Cave Hill, Belfast Lough, Galloway, Scotland |
| ENE | Holywood |
| E | Belfast Docks |
| S | Slieve Croob, Mountains of Mourne |
| SSW | Slieve Gullion |
| W | Lough Neagh |
| WNW | Sperrin Mountains |
| N | Slemish, Agnew's Hill, Antrim Mountains |

There is a nasty soft patch on the northern slopes of Divis and you would be best advised to traverse around the southern and western sides of the summit fence before attempting to descend northwards. As you walk down the rugged slopes of heather, look out for a groove in the ground which you should follow off to the left. This groove will lead you on to a boundary ditch and embankment, where a few wind-blasted thorn bushes are growing. This linear feature will lead you across a broad gap, until you start following a fence in the same general direction. If you cross the fence you can walk along a broad moorland crest until you reach Ballyhill Road on the next gap.

Cross over Ballyhill Road by crossing the fences on both sides of the road. Once across, start climbing gently up a sloping field, to reach a trig point beside a gate on top of a low hill. The trig point stands at 335m (1,100ft), and you pass it to walk down the other side of the hill. When you reach a gateway on the way down, keep to the left side of an old quarry, where roadstone is stored, to reach the main A52, or Ballyutoag Road. Turn right and follow this road a short way downhill, then turn left to follow the minor road known as Flush Road.

## The way to Belfast Zoo          *Allow 3 hours*

As you follow Flush Road uphill, there are no really significant gaps between the houses on the right-hand side of the road. When broad fields appear after the last of them, look out for a small step-stile on the right. You will find a vague path running across a field, then more step-stiles show the way up the slopes of Squires Hill. Although the summit reaches 374m (1,227ft), you do not need to pass too close to the summit masts. Keep well to the left of them and keep the stiles in line so that you will be led downhill through the fields, but beware of a very muddy area shortly before you reach the B95, or Upper Hightown Road.

Cross over the road and start to follow the access road towards a rather scruffy landfill site. Turn off this road to the right and follow a track which climbs between fences. As the track climbs, you should notice a young forestry plantation off to the right. Go through a gate as you pass the end of the plantation, then follow the track up to the head of a shallow moorland valley. When you reach the head of this valley, turn off the track to follow a path on the right. This path leads to a step-stile by a gate, from where you climb straight uphill for a short way. You will pass a small cairn on Cave Hill at 368m (1,207ft) before a slight descent leads to an ancient promontory fort protruding from the edge of the hill. From here, sweeping views take in practically all of Belfast's urban sprawl, and this point can prove to be very popular. Beware of the sudden drops in most directions, and spend some time discovering how many places you can identify clearly. It was at this point, known as McArt's Fort, that Wolfe Tone and the United Irishmen took their famous oath to free Ireland before the rebellion of 1798.

Cave Hill is the crowning glory of the Cave Hill Country Park, which includes the cliffs and woodlands all around Belfast Castle. The turrets and towers of the nineteenth-century castle, where three upper rooms have been set aside to house the Cave Hill Heritage Centre, can be seen below in clear weather. The Centre aims to explain something about the formation and significance of Cave Hill, tracing its history from its early years as a promontory fort to its present-day value as a public amenity. The hill takes its name from a series of small caves in the cliff, although these are not seen to their best advantage from Cave Hill itself. In earlier years the hill was called Ben Madigan after an Ulster king of the ninth century. It has also earned the nickname of Napoleon's Nose, owing to its distinctive profile as seen from many parts of the city. To help identify various features from the urban sprawl below, the OSNI Greater Belfast Street Map is a useful aid. In fact, this map is also useful to have at both the beginning and end of this walk.

Paths seem to converge on Cave Hill from all directions, and the one you use when leaving is that running roughly northwards along the top of the cliff edge. This path gradually drops downhill and passes through fences. You then drop further on to a scrubby wooded slope – the Hazelwood National Nature Reserve. You should notice an unusual array of wild animals as you come to the

end of this route – not every walk includes such exotic animals as giraffes and flamingos! A cobbley path and flight of steps lead down to the perimeter wall of Belfast Zoo. Keep left along the perimeter wall, and continue in this direction to reach the car park. If you can arrange for a lift, then someone could meet you at this point. The access road runs straight down on to the busy Antrim Road, where several Citybus services mean that you won't have long to wait for a bus back into Belfast. If, however, you want to end with refreshments, the Bellevue Arms is quite nearby.

## Alternative routes

### ESCAPES

The Belfast Hills are crossed by a number of roads, each of which offers useful escape routes. Even the access roads to the masts on Black Hill, Black Mountain and Divis can be used as escape routes. It makes sense to descend towards Belfast, where Citybus services are generally found in the suburbs. If you need an escape route towards the end, there are a couple of useful paths descending from Cave Hill towards Carrs Glen and Belfast Castle, but these will hardly get you to the end of your walk any quicker than continuing to Belfast Zoo.

### EXTENSIONS

As an upland walk, this walk through the Belfast Hills is just about as long as it possibly can be, and any extensions are therefore likely to be contrived. The route offered is virtually the same as the course of the Ulster Way, although this particular stretch has never been fully waymarked. If you extend the walk by continuing along the Ulster Way, then the route covers low-lying countryside around Belfast Lough and Three Mile Water, or around parts of the Lagan Valley. The creation of the Belfast Hills Regional Park might result in a greater network of routes becoming available to walkers, as well as an assortment of useful stiles and signposts.

17

# Route 2: LAGAN CANAL TOWPATH

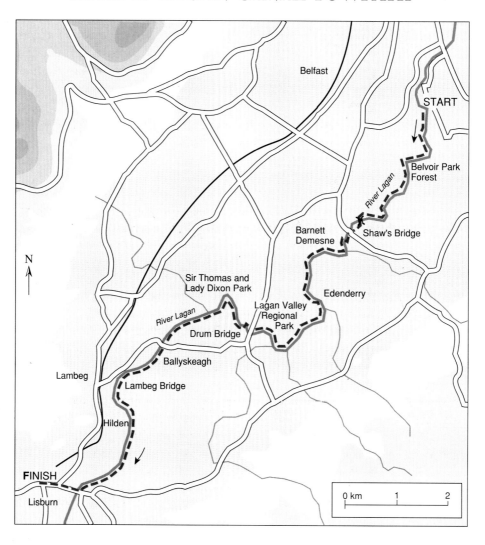

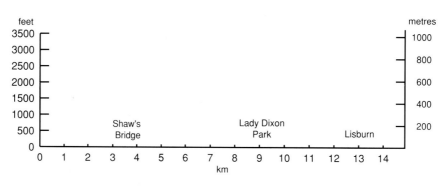

# Route 2: Lagan Canal Towpath

**TIME ALLOWANCE**   4 hours.

**STARTING LOCATION**
Lockview Road, Belfast.
OSNI Discoverer 15: GR 340713.
Large car park on Lockview Road.
Citybus 69 runs close to the start.

**FINISHING LOCATION**
Bus Station, Lisburn.
OSNI Discoverer 20: GR 265643.
Large car parks at the finish in Lisburn.
Frequent Ulsterbus services between Lisburn and
   Belfast.

**OVERVIEW/INTEREST**
Continuous towpath walk, suitable for children.
Access to other parts of the Lagan Valley,
   including parks and nature reserves.
Wonderfully wooded riversides.
Disused canal cuttings and old locks.
Includes a stretch of the Ulster Way.

**FOOTPATHS**
Level, easy walking from start to finish.
Paths are clear and obvious throughout; they are
   generally dry and covered in tarmac.
The towpath is well maintained throughout.

**STATISTICS**
**WALKING DISTANCE**   17km (10½ miles)
**TOTAL HEIGHT GAINED**   15m (50ft)
**PRINCIPAL HEIGHTS**   None

## The way to Shaw's Bridge          *Allow 1 hour*

You can reach the Stranmillis Road using Citybus
service number 69, and simply walk to the start of
the Lagan Canal Towpath on Lockview Road. The
Cutters Wharf is a popular riverside restaurant on
the western bank of the Lagan, and just beyond is
a large car park. If you walk to the far end of this
you will find a sheltered information board

showing the course of the Lagan Canal Towpath.
The River Lagan was made navigable piecemeal,
and after the construction of side-canals with
locks, the waterway was open as far as Lisburn by
the 1760s. There are many other places offering
public access alongside the River Lagan, such as
forests, parks and nature reserves. Feel free to
include these in your walk, but first check what
options are available to enable you to return to the
towpath without incurring any unnecessary road
walking. The Lagan Canal Towpath almost always
features a level, tarmac surface, often backed up
with small signs indicating the next destination up
or downstream. It is open to cyclists, but they are
requested to give way to walkers. You may also
find joggers and horse riders along the way, with
canoeists on the river itself. Specialist walking gear
and boots are not essential, although waterproofs
may still prove useful.

Leave the information board and follow a paved
path through an area of shrubbery. You do not
have immediate access to the Lagan Canal
Towpath, but have to pass a rowing club and tennis
courts first. The towpath is then aligned to the
River Lagan and you simply start to follow it
upstream. This is a well-wooded walk, so views are
necessarily limited to the river and its immediate
surroundings. If you navigate by anything, it is
likely to be by bridges, ticking them off on the map
as you pass them. As you turn a pronounced right-
hand bend in the river, there is a sewage works on
the opposite side, but you may be unaware of its
presence. There are some open fields on your side
of the river, known as the Lagan Meadows, while
the opposite bank features the mixed woodlands of
Belvoir Park Forest. A broad loop of the River
Lagan has here been severed by a short length
of canal, complete with towpath. The canal cutting
is overgrown, with any pools of water being quite
weed-grown. As you bend around another loop
of the river, you will pass a golf driving range, but
a tall fence should protect you from over-
enthusiastic patrons!

To stay true to the course of the Lagan Canal Towpath, cross the Red Bridge – which is, of course, painted red – and then cross a narrow, stone-arched bridge over another overgrown canal cutting. Turn right after this and continue alongside the old cut. The plain pathway allows you to look across to the Clement Wilson Park – a former factory garden now open to the public – and you will soon be led back on to the banks of the River Lagan. At this point, an elaborate system of weirs and chutes is used by canoeists, to the entertainment of many passers-by.

A short walk upstream takes you under the span of a busy, modern road bridge, before you reach the mellow stone arches of the much older Shaw's Bridge. Climb up a flight of steps to the left, then turn right to cross Shaw's Bridge. You will reach a car park and find another sheltered information board to study. Shaw's Bridge was originally a wooden structure allowing Cromwell to get his big guns across the River Lagan in 1655. The stone-arched bridge dates from 1709, but now carries only pedestrians as the traffic uses the new bridge.

## The way to Drum Bridge        *Allow 1 hour*

There is a signpost and gateway next to the information board at Shaw's Bridge. The signpost confirms that you are following a stretch of the Ulster Way, although you actually joined it earlier at the previous stone bridge. As you proceed upstream again, you will have the Barnett Demesne to your right, while across the River Lagan are the Minnowburn Beeches, a glorious sight in autumn, which are cared for by the National Trust. Although they are largely out of sight, you will be walking fairly close to many sports facilities, including the Mary Peters Running Track and the House of Sport (Sports Council for Northern Ireland). Again, you may be aware of a sewage works close to hand, but your attention may also be caught by the St Ellen Industrial Estate and the worker's village of Edenderry on the far bank. Gilchrist Bridge – a stout wooden footbridge – offers access to the village if required, but remember to return across it later to go upstream.

You will notice that the Lagan Canal Towpath is again routed alongside an overgrown cutting. You will pass a picnic site at the Eel Weir, and unless you keep your eye on the map you will be completely unaware of the looping course pursued by the River Lagan. The Malone Golf Course is close to hand on the right, while across the river are fields and occasional large houses. There is an old bridge that you pass beneath at one point. After walking around a broad bend in the river you will have a close-up view of Drum House, and will find yourself again following the banks of the river for a short while. The B103 is reached at Drum Bridge, and there is a restored lock-keeper's cottage nearby. There is no need to cross the busy road, as the towpath actually passes beneath it. The little village of Drumbeg, with its fine church and pub, is just a short way along the road, on the other side of the river. Many of the people who founded the city of Belfast are buried in the churchyard.

## The way to Lambeg Bridge        *Allow 1 hour*

After passing beneath the B103 at Drum Bridge, turn left to cross a footbridge over the River Lagan, then turn right to follow the river upstream. The Ulster Way, incidentally, does not cross the river, but heads into Sir Thomas and Lady Dixon Park, away from the Lagan Canal Towpath. You will be able to look across the river to the park, but in springtime you would need to enter it to appreciate its extensive beds of roses. The Lagan Canal Towpath follows the River Lagan for a while, but then detours away to the left. You may not be aware of it at first, but later you will realize that you are following another stretch of the old canal cutting. In fact, it becomes quite plain before you pass through a concrete tunnel beneath the busy M1 motorway.

After this noisy interlude, a dead straight stretch of the old canal begins to waver, and you pass beneath a modern high-level footbridge and an older road bridge. The road bridge is made of red sandstone, and features two high arches. One allows passage for the canal and the other accommodates the Lagan Canal Towpath. Continuing

*The weed-grown Lagan Canal and its towpath at a bridge near Ballyskeagh.*

along the towpath, you will pass alongside a factory wall before reaching Lambeg Bridge. The name Lambeg conjures up images of twelfth of July parades and big drums, but the so-called Lambeg Drums actually came to Ireland from Holland with William of Orange.

## The way to Lisburn                    *Allow 1 hour*

Just as you cross the road at Lambeg Bridge, you will be walking alongside a loop of the River Lagan, before switching almost immediately back on to the Lagan Canal Towpath as it follows the old canal cutting towards Lisburn. Although this final stretch remains tree lined, you will become more aware of houses, schools and old mill buildings. The mill at Hilden in particular dominates the waterside after you have passed another road bridge.

You are now approaching what used to be the heart of Ireland's great linen industry, but to be reminded of it you would need to visit the Irish Linen Centre in Lisburn. Do not be tempted to cross any of the footbridges on this final stretch, but stay on the southern bank of the river until you reach a broad road bridge. Turn right to cross

this bridge, then cross the busy road beyond, before walking straight up into the centre of Lisburn. The bus station is signposted from the pedestrianized part of the town centre. For the Ulsterbus service to Belfast, however, you might need to wait on Castle Street, just next to the Surf Mountain outdoor gear shop.

## Alternative routes

ESCAPES

This walk is already as low-level as it can get, so the only reason for wanting to escape is either because the weather is bad or because time is running short. Leave via the road bridges which cross the River Lagan. You can quickly pick up bus services if you head for bus stops away from Shaw's Bridge. If you abandon the walk at Drum Bridge, then you may have to walk back towards Belfast a short way before you can pick up a bus service on the Upper Malone Road. Leaving the route at Lambeg gives you a choice of nearby bus or rail services back to Belfast, but at that late stage you might as well complete the entire walk and finish in Lisburn.

EXTENSIONS

The Lagan Valley Regional Park is criss-crossed by paths, so that you have an entire network available to create alternative routes. The Lagan Canal Towpath remains faithful to the line of the River Lagan and its former canal cuttings. You could add loops to the towpath walk to take in parts of Belvoir Park Forest, Clement Wilson Park, Barnett Demesne, Minnowburn Beeches, the Giant's Ring Chambered Grave, and Sir Thomas and Lady Dixon Park, and make use of rougher paths on the opposite bank of the Lagan where these are available. There is an opportunity to extend the riverside walk further upstream at Lisburn, or further downstream through the new Laganside developments in Belfast, to end at the Lagan Lookout by the Lagan Barrier. If you decide that you want to head downstream and want to vary the route, then you can include the Botanic Gardens, Tropical Ravine, Palm House or the gardens of the Ormeau Park.

# Route 3: NORTH DOWN COASTAL PATH

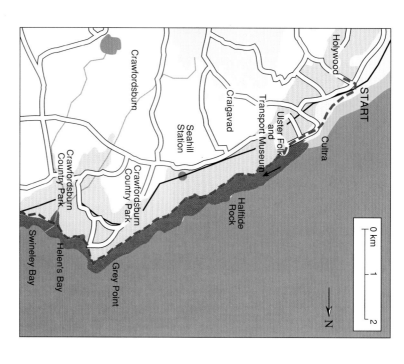

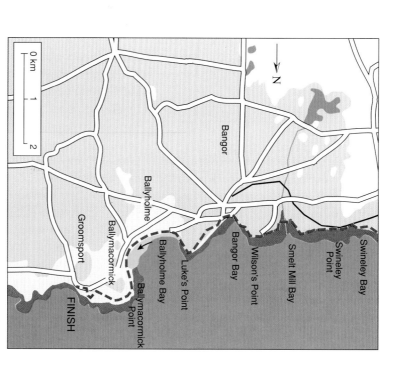

feet

1500
1000
500
0

Transport
Museum

Grey
Point

Bangor
Bay

Groomsport

0 1 2 3 4 5 6 7 8 9 10 11 12 13 14 15 16 17 18 19

km

# Route 3: North Down Coastal Path

TIME ALLOWANCE  5 hours.

**STARTING LOCATION**
The Maypole, Holywood.
OSNI Discoverer 15: GR 398793.
Parking available around Holywood as directed by
    signs.
Ulsterbus 1 and 2 serve Holywood and Bangor.
Northern Ireland Railway service to Holywood
    and Bangor.

**FINISHING LOCATION**
Groomsport Harbour.
OSNI Discoverer 15: GR 537836.
Parking available at Groomsport Harbour.
Ulsterbus 3 serves Bangor and Groomsport.

**OVERVIEW/INTEREST**
Easy coastal walking throughout, suitable for
    children.
Good coastal scenery and views.
Passes through the popular Crawfordsburn
    Country Park.
Plenty of heritage features, including the Ulster
    Folk and Transport Museum and Grey Point
    Fort.
Well served by public transport.

**FOOTPATHS**
Paths are generally clear and close to the shore.
Most have been surfaced and are quite dry.
Paths occasionally cross sandy beaches.
Short sections may be flooded by spring or storm
    tides.

**STATISTICS**
**WALKING DISTANCE**  20km (12½ miles)
**TOTAL HEIGHT GAINED**  100m (300ft)
**PRINCIPAL HEIGHTS**  None

## The way to Helen's Bay            *Allow 2 hours*

You can reach Holywood by car, following the busy A2 dual carriageway out of Belfast. Parking is available either side of the centre of town. Alternatively, forget about the car and use either Northern Ireland Railway or Ulsterbus services to get to Holywood. Ideally, you should start in the centre of Holywood, if only to admire the world's tallest permanent maypole at a crossroads. It rises like a ship's mast for 20m (70ft) and replaces earlier structures dating from at least 1700, when a ship ran aground on May Eve and its mast was used as a maypole. Follow the Shore Road down to the busy dual carriageway, cross over the road and go under a railway bridge to reach the shore of Belfast Lough. An Ulster Way signpost stands here, and you should turn right along the solid promenade path to begin this walk.

The concrete promenade path is equipped with benches, where you might pause to identify the Belfast Hills seen across Belfast Lough. Follow the path onwards, at first walking roughly parallel to the railway line. Later, the railway veers inland, while you continue across a stretch of grassy parkland. You may notice aircraft coming in and out of Belfast City Airport, or see high-speed ferries hurtling in and out of the lough. You pass a small pier and slipway at Cultra Avenue, and continue past the Royal Northern Ireland Yacht Club on Seafront Road. You will find that Seafront Road continues along the shore as a gravel track: the 'Private Road' sign applies only to vehicles, so follow the track onwards on foot. Rising for some distance inland is the Ulster Folk and Transport Museum – a vast open-air museum in the grounds of Cultra Manor displaying many fine buildings which have been rescued from ruin all around the countryside and rebuilt stone by stone. A visit is

*OVERLEAF:*
*The first low, wooded point reached on the coastal path beyond Holywood.*

highly recommended, but allow a whole day to explore properly. In any case, there is no immediate access to the Folk Park from the shore.

The coast path follows the top of a wall for a short way, then you pass the end of Glen Road. A concrete path beside garden walls leads to the next narrow shore road. The path continues alongside a tall safety fence bounding a golf course, then runs around a low, rocky, wooded point. If you look out across the lough you may see the Halftide Rock, which could have seals hauled out upon it. Cormorants are also in the habit of using the rock while hanging their wings out to dry. The path becomes pleasantly grassy as it continues alongside a tall wall; there are areas of shingle and rock before it passes close to a school and rises gently through an area of scrub and bracken. Later there is a fork in the path where you could cut the walk short by heading inland and uphill, joining a road and following it up to Seahill Station.

To stay on the coastal path, however, keep low and pass below the fence of the Seahill sewage treatment works. The path runs through an arched gateway, then a flight of concrete steps leads uphill over a wooded cliff, before another flight leads back down to the shore again. A gravelly path by a rocky shore then leads into the popular Crawfordsburn Country Park, one of the busiest countryside sites in Ireland. You pass a boathouse as you walk around a small bay, and also pass the end of a road which leads up into the village of Helen's Bay. Blue waymark arrows on posts indicate the coastal path through the Country Park, but you will hardly need them as the way ahead is so obvious.

Follow the path through a turnstile and continue along the top of a low cliff-line on the wooded Grey Point. A sign indicates a short diversion to the Grey Point Fort, a structure dating from 1904 which was placed here to defend Belfast Lough against invaders, serving for two World Wars. It is open to visitors at certain times. Carrickfergus Castle on the opposite side of the lough played a similar defensive role in earlier centuries, even witnessing the appearance of Paul Jones and the fledgling American Navy in 1778. A successful skirmish with HMS *Drake* in Belfast

Lough is widely regarded as America's first naval victory! The path continues around Grey Point and wanders through a wood before reaching another road running through Helen's Bay. Again, you have the option of cutting the walk short at this point by heading inland to a railway station.

## The way to Bangor   *Allow 1½ hours*

The promenade path around Helen's Bay is a popular short walk. You can enjoy the views across the lough, which now feature the peninsula of Islandmagee and a substantial part of the Rhinns of Galloway over in Scotland. A broad gravel track continues over a low, wooded point to reach the next part of the Crawfordsburn Country Park. If you have time, you can head inland to the Visitor Centre, or simply sample the short Meadow Walk or the Glen Walk with its waterfalls. The Visitor Centre has a restaurant on site. The Ulster Way, which you have been following so far, heads up through the glen to Crawfordsburn village, which has an Ulsterbus service. The North Down Coastal Path, however, continues towards Bangor and Groomsport.

After crossing a footbridge over the burn, the coast path passes a large, derelict house and leads around a rocky, wooded point to continue across a sandy beach. A high storm-tide could be a problem here, but normally the way is clear. After passing around the next wooded point, the path becomes concrete for a short way, then runs as a tarmac path around Swineley Point and past a golf course. Beyond Smelt Mill Bay, the path passes the end of Brompton Road and follows a tarmac path below a prominent tower.

After bending around a low cliff-line, the route approaches the seaside resort of Bangor. The harbourside features plenty of amenities for children, ample seating and a well-stocked marina. If you walk all the way around the harbour you will eventually reach the fine old Tower House where the Tourist Information Office is situated. Although Bangor is undoubtedly an old town, only fragments of its history survive, and to most visitors it has the air of a Victorian seaside resort.

## The way to Groomsport   *Allow 1½ hours*

Follow the promenade path out of Bangor, looking across Belfast Lough to spot the Mull of Kintyre and the Isle of Arran in Scotland. You then walk around the grassy Luke's Point and pass Ballyholme Yacht Club. A tarmac path continues around Ballyholme Bay, to reach a car park and children's play area.

You may need to walk at low tide as you head across the sands running close to a sea wall. This is only for a short while, as the path comes ashore again at the end of the wall.

You then enter a stretch of coastal heath and scrub managed by the National Trust at Ballymacormick Point. The path is variously grassy or gravelly, surrounded by gorse and brambles in places. Keep to it as it approaches Groomsport, which you enter using a narrow road, although you can follow a path all the way to the harbour if you wish. Groomsport is notable as the point where Schomberg landed in 1689 with 10,000 Williamite troops at his disposal. There is food and drink available in the village, as well as an Ulsterbus service back to Bangor for connections to Holywood and Belfast.

## Alternative routes

ESCAPES

Escape routes are hardly appropriate for such an easy and low-level coastal walk, but in foul weather you might like to know how you can bail out to a bus or train service. If you set out from Holywood and simply change your mind, then just turn around and walk back into town. Railway stations are located a short way inland at places such as Cultra, Seahill, Helen's Bay, Crawfordsburn, Swineley and Bangor. Ulsterbus services can be picked up at Cultra, Seahill, Crawfordsburn, Bangor and Groomsport. If you intend visiting the Ulster Folk and Transport Museum at Cultra, then you should abandon all hope of completing the walk in the same day, as there is simply too much to see on site.

EXTENSIONS

This is in fact the whole length of the North Down Coast Path, so it cannot actually be extended any further as a coastal path. However, because it is tied into the course of the Ulster Way, extensions are possible beyond both Holywood and Crawfordsburn. At the Crawfordsburn end you can climb through a delightfully wooded glen and admire its lovely little waterfalls before emerging at the Old Inn – an appropriate name for the oldest inn in Ireland! At the Holywood end, the Ulster Way climbs up a wooded slope in the Redburn Country Park, from where views extend all around Belfast Lough, taking in both the urban sprawl and the surrounding countryside. The Ulster Way is of course an enormously long route, so you have to set some sort of limit on any extension. Ulster wayfarers following the North Down Coastal Path from Crawfordsburn to Holywood then continue through the Lagan Valley and across the Belfast Hills, before heading for the Antrim Mountains and Causeway Coast.

# Route 4: SLIEVE DONARD

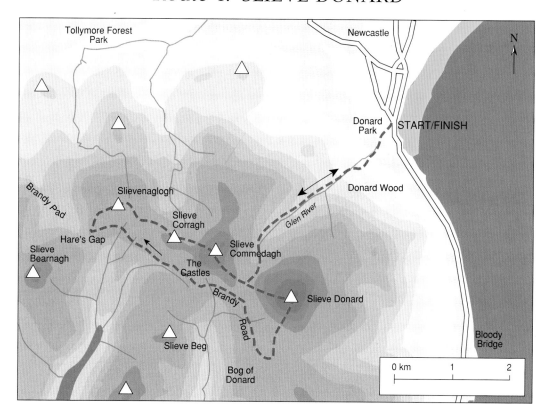

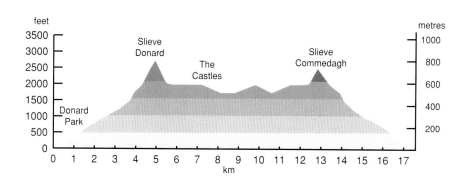

# 2

# HIGH MOURNES

## Route 4: Slieve Donard

**TIME ALLOWANCE**  8 hours.

**STARTING/FINISHING LOCATION**
Donard Park, Newcastle.
OSNI Discoverer 29, OSNI Mourne Country Map:
  GR 375306.
Large car park at Donard Park on the edge of
  town.
Ulsterbus 17, 20, 39, 237 and 240 serve
  Newcastle.

**OVERVIEW/INTEREST**
Starts close to the interesting Mourne Countryside
  Centre in Newcastle.
Popular climb to Ulster's highest mountain, with
  panoramic views.
Follows part of the Mourne Wall.
Includes an old smuggling path – the Brandy Pad.

**FOOTPATHS**
Paths are clear and dry for most of the route.
The Glen River Path has been reconstructed.
There is serious erosion on parts of the Brandy
  Pad.
Paths have been trodden on both sides of the
  Mourne Wall.

**STATISTICS**
**WALKING DISTANCE**  18km (11 miles)
**TOTAL HEIGHT GAINED**  1,250m (4,100ft)
**PRINCIPAL HEIGHTS**
Slieve Donard  850m (2,796ft)
Slieve Commedagh  767m (2,512ft)

### The way to Slieve Donard      *Allow 2 hours*

If you are in this area for the first time, then a visit to the Mourne Countryside Centre on the promenade in Newcastle is recommended. Interesting exhibits explain all about the Mountains of Mourne, and the Countryside Wardens who staff the Centre occasionally lead walks in the mountains, so they are worth approaching for help and advice. Percy French's famous song says that the Mountains of Mourne 'sweep down to the sea' – and indeed, as you look at Slieve Donard from the promenade, this is a most apt description. Parking is available not far off the promenade, and quite close to the Mourne Countryside Centre, at Donard Park. This large car park is situated adjacent to a sports field at the foot of the wooded slopes of Slieve Donard on the edge of town.

Leave the car park at the far wooded end, following a clear track which runs parallel to the Glen River. Although there is a network of forest tracks in Donard Wood, you should always remain within earshot, if not sight, of the Glen River. The path accompanies the river a short way upstream before you cross over Donard Bridge, then you head onwards up a rather rougher and steeper path to cross the next bridge at Craignagore. Continue upstream, and the well-trodden path will lead you out of the forest at a gateway. Although you still walk alongside the forest fence, you are now in the wilder upper reaches of the glen. Continue to follow the Glen River; you will notice how the path has been reconstructed in places where it was suffering erosion. Follow it across the headwaters of the river, then note how

29

large slabs of granite have been laid along the line of the path on the steeper slopes at the head of the glen. The National Trust, who recently acquired this part of Slieve Donard, arranged for the repair work to be done. Stay on the path, so as not to cause further damage to unstable slopes nearby. The path then reaches a gap in between Slieve Commedagh, to the right, and Slieve Donard, to the left. You will find yourself facing the monumental Mourne Wall – a drystone wall of Cyclopean proportions which actually runs for 32km (20 miles) across a dozen of the major summits in the Mountains of Mourne.

Turn left to follow the wall steeply uphill. This is a relentless uphill slog of some 260m (850ft), but the gradient does begin to ease a little as the summit is approached. There is no mistaking the summit of Slieve Donard, where a right-angled corner in the Mourne Wall features a stout stone tower made of squared blocks of masonry. The trig point stands at 850m (2,796ft) – and it stands on top of the tower! There is an untidy spread of stones as an apology for a summit cairn, reputed to be where St Domangard was buried. He gave his name to the mountain, which was previously known as Sliabh Slanga – Slanga being a son of Partholan, who came to Ireland after the Battle of Troy. The view is of course wide ranging, taking in the Mournes, Wicklow, Antrim, Scotland and the Isle of Man. In clear weather, it could be summarized as follows:

| | |
|---|---|
| E | Snaefell, Isle of Man |
| S | Howth Head, Dublin, Wicklow Mountains |
| SW | Slieve Binnian, Carlingford Mountain |
| WSW | Slievelamagan, Cooley Hills |
| W | Slieve Bearnagh, Slieve Meelbeg |
| NW | Slieve Commedagh |
| N | Slieve Croob, Belfast Hills, Antrim Mountains |
| NNE | Isle of Arran, Scotland |
| NE | Galloway Hills, Scotland |

*The Mourne Wall is an obvious feature to follow on Slieve Commedagh.*

Also of interest in the southern sector is the intricate nature of the fields in the area known as the Kingdom of Mourne. Every field has a name, and there are more fields than people. The Kingdom of Mourne was established when St Patrick threw his sandal from one end to the other of this lowland region – a distance of about 20km (12½ miles)! For a bird's-eye view of Newcastle, walk a short distance northwards across stony ground and make a beeline for the Lesser Carn. This burial cairn is the one you actually see from below, before you leave the promenade in Newcastle. When you have sampled this extra view, return to the summit of Slieve Donard to continue the walk.

## The way to Hare's Gap    *Allow 2½ hours*

Follow the course of the Mourne Wall roughly southwards down a steep slope which is mostly littered with boulders. When the wall and the ground start to level out at the foot of the slope, you will notice a stone step-stile built into the Mourne Wall. Cross over this chunky stile, so that you are on the western side of the Mourne Wall. You are now going to follow the course of the Brandy Pad as it contours around the mountainsides. This is an old smuggling path which was used to convey brandy and other contraband goods away from the eyes of the excisemen. Goods were generally brought in from the Isle of Man and landed secretly on the coast. The smugglers then carried their wares up alongside the Bloody Bridge River, along the Brandy Pad, down via the Trassey River, and away to Hilltown.

The route follows the Brandy Pad only as far as Hare's Gap. There is no problem following the path in clear weather, but in poor visibility it is possible to be drawn along other trodden paths running parallel, or along those which peter out on the mountainside. The Brandy Pad is becoming badly worn in places, and you should walk carefully so that you don't damage it any further. The path contours around the slopes of Slieve Donard at about 550m (1,800ft), and you should take care to bear left to continue beneath the rocky outcrops of The Castles. The spur path to the right leads back towards the head of the Glen River and gives you the option of an early descent.

The Brandy Pad offers remarkable views into the heart of the Mournes as it crosses the mountainside. There are views along the valley of Annalong Water, frowned upon by the rocky crest of Slieve Binnian. Later, the path climbs over a gap in the mountains between Slieve Commedagh and Slieve Beg. There is a short descent, which involves crossing a couple of minor streams where erosion is quite bad. You pass a rocky cleft which offers a few minutes of interesting exploration above the path. There are views along the length of the Ben Crom Reservoir, overlooked by the

*Walking on the Mourne Wall – possible, but not really recommended.*

proud peak of Ben Crom itself. There is a slight climb towards the end of the Brandy Pad to reach Hare's Gap. The gap lies in between the awesomely rocky peak of Slieve Bearnagh and Slievenaglogh. The Mourne Wall crosses the gap, and you will be walking in its company again.

## The way back to Newcastle   *Allow 3½ hours*

Turn right on Hare's Gap, but keep away from the Mourne Wall at first, as it climbs up an exceedingly steep and rocky slope. Pick your own way uphill, outflanking any difficult ground, then gradually drift back towards the wall. Grass and heather slopes are often punctuated by boulders as you cross the minor summit of Slievenaglogh. The wall continues across hummocky ground before climbing on to Slieve Corragh. The broad crest narrows later, and the ground to the north features pinnacles of rock. A steep pull leads on to Slieve Commedagh. Although not as steep or long as the earlier ascent of Slieve Donard, it nevertheless comes late enough in the day to feel just as tough! The Mourne Wall curves gracefully over the top of Slieve Commedagh, and features another stout stone tower which is a twin of the one on Slieve Donard. This is not on the true summit of the mountain, which actually stands a short way to the north-east at 767m (2,512ft), and is marked by a lonely burial cairn.

The descent from Slieve Commedagh is via the Mourne Wall. This drops fairly steeply and then levels out for a short while, before falling again. You will find that the wall leads you back on to the gap at the head of the Glen River. You need to cross the Mourne Wall at a stone step-stile to make sure that you are on the northern side. Take care to pick up the course of the reconstructed Glen River Path and follow this across the headwaters of the Glen River. You are, of course, retracing your earlier steps and all you need to do is to let the path lead you back through the gate into Donard Wood. The path descends through the wood, running parallel to the Glen River. Remember to cross the bridge at Craignagore, continue down the rougher path, and then cross Donard Bridge, before following the Glen River back to the car park at Donard Park on the edge of Newcastle. A full range of accommodation options, as well as places offering food and drink, are found throughout Newcastle.

## Alternative routes

ESCAPES

The most straightforward way off Slieve Donard in bad weather is to retrace your steps via the Mourne Wall and the Glen River Path. If you in fact cross the mountain, but decide against following the Brandy Pad, then you can descend via the Bloody Bridge River to the Bloody Bridge car park on the main A2 coastal road. Even if you do start to follow the Brandy Pad, you can always cut off it at an early stage to cross the gap and regain the Glen River Path. If you reach Hare's Gap and decide you can't face the high-level walk back over Slieve Commedagh, you can always follow the Trassey Track down to a small car park near Trassey Bridge. You then have the option of walking through Tollymore Forest Park on clear, low-level tracks to return to Newcastle. This last option is a long walk when you are trying to bail out of a difficult one, but worth consideration.

EXTENSIONS

The longest logical extension to any walk in the Mountains of Mourne is to consider a complete circuit of the Mourne Wall. This is long and tough, but highly recommended to walkers who know they possess the stamina and experience necessary to complete it. Any extension to the original route runs into problems getting back to Newcastle. Slieve Bearnagh almost demands to be climbed when you see it towering above Hare's Gap; you can either retrace your steps to continue with the walk, or descend to some other point and, by prior arrangement, make sure you can be collected. A rugged descent from Slieve Commedagh can take in the Cascade River, ending with a walk through Tollymore Forest Park. When the cloud hangs low and the air is laced with rain, you might actually prefer to be walking here, where at least the waterfalls would be worth seeing.

# Route 5:  SLIEVE BINNIAN

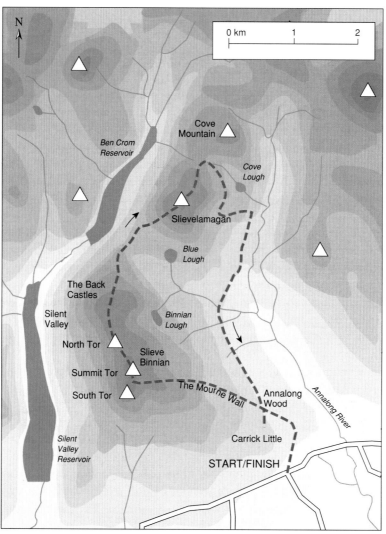

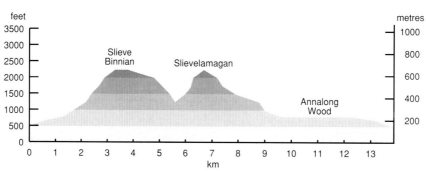

# Route 5: Slieve Binnian

**TIME ALLOWANCE**   6 hours.

**STARTING/FINISHING LOCATION**
Carrick Little car park, near Annalong.
OSNI Discoverer 29, OSNI Mourne Country Map:
    GR 345219.
Small car park at a crossroads.
Ulsterbus 34A passes in the summer months only.

**OVERVIEW/INTEREST**
Includes part of the Mourne Wall.
Reaches a commanding viewpoint.
Features a series of rugged summit tors.
Close to the Silent Valley.

**FOOTPATHS**
Low-level tracks are very clear; some upland paths
    are reasonably clear.
Slievelamagan is largely without paths.
No significantly wet or boggy areas.

**STATISTICS**
**WALKING DISTANCE**   14km (8¾ miles)
**TOTAL HEIGHT GAINED**   980m (3,215ft)
**PRINCIPAL HEIGHTS**
Slieve Binnian   747m (2,449ft)
Slievelamagan   704m (2,306ft)

## The way to Slieve Binnian       *Allow 2 hours*

The Carrick Little car park can be approached using the Heads Road either from Annalong or the Silent Valley. The car park can prove quite popular at weekends, and it occasionally becomes overcrowded so that cars spill out on to the road-sides. Please park considerately, and in such a way that you can make your escape afterwards. There is a clear track known as the Carrick Little Track running roughly northwards from the car park. You simply stride along this, looking ahead to the mountains and hoping for a fine day's walking. Notice the small fields along the way, which are surrounded by immensely bouldery boundary walls. The soil in these parts contains countless numbers of huge boulders, making it difficult to work. When a farmer wants to make a field, he has to bring in heavy machinery and have all the boulders excavated; then, using heavy machinery a second time, the boulders are balanced one on top of another to make the field boundaries. The effect is quite startling, and the gaps between some of the boulders are big enough for you to put your arm through, so the assumption must be made that they stay standing by faith alone!

Follow the Carrick Little Track as far as a gateway which is flanked by a stout stone step-stile. The Mourne Wall crosses the track at this point and offers the key to a safe and relatively easy ascent of Slieve Binnian. Relatively easy means that is is free of awkward rocky or boggy sections, but it is still a relentless ascent of some 530m (1,740ft). Pause for a while and note the encircling mountains, which include Chimney Rock Mountain, the dome of Slieve Donard and Slieve Commedagh. Turn left to start following the Mourne Wall uphill. The Carrick Little Track veers away from it before the ground starts to steepen by degrees. You will cross a couple of minor stone walls which run towards the more prominent Mourne Wall, and if you need excuses to pause for breath on the ascent, then take note of the unfolding panorama. Looking up ahead, you can see monstrous masses of granite arranged along the crest of the mountain, and huge boulders lie marooned on the mountainside. It might look fairly intimidating to cautious walkers, but the ground actually turns out to be reasonably easy to traverse. Instead of following the Mourne Wall straight towards the Summit Tor, veer away to the right and aim for a notch in the rocky summit crest. You then have the option of making a short, rocky scramble to gain the summit of Slieve Binnian at 747m (2,449ft). You will notice that the Mourne Wall doesn't actually cross the bare rock on top of Slieve Binnian, but its line was continued by a post-and-wire fence, the scant remains of which can still be traced. The view from the summit is extensive and features the following:

| | |
|---|---|
| N | North Tor, Slieve Bearnagh |
| NNE | Slievelamagan, Slieve Commedagh, Slieve Donard |
| NE | Chimney Rock Mountain |
| E | Snaefell, Isle of Man |
| S | Howth Head, Dublin, Wicklow Mountains |
| SW | Carlingford Mountain |
| W | Silent Valley, Eagle Mountain |
| WNW | Slieve Muck |
| NW | Lough Shannagh |
| NNW | Slieve Meelbeg |

Quite apart from viewing near and distant hills and mountains, the contrast between the chaotically jumbled and wild summit tors and the ordered neatness of the tiny fields in the Kingdom of Mourne is quite surreal. You should be able to pick out various lengths of the Mourne Wall as it snakes from summit to summit around the Mountains of Mourne, covering around 32km (20 miles) as it marks the gathering grounds of the Silent Valley and Ben Crom Reservoirs. When the Silent Valley was flooded to provide drinking water for Belfast, gangs of labourers were employed to construct the mighty Mourne Wall. On many remote stretches, some of them would camp out all through the week and return home only for the weekends. The handiwork of those unknown builders is commemorated in stone. The wall offers a faultless guide all the way around the Mountains of Mourne, so it is little wonder that so many walkers have come to rely on it while exploring these bleak uplands. In fact, some walkers do more than follow it, they actually walk along the broad cam stones on top of the wall, but this is not recommended as you might damage the wall, yourself, or both!

*Some of Slieve Binnian's rugged tors, and a view towards Slieve Donard.*

## The way to Slievelamagan

*Allow 2 hours*

You now leave the comfort and security of the Mourne Wall and strike out towards the heart of the range by traversing the crest of Slieve Binnian. This rugged top has been described as resembling the back of a stegosaurus – the dinosaur with a line of jagged armoured plates along its back! The armoured plates on Slieve Binnian are in fact massive, wrinkled tors of weatherbeaten granite – ranging from the South Tor, through the Summit Tor, to the Back Castles. Surprisingly, the walk along the crest of the mountain is achieved using quite a clear and easy path, which passes most of the tors on the mountain. In poor visibility, however, walkers crossing Slieve Binnian for the first time could find the summit crest a confusing place, and if approaching from Slievelamagan they might wonder which one is supposed to be the Summit Tor! The path runs downhill for a while, then begins to climb towards the North Tor.

This enormous, rugged excrescence frowns on mere walkers as they creep around its left side.

The downhill run from the North Tor is on ground which gradually steepens, and you are aiming to reach a low-slung gap at around 400m (1,300ft). You may need to scramble for a short way down a rock-step before you land on the gap, but this is part of the path and is not at all difficult if approached with care. The gap lies between the little Blue Lough and the larger Ben Crom Reservoir. If Slieve Binnian was enough for you, then you might consider an exit via the Blue Lough to rejoin the Carrick Little Track. If you want to take in another mountain, then the huge and heathery dome of Slievelamagan is directly before you. There is no real path to follow, just a vague line up the rocky, heather-covered slope. At least the ground is generally firm and dry. There is

*Walkers creep around the base of the monstrous North Tor.*

a full 305m (1,000ft) of steep and rugged climbing before you reach the obvious bouldery summit cairn at 704m (2,306ft). With Slieve Binnian now behind you, and a host of other mountains arranged in a circle from Slieve Muck to Chimney Rock Mountain, you should feel as if you are deep in the heart of the Mountains of Mourne. Although only a comparatively small range, they do give the appearance of being more extensive.

## The way back to Carrick Little  *Allow 2 hours*

You could continue further along this broad crest, crossing Cove Mountain and Slieve Beg to link with the course of the Brandy Pad, but that makes for a very long day's walk by the time you return to Carrick Little. Instead, you can descend roughly northwards to the gap which occurs before Cove Mountain, then swing to the right to descend towards Cove Lough. On this descent, remember that you are not actually heading for Cove Lough itself and keep well to the right of it, looking out for the beginning of a stony path which zigzags more southwards to link with a clearer track near a cliff face. You should notice a series of tracks scored across the valley of the Annalong River. Continue down across rugged ground, perhaps following the foot of the prominent cliff face, until you join the clearest track, which runs roughly parallel to the Annalong River but stays some distance above and away from it. Turn right to follow the track down through the valley. This track rises and falls at a gentle gradient and makes light work of the rugged ground that it crosses. After periods of heavy rain, a couple of stream crossings could leave you with wet feet, although normally these can be splashed through without problems. You will notice another track running in on the right-hand side, which is the path coming down from the Blue Lough. The Carrick Little Track runs alongside Annalong Wood and eventually reaches the gateway and stout stone step-stile noticed near the beginning of the walk, where the Mourne Wall crosses it. All that remains is to follow the Carrick Little Track back to the car park on the Heads Road.

## Alternative routes

ESCAPES

If you doubt your navigational abilities in poor visibility, you should only consider following the Mourne Wall up and down Slieve Binnian. The mountain has many hidden dangers, and is not a place to become lost or stranded. Mourne Wall also descends into the Silent Valley and passes close to the waterworks Visitor Centre. This descent is quite steep and rocky in places, and is not particularly recommended while you still have the option of following the Mourne Wall in the other direction to the Carrick Little Track. Once you commit yourself to following the crest of the mountain, your next escape options occur on the low-slung gap between the Blue Lough and Ben Crom Reservoir. A descent via the Blue Lough allows you to return to the Carrick Little Track early, while one towards the Ben Crom Reservoir gives access to the road-head in the Silent Valley. This latter option could be considered in an emergency, and during the summer months there may be a shuttle bus service running between the reservoir dam and the Visitor Centre, where the nearest telephone is located.

EXTENSIONS

Apart from rising to the challenge of following the Mourne Wall all the way around the High Mournes, there is really only one logical extension to this walk: simply to continue along the crest of the range to cross Cove Mountain and Slieve Beg. This will lead you towards the Brandy Pad – the old smuggling path across the Mountains of Mourne. At this point your options are many, but each one has the effect of extending your day's walking drastically. You could descend from the Brandy Pad into either the valley of the Annalong River or the Silent Valley. You could also follow the Brandy Pad to either the Bloody Bridge or the Trassey Bridge, assuming that someone could meet and collect you at those points. Alternatively, you could reach for the heights again by contemplating ascents of Slieve Commedagh and Slieve Donard. These extra ascents would take you so close to Newcastle, where you could be met.

# Route 6: SLIEVE BEARNAGH

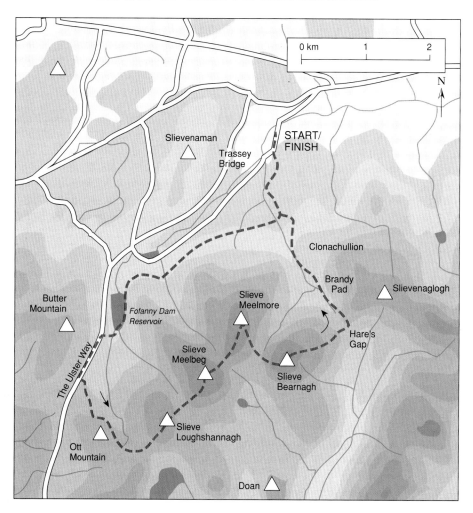

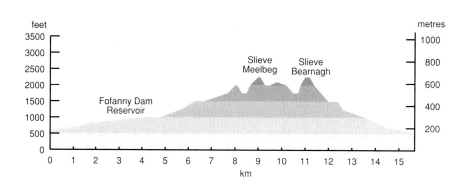

# Route 6: Slieve Bearnagh

**TIME ALLOWANCE** 7 hours.

**STARTING/FINISHING LOCATION**
Cecil Newman car park, Trassey.
OSNI Discoverer 29, OSNI Mourne Country Map:
  GR 312314.
Small car park near Trassey Bridge.
Ulsterbus 34 runs near Trassey.

**OVERVIEW/INTEREST**
Includes part of the Mourne Wall.
Features splendid views of the Mountains of
  Mourne.
Impressive summit tor on Slieve Bearnagh.
Includes a stretch of the Ulster Way.
Close to Tollymore Forest Park.

**FOOTPATHS**
Paths are clear and dry for most of the route.
The Mourne Wall is an obvious feature to follow.
Care is needed on steep paths on Slieve Bearnagh.
There is erosion on paths near the Hare's Gap.

**STATISTICS**
**WALKING DISTANCE** 16km (10 miles)
**TOTAL HEIGHT GAINED** 970m (3,180ft)
**PRINCIPAL HEIGHTS**
Slieve Loughshannagh 620m (2,030ft)
Slieve Meelbeg 708m (2,310ft)
Slieve Meelmore 680m (2,237ft)
Slieve Bearnagh 739m (2,394ft)

## The way to the Ott Track
*Allow 2 hours*

Slieve Bearnagh is readily recognized in views all around the Mountains of Mourne, its summit generally being seen as a rugged peak of rock, or even as a tower of rock in some profiles. In some views it may look a daunting prospect, and yet most hillwalkers would have little trouble crossing it. To reach the topmost point, however, requires more serious hands-on scrambling, although cautious walkers don't actually need to grapple with the rock. The course of the Mourne Wall allows for fairly easy route-finding over the mountains, and the low-level Ulster Way can also be used to create a varied circular walk.

Start at the Cecil Newman car park near Trassey Bridge, not far off the B180 road at the western end of Tollymore Forest Park. Cecil Newman is noted on a memorial boulder at the entrance to the car park as a 'Friend of Mourne'. When you leave the car park, turn left up a minor road, passing an Ulster Way signpost to reach a gateway on the left. A plaque marks the start of the Trassey Track, and you cross a step-stile beside the gate to start walking along a stony path. You walk beside a forest and pass through two swinging gates before the track leads out on to the lower slopes of the mountains. Turn right to follow a wall which contours around the mountain slopes, and which is followed by the Ulster Way.

This path leads to a step-stile, where a flight of stone steps leads across a small stream. As you climb up from the stream, an Ulster Way marker post directs you towards another path which contours around the next slope. The path is actually on top of a pipeline, which occasionally shows above the ground and which can be traced to the Fofanny Dam. At this point, you can cross a footbridge. Don't cross the dam, but turn left and walk along the top of an embankment beside the reservoir. At the head of the reservoir, follow the edge of a forest uphill and cross a step-stile to land on a minor road. Turn left to follow the minor road uphill, gaining better views of the mountains you will be climbing over the next hour or so. Then follow the road up as far as a small car park next to a Down District Council sign, near the beginning of the Ott Track.

## The way to Slieve Bearnagh
*Allow 3 hours*

Turn left to leave the minor road at a step-stile near a gate. The Ott Track proceeds clearly across the slopes of Ott Mountain, and at a junction you will

41

find that a yellow arrow painted on a boulder steers you to the right. Simply follow the Ott Track until it expires, and aim to continue its direction using a rather vaguely trodden path. If you lose this in an area of peat hags or on the higher, more heathery slopes, it doesn't matter too much. If you climb roughly eastwards, then you will reach the very obvious course of the Mourne Wall, where you turn left. Follow the Mourne Wall steeply uphill on to Slieve Loughshannagh, reaching the summit of the mountain at 620m (2,030ft).

The Mourne Wall runs roughly north-eastwards from Slieve Loughshannagh, descending steeply to cross a gap which bears an amount of rain-washed sand. The next ascent is a steep climb of around 200m (655ft) over short grass and heather, featuring scattered boulders of granite. There is a pronounced right-angled bend to the right as the Mourne Wall crosses the summit of Slieve Meelbeg at 708m (2,310ft). A short, but steep, descent leads quickly down to the next gap. A gentler ascent comes in two stages as you proceed towards Slieve Meelmore, the two parts separated by a more level shoulder. The Mourne Wall crosses over the broad crest of Slieve Meelmore at 680m (2,237ft), and you continue along the wall to reach a prominent stone tower at a dog-leg corner. This tower has twins on the summits of Slieve Commedagh and Slieve Donard, and despite a sternly worded

*The Mourne Wall is the safest feature to follow on Slieve Bearnagh.*

plaque advising that trespassers will be prosecuted, you are in fact welcome to walk on the mountain. The plaque is of historical interest only, dating from the early days of water catchment in the Silent Valley, when visitors were actually barred from the area lest they cause contamination to the water supply.

The Mourne Wall crosses the steep slopes of Slieve Meelmore diagonally. The ground is rough and bouldery, but there are no real problems on the way down to the next gap. When you land here, cross over on to the southern side of the Mourne Wall before climbing on to the slopes of Slieve Bearnagh. You will need to keep well to the right of some steep granite slabs as you climb above the gap, but once above them you can drift back towards the wall and follow it further uphill. The wall climbs steeply uphill, and levels out briefly on the shoulder of Slieve Bearnagh. There is a rocky tor off to the right, but on the next ascent you reach a truly monstrous excrescence. The Mourne Wall runs up to this monolith of granite, but if you are a cautious walker you do not need to climb over it. Keep to the right of the tor and you will find a fairly well-trodden path passing it. The summit of Slieve Bearnagh rises to 739m (2,394ft) and offers a fine view around the Mountains of Mourne and far beyond, as follows:

| | |
|---|---|
| N | Slieve Croob, Belfast Hills |
| NE | Slievenaglogh |
| E | Slieve Commedagh, Slieve Donard |
| ESE | Cove Mountain, Chimney Rock Mountain |
| SE | Slievelamagan |
| S | Slieve Binnian, Silent Valley |
| SW | Doan, Slieve Muck |
| W | Slieve Meelbeg |
| NW | Slieve Meelmore, Sperrin Mountains |

## The way back to Trassey          *Allow 2 hours*

The safest and most straightforward way down from the summit of Slieve Bearnagh is of course to follow the Mourne Wall downhill. The slope is steep and bouldery, and you need to be careful before landing on the Hare's Gap, as there are steep slabs of granite which appear quite suddenly. The Mourne Wall breaks briefly at this point, where it is replaced by a stretch of fencing. You need to outflank this sudden drop by keeping well to the right of the wall. If you come down on the correct line, you will find a flight of recently constructed stone steps leading down to Hare's Gap, saving you from picking a way down the broken, rocky slope. There is an iron gate in the Mourne Wall on Hare's Gap, where the Brandy Pad exits from the mountains towards Trassey. You will be following the course of this former smugglers' path downhill to Trassey.

Go through the gate and pick your way down into the valley. The path goes down a bouldery slope, where you can later pick up a clearer path that crosses the Trassey River. Soon after, you have to cross over again, to follow a broad track further downstream. Crossing the river in normal flow is simply a matter of splashing across, but in heavy rain it might be swollen, in which case you should keep to one side without crossing. The Trassey Track pulls away from the river as it leaves the valley, and as you walk out on to the more gentle lower slopes of the mountains, you will be led to a swinging gate next to a larger gateway near a stone

sheepfold. All you now need to do to is to retrace your earlier steps along the enclosed part of the Trassey Track, passing a forest to return to the Cecil Newman car park near Trassey.

## Alternative routes

### ESCAPES

If the weather is against you after starting this walk, you might as well restrict your wanderings to following the low-level course of the Ulster Way. If you do venture into the mountains, your navigation is made fairly easy once you are following the course of the Mourne Wall. Escapes from the Mourne Wall are best made from the gaps between the mountain summits. You can escape easily enough from the gap in between Slieve Loughshannagh and Slieve Meelmore; the next escape is from the gap in between Slieve Meelbeg and Slieve Bearnagh. Once you commit yourself to the steep and rocky slopes of Slieve Bearnagh, you should follow the course of the Mourne Wall carefully across the mountain: any other course could lead you on to steep, rocky and dangerous ground. Beyond Slieve Bearnagh is Hare's Gap, from which point you will be completing the full route by descending via the Trassey Track.

### EXTENSIONS

The most ambitious extension to this walk would be to complete the full circuit of the Mourne Wall, which crosses a dozen major summits as it snakes for about 32km (20 miles) around the Mountains of Mourne. This circuit is best started from and finished at the Silent Valley, and it is an expedition to be reserved for tough walkers with plenty of time and stamina to complete the trek. Lesser extensions can be made by including Slieve Muck and Carn Mountain when you first climb into the mountains via the Ott Track, or by adding Slieve Commedagh and Slieve Donard on to the end of the walk. You would probably find it best to alter the finish of the walk if you extend it by any distance, possibly by descending via the Glen River Path and returning through Tollymore Forest Park, or making some other arrangement to be collected.

# Route 7: SLIEVE MUCK

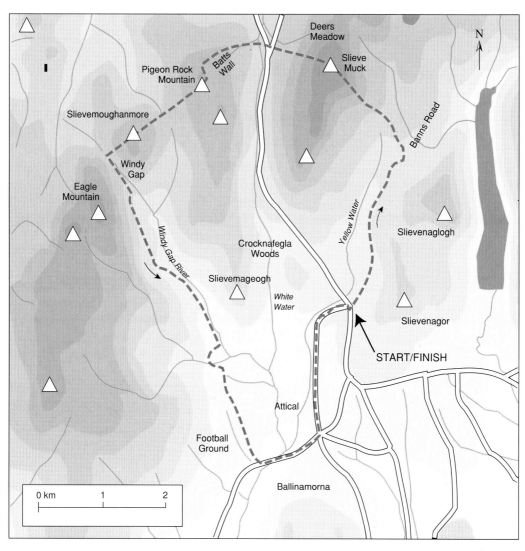

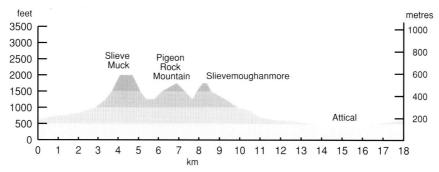

# Route 7: Slieve Muck

**TIME ALLOWANCE** 7½ hours.

**STARTING/FINISHING LOCATION**
Banns Road, near Attical.
OSNI Discoverer 29, OSNI Mourne Country Map:
   GR 285215.
Small car park off the B27 near Attical.
Ulsterbus 34A passes in the summer months only.

**OVERVIEW/INTEREST**
Fine mountain walk, with splendid views of the
   Mountains of Mourne.
Includes part of the Mourne and Batts Walls.
Includes the highest stretch of the Ulster Way.

**FOOTPATHS**
Low-level tracks are very clear and dry.
High-level paths are aligned to obvious walls.
Some boggy areas show signs of erosion.

**STATISTICS**
**WALKING DISTANCE** 20km (12½ miles)
**TOTAL HEIGHT GAINED** 895m (2,935ft)
**PRINCIPAL HEIGHTS**
Slieve Muck 673m (2,198ft)
Pigeon Rock Mountain 534m (1,753ft)
Slievemoughanmore 559m (1,837ft)

*ABOVE:*
*Looking back along Batts Wall to the distant peak of Slieve Bearnagh.*

*OVERLEAF:*
*Straight as a die – Batts Wall, with Slievemoughanmore and Eagle Mountain.*

## The way to Slieve Muck
*Allow 2 hours*

The car park for this walk is only just off the B27 near the village of Attical, but it is easily missed. Look out for it near the point where Attical Road joins the B27. This is not the same as Attical Bog Road, which is the road actually signposted for the village. The car park is at the foot of the Banns Road, the name of the track which you will use to reach the mountains on this walk. Simply follow the stony track past the lower enclosures, and proceed into more rugged open country after passing through a gate. The Banns Road continues as an obvious stony track across the bouldery moorland slopes, and the great bulk of Slieve

Muck rises to the left, across the course of the Yellow Water. You will notice a fairly prominent stone wall leading off to the left towards Slieve Muck, but don't be tempted to follow it. Instead, follow the Banns Road until you reach an iron gate in the Mourne Wall. Do not go through the gate, but enjoy the view towards the dam of the Ben Crom Reservoir. Ben Crom and Doan raise their

45

attractively rocky peaks to the left of the dam, with the awesome peak of Slieve Bearnagh seen further beyond this.

Turn left to follow the course of the Mourne Wall uphill. Unfortunately, in this area the wall does not assume the classic proportions which might be noticed on other walks, but it remains a clear and obvious feature offering a faultless guide up the rugged slopes of Slieve Muck. The ascent of Slieve Muck from the gate on the Banns Road is about 380m (1,245ft). As you begin to follow the wall towards Slieve Muck, you should notice a vague track which, although it drifts away from the wall, offers a reasonably good walking surface for a while. Later, you can follow the wall more closely. The heather-covered, bouldery slope steepens so much that one section of the Mourne Wall was never built, and the gap was filled with a length of post-and-wire fencing. You will need to keep well to the left to climb this part of the slope. The ground continues to rise steeply, and later more gently. There is another steep and rocky climb, where the wall is again replaced by a short length of fencing, but this is quickly passed and the ground gradually begins to level out. The upper slopes of Slieve Muck bear very short grass and a few patches of stones. The trig point will be found away to the left of the Mourne Wall, standing at 673m (2,198ft).

The view from the summit of Slieve Muck is very good in respect of the Mountains of Mourne, but even in clear weather, more distant views will be seen only over the shoulders of other peaks. Look out for some of the following:

| | |
|---|---|
| N | Belfast Hills |
| NNE | Slieve Loughshannagh, Slieve Meelbeg |
| NE | Slieve Bearnagh |
| ENE | Slievelamagan, Slieve Donard |
| ESE | Slieve Binnian |
| S | Knockchree, Howth Head, Wicklow Mountains |
| SW | Carlingford Mountain |
| WSW | Eagle Mountain |
| W | Pigeon Rock Mountain |
| NW | Cock Mountain, Sperrin Mountains |

## The way to the Windy Gap     *Allow 2½ hours*

The Mourne Wall heads northwards along the crest of the mountain. However, you take another wall running roughly westwards. This runs downhill fairly steeply. The only problem on the descent is a short, greasy rock-step which appears suddenly on the lower parts of the slope, but this is easily side-stepped to the left. When you reach the bottom, cross a step-stile and then the B27 at Deers Meadow. Walk across a rushy, triangular patch of ground and cross a minor road, then another step-stile. You are now following a stretch of the Ulster Way, and should spot the 'walking man' waymark as you cross the roadside stile.

Batts Wall runs straight uphill, though at a reasonable gradient over easy ground. The total ascent from the road to the summit is 165m (540ft). The wall bends to the left on the ascent, then makes a sudden right-angled turn to the left on the 534m (1,753ft) summit of Pigeon Rock Mountain. As the wall leaves the summit and runs downhill, there is a sudden bend to the right, before it runs straight down to a low-slung gap. The downhill stretch is fairly easy, although there are some small patches of bog. After crossing the gap, a steep ascent of around 160m (525ft) leads on to Slievemoughanmore. The Ulster Way reaches the highest point in its course as it follows Batts Wall across the summit of the mountain, but walkers who detour away from the wall will be able to reach the summit cairn at 559m (1,837ft). This point offers a splendid view northwards which simply isn't available if you walk only alongside the wall. Follow Batts Wall down from Slievemoughanmore, straight down to the Windy Gap, where you turn left to cross a step-stile at a wall junction.

## The way back to the Banns Road

*Allow 3 hours*

After crossing the step-stile, simply start following another wall roughly south-eastwards down across a slope. The narrow path beside the wall soon joins a much broader and clearer track running down from an old granite quarry. As you continue down the valley of the Windy Gap River, you pass beneath boilerplate slabs of granite on the slopes of Eagle Mountain. The track you are following sometimes has a gravelly surface or bears short grass, but occasionally it features split granite setts for short lengths. One small stream crossing the track is actually culverted beneath a row of setts. After passing beneath a rugged, gully-slashed cliff face, the track levels out in an area of boulders.

You will find yourself running quite close to the Windy Gap River, but avoid the temptation to cross a footbridge. Looking across the river, however, you will notice a stand of attractive pines planted on the slopes of Slievemageogh. A small sign points out that a lane ahead is private, and advises walkers how to proceed. You will need to keep well to the right of a white house seen ahead, following a boundary wall across bouldery, boggy ground until you have passed the building. You will then find yourself alongside a river, which you cross using a footbridge a short way downstream.

Ahead is a stony track, which you follow onwards. The track runs over a rise, and you will be treated to a fine view of the mountains you have climbed during the day, as well as noting the presence of Slieve Binnian's rugged crest of granite tors, and the monstrous towering tor on the summit of Slieve Bearnagh. When the track begins to run downhill, it passes a water treatment works and proceeds as a narrow tarmac road. You will later notice Holy Cross Park – a Gaelic football pitch – just before you join a minor road. Turn left to follow this minor road towards the village of Attical. The road crosses a bridge over White Water before reaching the village.

Attical is quite small, and you simply turn left along the road in between the Roman Catholic chapel and the village shop. This is Attical Road, which runs roughly northwards to pass a few houses and farms. It later bends to the right and runs up to join the B27. Simply turn right to follow the road straight back to the car park at the start of the Banns Road. There are a couple of bed & breakfasts nearby if you are intending to stay in the area. You will have seen their signs while walking the tarmac sections of this route.

## Alternative routes

ESCAPES

If you start the ascent of Slieve Muck and need an escape route, the best thing you can do is to turn around and abandon the entire walk. If you have crossed Slieve Muck and cannot continue with the walk for any reason, then bail out by following the B27 southwards from Deers Meadow to return to the Banns Road near Attical. You could probably get a lift from a passing motorist if your need was particularly urgent, although the road walk through the mountain pass is quite scenic. Once you have crossed Pigeon Rock Mountain, you could exit via the next gap, but it would make more sense to continue over Slievemoughanmore and complete the walk by following the broad, clear quarry track down from the mountains.

EXTENSIONS

The two most logical and challenging extensions to this route would involve following either the Mourne Wall or Batts Wall onwards. The Mourne Wall describes a complete circuit around the Mountains of Mourne, covering over 32km (20 miles) as it crosses a dozen major High Mourne summits. Batts Wall can be traced over the Low Mournes, crossing Eagle Mountain and Shanlieve before reaching the head of Rostrevor Forest. If you simply wish to extend the circuit given in the route description, then consider staying high around the northern side of the Spelga Dam, instead of simply crossing the Deers Meadow on the southern side. This extra loop would amount to a considerable extension, being rugged underfoot even if not very high.

# Route 8: EAGLE MOUNTAIN

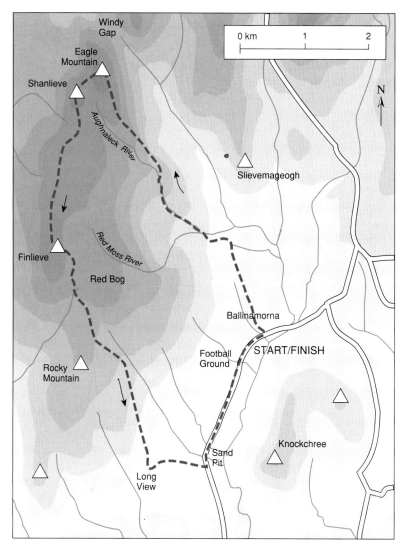

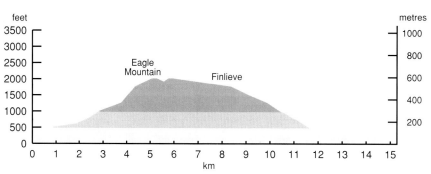

# 3
# LOW MOURNES

## Route 8 : Eagle Mountain

**TIME ALLOWANCE** 5½ hours.

**STARTING/FINISHING LOCATION**
Holy Cross Park, near Attical.
OSNI Discoverer 29, OSNI Mourne Country Map:
  GR 260191.
Small parking spaces by the Sandy Brae.
No bus service.

**OVERVIEW/INTEREST**
Interesting network of old bog roads.
Broad moorland crest with fine views from the
  several summits.
Includes a stretch of Batts Wall.

**FOOTPATHS**
Low-level paths and tracks are clear.
Care is needed in selecting high-level paths, and
  there are no paths over the highest moorlands.
Higher parts can be quite boggy.

**STATISTICS**
**WALKING DISTANCE** 16km (10 miles)
**TOTAL HEIGHT GAINED** 650m (2,130ft)
**PRINCIPAL HEIGHTS**
Eagle Mountain 638m (2,084ft)
Shanlieve 627m (2,056ft)
Finlieve 579m (1,889ft)

## The way to Eagle Mountain
*Allow 2 hours*

Take great care parking at the start of this walk.
There is a private car park attached to the Gaelic
Football ground at Holy Cross Park, but only use
this with permission. There are small spaces

alongside the Sandy Brae road, but park off the
road and do not obstruct any gateways or
driveways. Do not block access to the water
treatment works either. If in doubt, ask for
permission to park.

You start this walk by following the Sandy Brae
road away from Holy Cross Park. The road is
narrow and surfaced with tarmac as far as the
water treatment works, then it continues as a
gravel road. There are some fine views towards the
High Mournes from a couple of rises along the
road. Looking ahead, you will be aiming to climb
Eagle Mountain, Shanlieve and Finlieve, which
are all arranged along the high crest to your left.
Follow the gravel road almost to the last buildings,
but leave the road before you actually reach them.
You will find a grassy track on the left, but if you
reach any of the buildings, or get as far as a
footbridge, then turn back a short way to locate the
grassy track.

The track runs gently uphill and proceeds along
the line of a fence for a while. Go through a gate
in this fence and follow the line of the track
onwards. Cross the Red Moss River at a bouldery
ford and note how the track is now deeply cut into
the rugged moorland slope. Invasive bracken
occurs in patches among the heather, but the track
steers a way through it all. Cross another stream,
follow the track onwards and upwards, and then
cross the Aughnaleck River. A short climb leads
above the river, before the track bends to the left
to continue uphill. The course of the track becomes
more and more vague, but you should be able to
trace it to a point where a few granite setts have
been cut from an outcrop. In any case, the track is

now running at a high level and either proceeds along the heathery moorland crest, or follows a line of cliffs overlooking the valley. Whatever vague path you find among the heather and boulders will eventually peter out, and the cliff-line you are following will eventually give way to the final gentle climb on to the heathery dome of Eagle Mountain. There is a bouldery cairn on the 638m (2,084ft) summit. At this point you can pause and sample the view, which is reasonably extensive on a clear day and includes some of the following:

NE      Slievemoughanmore, Pigeon Rock
        Mountain
ENE     Slieve Muck, Slievelamagan, Slieve
        Donard
E       Slievenaglogh, Slieve Binnian.
SSE     Knockchree
SSW     Finlieve
WSW     Shanlieve
W       Slieve Gullion
NW      The Sperrin Mountains

## The way to Finlieve                    *Allow 1 hour*

There is no problem starting the high-level walk from Eagle Mountain to Finlieve in any weather, but in poor visibility the journey can quickly become quite difficult for all but competent navigators. To get from Eagle Mountain to the neighbouring summit of Shanlieve, simply follow Batts Wall across the gentle gap between the two summits. There is an accumulation of rain-washed sand on the heathery gap, before the wall leads up on to Shanlieve. Simply bear to the left of a corner on the wall to reach the summit cairn at 627m (2056ft). The view looking westwards is rather better from the summit of Shanlieve than it is from Eagle Mountain.

There is no path or any sort of useful guide between the summit of Shanlieve and the distant hump of Finlieve. In the intervening space is a broad and boggy moorland crest liberally covered with a decaying blanket bog riven into hags and groughs. By heading roughly southwards from

Shanlieve you will be led on to a broad, gentle gap where most of the peat has washed away to leave a firm surface of stones. Once across the gap, however, you will start crossing the boggy part of this upland walk. There is no easy way through it all, although you could try following some of the peaty channels if you think they are going your way. There are a couple of areas where stony ground provides a firmer footing, but you will either hit or miss these depending on your exact course. You must persevere, and once you are across this broad and boggy hump the ground becomes much better for walking. The final climb on to the gentle hump of Finlieve is accomplished on a firm, grassy surface. There is a small cairn on the top of the hill at 579m (1,889ft). Views towards the mouth of Carlingford Lough and beyond to Dublin and the Wicklow Mountains are quite good, and if the weather is good you might like to pause for a while on this quiet summit.

## The way back to Holy Cross Park

*Allow 2½ hours*

Head roughly south-eastwards to leave the summit of Finlieve and you will drop down a grassy slope towards the Red Bog. This is a cutaway bog now reverting to nature, but leading away from it you can still discern the old bog roads. Simply link with the most obvious one of these and start following it down the broad moorland slopes. It eventually straightens itself and becomes a plain and obvious line to follow. The track descends across the slopes of Rocky Mountain and is eventually deflected to the right when it encounters field boundaries further downhill. Keep following the path until you have to go through a gate. The track is now more stony and it runs downhill enclosed by fences or walls, or is flanked by masses of gorse. When it eventually lands on a tarmac road it does so beside a house called Long View.

Turn left along the narrow tarmac road here and let the road lead you around a bend to the right. Walk straight along the road past fields and farms until you reach a junction with a slightly wider tarmac road. Turn left here and start walking back towards Attical. You will pass the entrance to a gravel pit, as well as many more farms, houses and small fields. The road is straight for a while, but when it does start to bend to the right you are quite close to the end of the walk. Holy Cross Park and the Sandy Brae road will be found off to the left.

## Alternative routes

### ESCAPES

In foul weather or poor visibility, the chances for dodgy navigators to go astray on the higher parts of this walk are increased. You could probably reach the summit of Eagle Mountain simply by continually climbing uphill from the end of the access paths. If you require firm guidance beyond this point you would be well advised to follow Batts Wall down to the Windy Gap, and then follow the course of a wall and an old quarry track back towards the Sandy Brae road. Once you commit yourself to following the broad and boggy moorland crest you should stick with it until you can follow the bog roads off the slopes of Finlieve.

If you want to cut out some of the road walking at the end of the route you could try linking with the course of the Red Moss River and following it downstream, to land back on the Sandy Brae where you left it earlier.

### EXTENSIONS

For a good, long extension to this walk you would be advised to trace the route in the opposite direction, then keep a close eye on the amount of time you can spare for a long walk. When you reach the summit of Eagle Mountain, you could follow Batts Wall over Slievemoughanmore and Pigeon Rock Mountain, and maybe continue over Slieve Muck to link with the course of the Mourne Wall as well. In fact, Batts Wall could also be followed in the other direction to reach the head of Rostrevor Forest, or you could head off in that direction before attempting to traverse a high-level route towards Slieve Martin. It is also possible to construct circular walks over these summits from either the Kilbroney or Leitrim sides of the range.

*The dome of Eagle Mountain as seen from the village of Attical.*

# Route 9: SLIEVE MARTIN

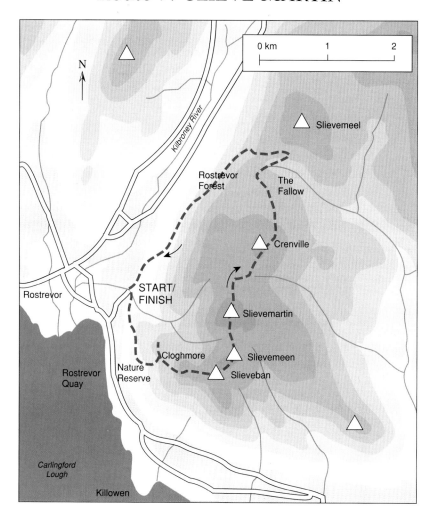

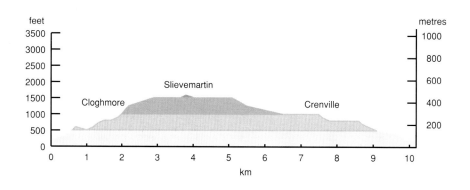

# Route 9: Slieve Martin

**TIME ALLOWANCE** 4½ hours.

**STARTING/FINISHING LOCATION**
Rostrevor Forest, Rostrevor.
OSNI Discoverer 29, OSNI Mourne Country Map:
  GR 185180.
Large car park in the forest.
Ulsterbus 39 serves Rostrevor.

**OVERVIEW/INTEREST**
Passes through the important Rostrevor Oakwood
  National Nature Reserve and Rostrevor Forest,
  with short waymarked trails.
Features Cloghmore – a spectacular 40-tonne
  boulder.
Fine views around Carlingford Lough.
Includes a short stretch of the Ulster Way.

**FOOTPATHS**
Low-level forest tracks are firm and clear.
Upland paths vary from clear to vague.
Some upland stretches have no paths.

**STATISTICS**
**WALKING DISTANCE** 12 km (7½ miles)
**TOTAL HEIGHT GAINED** 530m (1,740ft)
**PRINCIPAL HEIGHT** Slieve Martin 485m (1,597ft)

## The way to Slieve Martin                    *Allow 2 hours*

Slieve Martin rises dramatically from the waters of
Carlingford Lough near Rostrevor, or as Percy
French might have put it, the slopes of the
mountains 'sweep down to the sea'. It is unfortunate that they are covered in forest, as this
gives an impression of dullness and uniformity. In
fact, there is an interesting ancient oakwood on
the lower slopes, which is protected as an
important National Nature Reserve, and the higher
forest is soon left behind. A moorland crest offers
good walking and fine views before the route again
enters forest, and even then there are views across
the valley of the Kilbroney River. The route is fairly
short but it can be extended, although this would
result in a longer return through the forest if
tarmac roads in the valley are to be avoided.

Rostrevor Forest is signposted from the main A2
just outside Rostrevor village, and you should park
as directed by signs along the access road. There
are information boards and a café immediately
available at the car park. Walk back downhill from
the car park to reach the Forest Office, and then
turn left to pass in front of it. Just beyond the office
is a path on the left signposted for Rostrevor
Oakwood. There are also marker posts bearing
black and yellow arrows, denoting two of the
shorter waymarked trails in the forest. The path
passes an old quarry before you need to turn left
along a broader track. A large sign indicates that
you are entering the Rostrevor Oakwood National
Nature Reserve, while a smaller sign points the
way to Fiddler's Green. This broad path zigzags up
the richly wooded slope and reaches the grassy
clearing known as the Fiddler's Green. There is a
sign confirming that you have reached this point,
as well as a bench if you want to rest at this stage
in the climb. Notice how the trees of the Rostrevor
Oakwood suddenly give way to forest trees at this
particular point.

When you continue above Fiddler's Green, you
will reach a forest track and you should turn right.
Immediately after crossing a gentle rise on this
track, turn left to follow a narrower, grassy path
uphill through the forest. The gradient is steeper,
but you will soon reach the edge of the forest and
proceed on to gentler and more open slopes
beyond. Bear to the left across the open ground,
passing a few low outcrops of rock, or small
boulders, before reaching Cloghmore. This 40-
tonne boulder is perched on a brow overlooking
Rostrevor, Warrenpoint and Carlingford Lough,
and it is worth a few moments of your time to see
it. Many previous visitors have carved or painted
their names upon the rock, but it is hoped that
readers will resist the temptation to leave their
mark! The Cloghmore boulder is a feature which

*Cloghmore – the spectacular boulder perched high above Rostrevor Forest.*

you will later be looking down upon from the top of Slieve Martin. According to legend, the boulder was hurled across Carlingford Lough by Fionn MacCumhail at a rival giant.

Retrace your steps from Cloghmore, but do not go back into the forest. Instead, follow a narrow path which zigzags up a steep slope in between a clear-felled area to the left and a mature stand of trees to the right. Further up the slope, the narrow path follows the line of a tumbledown stone wall and a fence. As you follow this course, you will first be treated to views of Carlingford Lough, and then be led downhill a short way to touch a clear path briefly at the top edge of Rostrevor Forest. As soon as you hit this path, leave it to the right to follow a rather vague path uphill. A marker post bearing a black arrow confirms the course you should take. The vague path drifts away from the fence and reaches the summit of Slieve Martin. A trig point is surrounded by a scattering of stones at 485m (1,597ft). The clear-felling on the lower slopes of Slieve Martin is a mess, but at least it has opened up the views, and when the next stands of forest become well established the scenes of

devastation should be obscured. Further afield, the views are rather more attractive. A round-up of near and distant features could include:

| | |
|---|---|
| NE | Eagle Mountain, Slieve Muck |
| ENE | Slieve Donard, Slieve Binnian |
| SSW | Carlingford Mountain |
| S | Howth Head, Dublin, Wicklow Mountains |
| W | Clermont, Cooley Hills |
| WNW | Slieve Gullion, Camlough Mountain |
| NW | Sperrin Mountains |

## The way back to Rostrevor  *Allow 2½ hours*

Leave the trig point on Slieve Martin and walk back towards the fence, then turn left to follow the fence northwards. You will be walking on predominantly heather-covered ground, while across the fence it is grassier. When you reach a junction of fences, turn right to continue along a forest fence. As you follow the fence, the trees on the left suddenly thin out, so that you can turn left and walk along an unplanted swathe. The grass is tussocky and there are hidden holes in the ground, but you will find a line of old fenceposts to follow across the ruggedly vegetated slopes of Crenville. Soon after this fence-line starts to descend, and where it runs more closely to a stand of trees, you should drift to the left away from it. You will cross an unplanted area which features even more tussocky grass. The idea is to reach a forest track leaving the area known as The Fallow. Young trees have been planted near the track, but even when these are growing higher there will still be space to reach it. Once you land on the firm gravel track, the hard part of the walk is over. The return to the car park is entirely along forest tracks.

Turn right to follow the track, and keep right to enter a taller stand of forestry. At the next junction, turn left to follow a track on the edge of Rostrevor Forest, looking on to the slopes of Slievemeel. By the time the track runs downhill and bends to the left, you can enjoy a view along the length of the valley of the Kilbroney River. Simply continue downhill along the forest track, passing from an area of fairly young trees into a more mature part of Rostrevor Forest. Keep to the right at two junctions with other forest tracks, until you reach a barrier gate and a narrow tarmac road. Turn left along the tarmac road, passing another barrier gate, and keep low to return to the car park where you started. Although there is a café in the forest, you will find that nearby Rostrevor offers good refreshments, and there are places to stay in and around the village.

## Alternative routes

ESCAPES

The wooded and forested slopes rising above Rostrevor can shelter walkers from the weather whenever it becomes more severe on the higher, more open slopes. It is possible at places such as the Cloghmore boulder and on the summit of Slieve Martin to switch back on to forest tracks and take a route back down to the car park. In fact, by using a higher car park in the clear-felled part of the forest, you could cut the ascent of Slieve Martin to a minimum. Once you head through the forest across the tough and tussocky slopes of Crenville, continue with the route as described.

EXTENSIONS

If you are staying in the village of Rostrevor, a short extension to the route simply involves walking through the attractive Kilbroney Park to reach Rostrevor Forest. At the other end of the scale, the high-level portion of the route could be extended over Slievemeel, or even as far as Shanlieve and Eagle Mountain. If you go this far, you could descend along the course of Batts Wall and follow the forest tracks used by the Ulster Way to return to the car park at the opposite end of Rostrevor Forest. If you want to sample a challenging walk from one end of the Mournes to the other, then providing you have the necessary skills and stamina you could try to keep to a high-level course all the way from Rostrevor to Newcastle. Your first summit would be Slieve Martin, and if you were fortunate your last summit could be Slieve Donard much later in the day. The courses taken by Batts Wall and the Mourne Wall would all feature very strongly on this type of high-level walk.

*The summit of Slieve Martin, overlooking Carlingford Lough.*

# Route 10:  SLIEVE GULLION

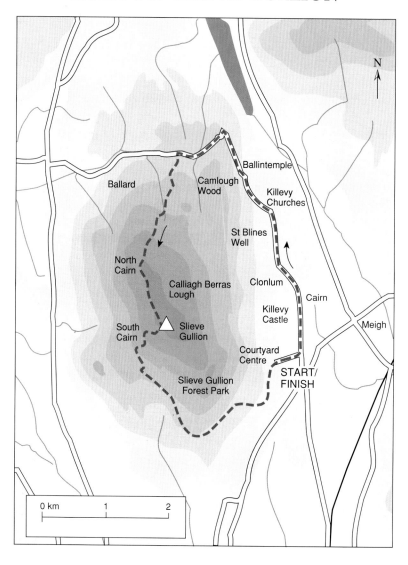

Ballintemple

Ballard

Camlough Wood

Killevy Churches

St Blines Well

North Cairn

Calliagh Berras Lough

Clonlum

Cairn

South Cairn

Slieve Gullion

Killevy Castle

Meigh

Courtyard Centre

START/ FINISH

Slieve Gullion Forest Park

0 km      1      2

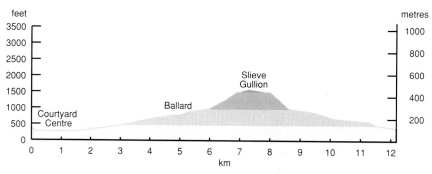

feet                                                        metres

3500                                                        1000

3000

2500                                                        800

2000                          Slieve
                              Gullion                       600

1500
                                                            400
1000        Courtyard          Ballard
500         Centre                                          200

0
    0   1   2   3   4   5   6   7   8   9   10  11  12
                            km

# 4
# ULSTER BORDER COUNTRY

## Route 10: Slieve Gullion

**TIME ALLOWANCE**  5½ hours.

**STARTING/FINISHING LOCATION**
Slieve Gullion Courtyard Centre.
OSNI Discoverer 29: GR 042196.
Large car park at the Centre.
Ulsterbus 43 serves Meigh.

**OVERVIEW/INTEREST**
A land of myths and legends, including
   Cuchulainn and Fionn MacCumhail.
Takes in Slieve Gullion Forest Park and Courtyard
   Centre.
Ascends one of Ireland's most revered mountains,
   with extensive views from the summit.
Features numerous archaeological remains and a
   geological curiosity – the Ring of Gullion.

**FOOTPATHS**
Low-level roads and forest tracks are clear.
Hill paths can be well trodden, vague or absent.
The line of descent is badly eroded in places.

**STATISTICS**
**WALKING DISTANCE**   13km (8 miles)
**TOTAL HEIGHT GAINED**   475m (1,560ft)
**PRINCIPAL HEIGHT**   Slieve Gullion   573m (1,894ft)

### The way to Ballard
*Allow 2 hours*

Slieve Gullion has its place in the early mythology
of Ireland, and derives its name from Cullan the
Smith. Cullan's fierce hound was killed by the
young boy Setanta, who then took the hound's
place and became known as the Hound of Cullan

– or Cuchulainn – Ireland's most notable warrior
hero. The Slieve Gullion Forest Park is well
signposted from many roads around Newry and
South Armagh. Follow these signs and you will be
led towards the village of Meigh, close to the
entrance to the Forest Park. The access road leads
to a large car park near the Courtyard Centre.

If you want information about Slieve Gullion
and the Forest Park, then start at the Courtyard
Centre. This building includes an exhibition area,
craft workshops, restaurant, self-catering accommodation and facilities for school groups. A couple
of short nature trails leave the Courtyard Centre
and these are well used. A lengthy looped Forest
Drive is available on the southern and western
slopes of Slieve Gullion, and part of this will be
encountered on the walk. The Forest Drive is also
used by people who want to climb Slieve Gullion
the easy way, as there is a clear path to the summit
from a high-level car park. The walk described
below is a lengthier circuit around the base and
along the crest of Slieve Gullion.

Leave the car park by following the road marked
'Exit' and head down to a crossroads before
turning left. Follow a minor road roughly
northwards to Clonlum, where you can inspect a
chambered cairn just to the right of the road. On
the left side of the road you will catch a glimpse of
the large house known as Killevy Castle. Continue
through a minor crossroads past houses and farms.
Look uphill to the left and you should spot the
whitewashed St Bline's Well on the slopes of Slieve
Gullion. More obvious are the ruins of the Killevy
Churches, where two churches have been joined
together just to the left of the road. This is a curious

structure, as the churches were actually built centuries apart.

The road forks just beyond the Killevy Churches, and you should keep left and follow a minor road uphill to pass a forested slope. As you climb, the view begins to open up across a wide area of fields surrounded by rugged little hills, marred only by the presence of army observation towers and masts. The road forks again and you should keep left to climb uphill more steeply for a short while. It then emerges from the forest at a small car park and picnic site, and you continue to the highest stretch of the road, where you will find a ruined farmstead on the right and another one a short way ahead on the left. You can leave the road at this point by going through a gate on the left.

## The way to Slieve Gullion          *Allow 2 hours*

After passing through the gate, a clear track leads you across a large field and then through another gate. The track then proceeds as a ribbon of short, green grass up slopes of deep heather. You will pass a metal waymark arrow welded on to the top of a bar set into the ground. This is one of a series of four which you might spot while you are climbing Slieve Gullion. Treat them with a little suspicion, as some of them are easily turned around and you are therefore at the mercy of any walkers who have gone before you! In fact, there should be no problem following the grassy track uphill, but it does eventually expire in deep heather on a steep slope. You then have to pick a way uphill without the benefit of a clear path, passing a couple of low rocky outcrops as the ground steepens. If you need an excuse for a rest, then the view northwards is expanding all the time. Ultimately, you will reach a sprawling burial cairn known as the North Cairn, and at this point you might as well pause for a rest.

You may have found a narrow and rather vague path on the ascent, but you should find a much clearer path along the crest of Slieve Gullion. In mist, you can rely on a line of fenceposts to lead you to the small pool called the Calliagh Berras Lough. The warrior Fionn MacCumhail had the unfortunate experience of being lured into the

pool, whereupon he emerged as a wizened, white-haired old man. His warrior friends had to dig into the summit cairn on Slieve Gullion to find the Calliagh Berras, the woman who had caused the enchantment. She was forced to restore Fionn to his original state, but his former head of red hair remained white. If you keep around the left-hand side of the pool you will drift away from the fenceposts and you should then pick up a reasonably well-trodden path through heather and boulders to reach the main summit.

The huge burial cairn on Slieve Gullion is known as the Calliagh Berras House, and it bears a trig point and view indicator at 573m (1,894ft). You have the option of crawling into the burial chamber via a passageway in the side of the cairn. A skylight allows light to enter, so that you can see around the inside without the aid of a torch. The distant view is remarkably extensive, but the arrangement of the rugged little hills of the Ring of Gullion is more intriguing. On a clear day you should be able to spot most of these features:

| | |
|---|---|
| N | Lough Neagh |
| NNE | Camlough Mountain |
| NE | Slieve Croob |
| ENE | Mountains of Mourne |
| E | Slieve Martin |
| SE | Cooley Hills, Carlingford Mountain |
| SSE | Hill of Howth, Dublin |
| S | Wicklow Mountains |
| SSW | Croslieve, Slieve Bloom Mountains |
| W | Cuilcagh |
| WNW | Slieve Beagh |
| NW | Sperrin Mountains |
| NNW | Slieve Gallion |

The Ring of Gullion is a peculiar geological formation which was caused during a period of volcanic upheaval. A cylindrical section of the earth's crust, measuring some 11km (7 miles) across, foundered and began to sink. All around the circular fracture zone, molten rock rose to fill the space. Slieve Gullion's dome of granite is therefore now left at the centre of a rugged 'ring dyke' which has resisted erosion and now appears as a circular range of little mountains. The little

*A prow of rock offers a viewpoint on the northern slopes of Slieve Gullion.*

peaks around the Ring of Gullion include: Courtney Mountain, Sturgan Mountain, Camlough Mountain, Cloghoge Mountain, Fathom Mountain, Anglesey Mountain, Clermont, Feede Mountain, Slievebolea, Cofracloghy, Tievecrom, Croslieve, Slievebrack, Mullaghbane Mountain, Carrigans Hill and Slievenacappel.

## The way back to the Courtyard Centre

*Allow 1½ hours*

If you locate the entrance to the chamber inside the summit burial cairn on Slieve Gullion, then you only need to start walking downhill on that side of the cairn to locate the path leading down from the summit. This is a clear line trodden through the rugged slopes of rock and heather, and in places it is becoming quite badly eroded. You will pass a shelter which has been built into the side of the hill, and then continue downhill until you reach a fence. Turn left and cross the fence using a step-stile. Walk down a clear track into the forest, passing another shelter and turning left along the narrow tarmac road of the Slieve Gullion Forest Drive. The Forest Drive gradually turns around the southern side of Slieve Gullion, running roughly south-eastwards and north-eastwards. When it descends through a clear-felled area, look out to the right and you will spot another narrow road running parallel below. If you look carefully, you will spot a very short path dropping down to the lower road. You can take this path and then turn left along the lower road. The lower road runs more steeply downhill and eventually swings left to return to the Courtyard Centre.

## Alternative routes

### ESCAPES

Once you are committed to climbing Slieve Gullion, you might as well continue with the walk and descend using the clear path. Direct descents towards the Courtyard Centre are to be discouraged, as they either lead into dense stands of trees or on to difficult ground where clear-felling has occurred. If time is pressing and you are determined to climb Slieve Gullion, follow the Forest Drive by car until you emerge from the trees at a high-level car park. You can easily make the shortest possible ascent to the summit from the roadside, and enjoy the view.

### EXTENSIONS

Slieve Gullion is a solitary mountain, and so cannot easily be linked with other heights. There are certainly tougher ascents – either climbing above St Bline's Well or using lengthy firebreaks on the forested western slopes. Any attempt to move away from Slieve Gullion will involve lengthy road walks. The eye is naturally led around the rugged peaks of the Ring of Gullion, but walkers who attempt to make a tour around the Ring will find that walls, fences, forestry, rock, bog, deep heather, gorse and brambles soon bring progress to a halt. There are plans to open up a few short walks on the little hills of the Ring of Gullion, and in time it might be possible to enjoy longer walks. The nearest easily walked range of hills would be the Cooley Hills and Carlingford Mountain, and explorations are recommended.

# Route 11: SLIEVE BEAGH

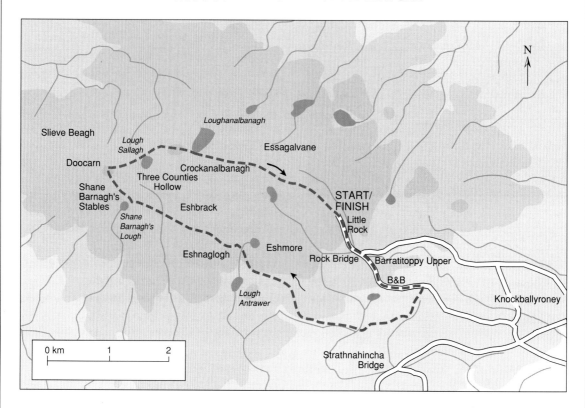

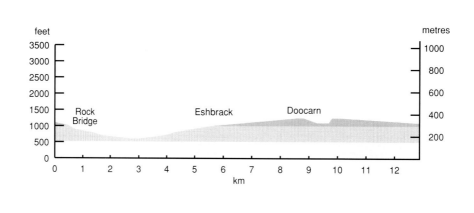

# Route 11: Slieve Beagh

**TIME ALLOWANCE**   4½ hours.

**STARTING/FINISHING LOCATION**
Barratitoppy Upper, near Knockatallan.
OSNI Discoverer 18, GR 562427.
Small parking space by the roadside at Little Rock.
No bus services.

**OVERVIEW/INTEREST**
Land of myth and legend, featuring Shane
   Barnagh's Stables.
Extensive open moorlands with high-level bog
   roads, and wide-ranging views.
Relatively unexplored.

**FOOTPATHS**
Minor roads and bog roads are firm and dry.
No paths cross the extensive moorlands.
The higher parts can be wet and boggy.

**STATISTICS**
**WALKING DISTANCE**   13km (8 miles)
**TOTAL HEIGHT GAINED**   240m (785ft)
**PRINCIPAL HEIGHT**   Doocarn   380m (1,255ft)

## The way to Eshnaglogh

*Allow 2 hours*

Slieve Beagh is a remote, rolling moorland largely surrounded by forestry plantations. The counties of Monaghan, Fermanagh and Tyrone meet in Three Counties Hollow close to the highest point on the moorland – the broad rise known as Doocarn. This is bleak and unfrequented country, and yet it has an important place in Irish mythology. When Noah set sail in his famous Ark, there was another vessel carrying Bith, Ladra, Fintan, the princess Cesair and her 50 handmaidens. This alternative ark reached Ireland, where the 50 handmaidens were shared out among the three men. Bith complained that he was one woman short, but he later achieved fame by being the first man to die in Ireland. Slieve Beagh was named after him. In early Christian times, St Dympna was on the run from her father, who wanted to marry her, and she crossed Slieve Beagh on her way from Clogher to Tydavnet. She eventually reached Geel, in Belgium, where her father caught up with her and promptly beheaded her. Nowadays, Tydavnet is twinned with Geel, and so there are probably more Belgians aware of Slieve Beagh than elsewhere in the world!

Finding your way to the start of this walk can be difficult. You should use either the R186 from Monaghan or the B83 from Clogher – roads which were formerly severed at the Border but are now open for through traffic again. This was once the main Dublin to Derry coach road. Follow a sign for Knockatallan, then navigate carefully along minor roads to reach Barratitoppy Upper. There is a solitary bed & breakfast beside the road near Lough Meenish. If you are accommodated there you will be able to park on-site, but if not you should proceed up the road, through a forest, across the Rock Bridge, and then keep left and park by the Little Rock – the first patch of rock high up on the right-hand side of the road. If you can navigate your way thus far, then you should be able to cope with the actual walk!

Follow the road back downhill on foot, cross the Rock Bridge and continue along the road through the forest until you pass the bed & breakfast near Lough Meenish. A little further down the road, turn right along a clear track and follow this past a straggle of farm buildings until you reach the next minor road. Close all gates after you – especially the last one leading on to the road. Turn right to follow the minor road uphill, climbing from fields into an area of high moorlands. You will pass a small quarry before the tarmac on the road becomes quite badly potholed. Pass the lonely Lough Antrawer and continue along the rough track, bearing left at a junction of tracks, and walk to a turning space at the end of the track at Eshnaglogh. Beyond this point you will be walking across bleak, open, rugged moorlands where in poor visibility you will need to be a competent navigator. In clear weather, you still need to take great care over route-finding, but at least you will be able to enjoy the far-reaching views.

## The way to Doocarn                    *Allow 1 hour*

Walk roughly north-westwards over the moorland, crossing an area where turf has been cut from the bog, but later reaching an uncut area. You will need to forge through deep, tough, tussocky vegetation as you cross a shallow valley. There are a few slender little trees and shrubs growing here. You will cross the Border as you make your way through this valley, although the actual line may not be quite the same as a post-and-wire fence which you also need to cross. As you switch from Monaghan to Fermanagh, the heathery ground is a little easier to negotiate, although some high stepping is still required in places. Head across the moorland rise to locate the lonely little moorland pool of Shane Barnagh's Lough. Shane Barnagh is reputed to have been a 'rob from the rich and give to the poor' type of rapparee (freebooter), and as he was killed without revealing his hidden hoard it is widely believed to be somewhere deep in the lough. The map also notes Shane Barnagh's Stables, which turns out to be a long gash in the underlying gritstone. As this feature appears quite suddenly without prior warning, it is safe to assume that someone could have laid low and not have been easily observed by anyone else who happened to be crossing Slieve Beagh.

Ahead you can see the remains of a high-level forestry plantation. Although the going underfoot is still quite tough, you will find the easiest course is to walk just to the left of the plantation. The few trees which survive on this exposed moorland plot are hardly thriving, and most have been reduced to bleached skeletons. When you pass the last of the trees, aim for anything which looks as if it might be the summit of Doocarn at 380m (1,255ft). The immediate scene is remarkable – rather like being adrift on a rolling ocean of moorland. If you study your map very carefully, you can try to work out which humps or bumps are in Monaghan, Fermanagh and Tyrone.

Identifying the exact location of the county boundaries in Three Counties Hollow takes even more skill. Looking at the wider prospect, the view is indeed extensive, as Slieve Beagh is such an isolated crest of moorland. In very clear weather, you should be able to enjoy a remarkably distant panorama which could include:

| | |
|---|---|
| N | Mullaghcarn, Inishowen Peninsula |
| NNE | Sawel, Sperrin Mountains |
| NE | Antrim Mountains |
| ENE | Belfast Hills |
| E | Slieve Croob |
| ESE | Slieve Gullion, Mountains of Mourne |
| SSE | Wicklow Mountains |
| S | Slieve Bloom Mountains |
| WSW | Cuilcagh |
| W | Belmore Mountain, Truskmore |
| NW | Donegal Highlands |

## The way back to Barratitoppy

*Allow 1½ hours*

You leave Doocarn by walking roughly westwards towards the shining pool of Lough Sallagh. As you make your way over a broad and boggy depression you are crossing the boundary between Fermanagh and Tyrone. The Border between Monaghan and Tyrone actually runs through the lough, and you will find the walking easier if you keep well to the left of the lough and stay in Tyrone for a while longer. Aim to walk along the broad moorland crest, which may or may not bear a slender mast next to a wooden hut (the whole assembly has a temporary look about it). After crossing a couple of broad moorland rises you will pass the head of Loughanalbanagh, then climb a short way up the rugged slopes of Crockanalbanagh. Looking at the map, it seems fair to say 'walk towards the northern side of Lough Galluane', but in fact the former lough is completely grassed over and no longer exists. However, you can still make out its curved shape where the level grass meets the more rugged moorland slopes surrounding it. Another thing which helps to identify this spot is the fact that turf-cutting has taken place on the moorland gap just to one side of the former lough. You should walk through the cuttings, and in doing so you will cross the Border between Tyrone and Monaghan. Look for the tracks of vehicles on the bare black peat and hope that they lead you straight on to the end of a firm bog road. When you have located this road, simply walk along its gravelly top and continue south-eastwards until you hit a minor road. Keep right and you will be led straight back to the Little Rock where you parked at the start of the walk.

## Alternative routes

### ESCAPES

The only real escape from Slieve Beagh is either not to go out on to the open moorlands, or simply to turn around and retrace your steps if you find that the vegetation or boggy areas are becoming too difficult. Do not venture on to these bleak moorlands in poor visibility unless you are proficient with a map and compass. If you lose your way on Slieve Beagh you could end up floundering aimlessly among extensive bogs, amongst other hazards.

### EXTENSIONS

These broad moorland slopes offer the scope for much longer walks than the simple circuit described. As there are no really prominent ridges or summits, you can walk in virtually any direction without feeling that you are losing too much height. You could gain access to the open moorlands by choosing either bog roads or forest tracks – and there are plenty which lead on to these extensive slopes. You could either aim to complete an extended circular walk, or make a more challenging traverse across the entire length of Slieve Beagh. You could link the lonely moorland loughs like a string of shining gems, or make an enormous looped walk by including the course of the Ulster Way as it uses forest tracks and some minor roads on the northern slopes of Slieve Beagh.

*At Shane Barnagh's Stables overlooking Shane Barnagh's Lough.*

# Route 12: THE PLAYBANK

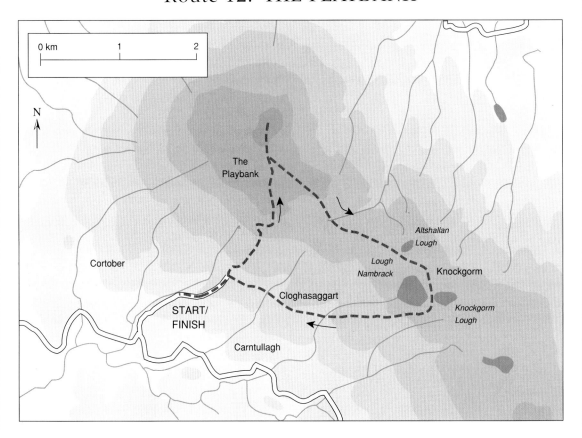

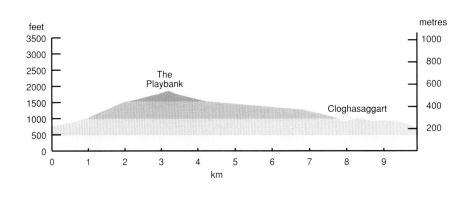

# Route 12: The Playbank

**TIME ALLOWANCE**   4½ hours.

**STARTING/FINISHING LOCATION**
Cortober, near Ballinagleragh.
OSNI Discoverer 26: GR 021236.
Small parking spaces by the roadside.
No bus service.

**OVERVIEW/INTEREST**
Splendid, rugged moorland crest.
Fine views around the North West.
Heart of ancient Breffni.

**FOOTPATHS**
Clear track running on to the high moorlands.
Pathless moorland terrain, with some boggy areas.
A number of fences to be crossed later.

**STATISTICS**
**WALKING DISTANCE**   11km (7 miles)
**TOTAL HEIGHT GAINED**   360m (1,180ft)
**PRINCIPAL HEIGHT**   The Playbank 542m (1,787ft)

## The way to The Playbank          *Allow 1½ hours*

You will need your map to hand to navigate to the start of this walk. First you will need to reach Ballinagleragh on the R207 between Dowra and Drumshanbo, not far from the shores of Lough Allen – the first large lough on the mighty River Shannon. A network of minor roads climbs uphill to the east of Ballinagleragh, and you will need to find your way through them until you are following a high-level dead-end road at Cortober. There are only a couple of parking spaces beside this road, so park considerately and do not block any access points to farms or fields. This is a quiet area and you are unlikely to have much competition for parking space. The actual grid reference given is a point where a track branches off the road, and if you go much further up the road you may need to turn around and drive back a short way along the road.

When you start the walk, you simply follow the narrow road uphill until it becomes a clear track running onwards. It is enclosed at first, and runs along the crest of a spur which leads towards the higher moorlands. After passing through a final gate, you are on an open moorland slope, with The Playbank directly in front of you. The track is still fairly easy to discern, although in places it is little more than a rushy path, and if you keep following it uphill it bends to the left, then sharply to the right, to climb on to the top of a rocky brow. Beyond this point, the line of the track disappears on the heathery moorland slope. However, if you keep walking roughly northwards you will be on course to reach the summit of The Playbank. You will be walking through heather and bog, sprinkled with a few boulders and featuring a couple of low outcrops of rock. There is a trig point on the summit at 542m (1,787ft) and some older maps refer to the area as The Playground. Whether you call it Playbank or Playground, it is an unusual name, and one which refers to the ancient Celtic festivities which used to take place on the hillside around midsummer – Lughnasa in the Celtic calendar. You are in the heart of ancient Breffni, where pre-Christian traditions lingered longer than in most other parts of Ireland. You can sample the view, which stretches all around the north-west of Ireland to include:

| | |
|---|---|
| ENE | Cuilcagh |
| ESE | Benbrack |
| S | Slieve Anierin |
| SW | Arigna Mountains |
| W | Ox Mountains |
| NW | Lackagh, Truskmore |
| N | Blue Stack Mountains |

For a rather different kind of view, head for the prominent cairn which overlooks the northern slopes of The Playbank. From this point you will only be able to enjoy the northern prospects, but there is a greater sense of depth created by the

cliffs, which fall away from the moorland edge quite suddenly. If you let your eye wander along the foot of the cliffs you will notice that the ground below is very disturbed, and it seems that a portion of a former cliff has sheared away and come to rest mostly intact at the foot of the present cliff-line. You might also notice that other portions of the present cliff appear to be in an unstable state, and your wanderings should therefore be conducted warily. You can either walk back up to the summit trig point on The Playbank to continue, or explore along the northern cliff-line before returning to the summit.

### The way to Knockgorm          *Allow 1½ hours*

Walk southwards to leave the summit of The Playbank, then begin to drift south-eastwards to keep on the broad, hummocky moorland crest. There are low outcrops of rock to pass and quite a few boulders in the heather. If you keep well to the left you can walk alongside a cliff-line for a short while, but do not follow it too far or you will be pulled off course. There is a fence which crosses

*A cairn close to the summit offers a fine view northwards from The Playbank.*

the broad crest, and if you keep well to the right of it you can pass around its end on the edge of a low cliff. A forest climbs almost to the moorland crest, and you can walk alongside it while it runs at this level. When the forest fence turns right and runs towards Lough Nambrack, you should keep high for a while longer to follow a low ridge of rock, passing little Altshallan Lough and walking around the eastern side of Lough Nambrack. In effect, you will be crossing tussocky moorland in between Lough Nambrack and Knockgorm Lough. After passing between the two loughs, walk roughly westwards across a rugged moorland slope.

### The way back to Cortober          *Allow 1½ hours*

Returning to the point where you started this walk is basically a matter of heading westwards and keeping fairly close to the forest, but the area has been divided up by post-and-wire fencing, so look ahead and choose a route which doesn't require too many fences to be crossed. There is a stream running out of the forest which has carved itself a particularly steep-sided ravine, and you will need to scout along the rim of this before choosing a good route across. If you aim for the lowest corner of the forest beyond the ravine, you will cross the access track leading into the trees. Walk roughly north-westwards along the perimeter of the forest, then cross another small river. As you climb up from it, head towards a conspicuous flat slab of rock. You can see from the stones supporting it that it is an artificial structure. The place-name Cloghasaggart (Priest's Stone) on the map suggests that it is in fact a Mass Rock dating from Penal times, when Roman Catholics could worship only in remote and unfrequented areas. From where the priest would be standing there is quite a wide-ranging view, but the congregation would be down in a dip and effectively out of sight of prying eyes. After following a prominent fence-line straight onwards across the moorland slope, you will reach the gateway which first gave you access to the open moorlands. Turn left to go through the gate, then simply follow the track downhill to join the narrow tarmac road where you parked your car.

## Alternative routes

ESCAPES

There are no real escape routes off The Playbank, apart from turning around and retracing your steps. If you find you are exhausted after passing Lough Nambrack, you can avoid hurdling fences towards the end of the walk by descending into the valley of the Yellow River and following minor roads back towards the starting point via Sranagarvanagh. It might take you longer, and it certainly measures further, but it would be easier. Do not be tempted to thrash a way through the forest in the hope that you will be able to link with the forest access track, as it simply isn't worth the effort and the trees are closely packed together.

*On the northern cliffs of The Playbank, where a little care is needed.*

EXTENSIONS

The walk over The Playbank and Knockgorm is quite short, and extensions to the route can be as long as you like. By keeping to the broad moorland crest you can follow the Cavan and Leitrim county boundary, which is also the Ulster and Connacht border, towards Poulglass. If you don't want to return by road, you could continue well into Leitrim by crossing the broad and bleak slopes of Slieve Anierin. By descending towards Drum-shanbo you could pick up the waymarked Leitrim Way, which is no more than a road walk leading back towards Ballinagleragh. This is a long day's walk, taking you out of Ulster and into Connacht. To stay in Ulster, you could cross Benbrack and the Glan Gap to climb on to the broad moorland shoulders of Cuilcagh, but you will need to be a strong walker with plenty of time and energy to spare for such a long and difficult walk. Unless you arrange to be collected at some other point, you would need to be walking for a long time to return to your starting point.

# Route 13: CUILCAGH

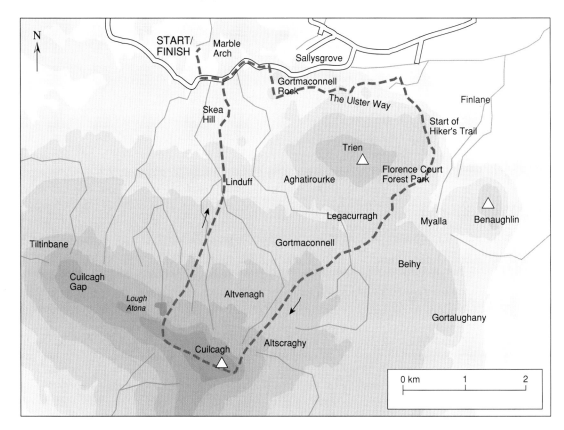

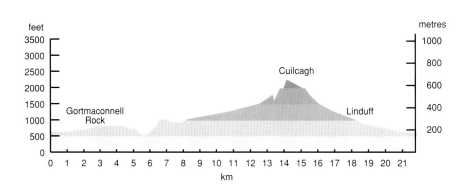

# 5

# FERMANAGH LAKELANDS

## Route 13: Cuilcagh

**TIME ALLOWANCE**   9 hours.

**STARTING/FINISHING LOCATION**
Marble Arch Caves.
OSNI Discoverer 26: GR 122344.
Large car park.
No bus service nearer than Florence Court.

**OVERVIEW/INTEREST**
Starts at the best show caves in Ireland.
Wilderness moorland walking and spectacular
   rock formations.
Extensive views from the summit, and down to
   beautiful Lough Atona.
Includes the Hiker's Trail and part of the Ulster
   Way.

**FOOTPATHS**
Lower-level paths and tracks are clear.
Upland terrain is largely pathless moorland.
Can be quite muddy or boggy in places.
The Ulster Way and Hiker's Trail are waymarked.

**STATISTICS**
**WALKING DISTANCE**   24km (15 miles)
**TOTAL HEIGHT GAINED**   700m (2,300ft)
**PRINCIPAL HEIGHT**
Cuilcagh   665m (2,188ft)

### The way to the Hiker's Trail          *Allow 3 hours*

Park at the Marble Arch Caves. If you decide to
explore the caves, you will almost certainly not
have time to climb Cuilcagh afterwards. However,
you will have every excuse to make a second visit,
as the caves are well worth seeing. The standard
tour leaves the Visitor Centre and descends into a
hole via a flight of steps. The first part of the
passageway is flooded, with access only by boat.
After that, you walk along specially constructed
paths and marvel at the illuminated cave formations. There is no need to retrace significantly from
the end of the show cave, as a flight of steps leads
back up to the Visitor Centre. All highly recommended – but for some other time. Cuilcagh
beckons the walker onwards, but if the Visitor
Centre restaurant is open you might start the day
with something to eat and drink.

Follow the access road up and away from the
Visitor Centre. Turn left along a minor road called
the Marlbank Scenic Loop. This runs through
limestone country, passing a signpost for a hilltop
viewpoint at Gortmaconell. You should stay on the
road, following it downhill for a while. Look out
for an Ulster Way marker off to the right at a
gateway, and leave the road at this point. The
Ulster Way is rather sparsely marked, so you
should always look ahead for the next waymark
post. The route climbs up a scrub-covered slope
and emerges into more open country behind
Gortmaconnell Rock. You eventually reach a
rather wetter upland area, where you turn left and
proceed across a muddy slope.

There are fences and ditches to cross, and you
will later reach drier ground beyond, where you
pass through a gap beside a limestone knoll. The
Ulster Way reaches the edge of Florence Court
Forest and follows a track downhill for a while.
However, a path running off to the right takes the
route back up to the edge of the forest again.

71

Follow a rugged path along the top side of the forest until you reach a stile and a noticeboard for the Hiker's Trail. This is a waymarked route to the summit of Cuilcagh, but although the marker posts do offer an aid to navigation, you should still take care over route-finding and remember that the open moorland slopes are quite rugged. In poor visibility the terrain can seem featureless.

## The way to Cuilcagh                    *Allow 3 hours*

The Hiker's Trail starts by crossing a pockmarked and scrub-covered slope – the humps and hollows are a feature of the limestone bedrock. You should always be looking ahead to spot the next tall yellow marker post which indicates the route. These are quite widely spaced and it is possible to lose sight of one of them before spotting the next in line. The hummocky limestone terrain at Legacurragh soon gives way to an open moorland slope, which rises in great swellings and generally features a view ahead towards Cuilcagh. Do not imagine that this slope will convey you gradually towards the summit, however, as there are a couple of streams to cross which are hidden away in folds of the moorland. You will normally be able to hop across these streams, but after periods of heavy rain they might be quite swollen.

The waymark posts do not in fact lead you all the way to the summit, but they almost do. The gradient begins to increase at Altscraghy, then the last marker post is passed before the ground suddenly rears up sharply. The final pull up to the summit is on a short, but relentlessly steep, slope which will probably leave most walkers puffing and blowing. Once the ground begins to level out, look ahead to spot a huge, bouldery summit cairn. This is actually a burial cairn and serves as a landmark throughout the surrounding countryside. A trig point has been planted on top of the cairn at 665m (2,188ft).

If you reach the summit on a clear day, then you will be rewarded with an exceptionally wide-ranging view which seems to take in most of Ulster and stretches well into the plains in the middle of Ireland. Small wonder that in the early days of the

Ordnance Survey the summit of Cuilcagh should have been chosen as a sighting point in the primary triangulation of Ireland. Sightings were taken throughout the day, and even at night using special 'limelights', and the longest sighting ever recorded in Ireland was from Cuilcagh to Keeper Hill, near Limerick city! A summary of the view might include the following:

| | |
|---|---|
| N | Belmore Mountain |
| NNE | Inishowen Peninsula |
| NE | Sperrin Mountains |
| ENE | Slieve Beagh |
| E | Mountains of Mourne |
| ESE | Slieve Rushen |
| SE | Wicklow Mountains |
| SSW | Benbrack |
| SW | Bencroy, Slieve Anierin |
| WSW | The Playbank, Arigna Mountains |
| W | Ox Mountains |
| NW | Truskmore |
| NNW | Donegal Highlands |

## The way back to Marble Arch Caves
*Allow 3 hours*

You will probably have realized that even following the waymark posts on the Ulster Way and the Hiker's Trail is not a foolproof way of navigating across the rugged slopes of Cuilcagh. You still need to rely on the map, and this is especially the case in poor visibility. Once you reach the summit of Cuilcagh, you will need to make a decision about the rest of your route. In poor visibility, or if there is a risk of running into the night, you might consider returning via the Hiker's Trail. This, as you already know, is a long and rugged walk, which is not accomplished much faster even heading downhill. In clear weather, if you are still feeling fit, it is worth traversing the summit ridge and heading more directly back towards the Marble Arch Caves, but remember that this is largely pathless moorland terrain.

*Overlooking Lough Atona and a distant view of Belmore Mountain.*

*Towering blocks of rock are piled high above Lough Atona on Cuilcagh.*

Aim to follow the summit crest roughly west north-west. You will be following closely the county boundary between Fermanagh and Cavan, which is also the line of the Border. It all looks the same – boulders, grass, gravelly patches and isolated peat hags. There are no aids to navigation, but in clear weather the way forward is fairly obvious and you can enjoy the wide-ranging views as you travel. You may find it best to walk along the top of the steep slope overlooking the northern

slopes of Cuilcagh. This edge becomes increasingly rocky and is an attractive subject for photographers. You might like to stand on a rocky prow and survey the northern slopes of Cuilcagh. Look out for the lovely little Lough Atona, filling a heathery hollow at the foot of the cliffs.

You should be thinking about making your descent around this point. The moorlands are broad, featureless and almost entirely pathless, and you should aim to identify the end of a track roughly north north-east at Linduff. If you can reach this track, you will find the easiest way to end this difficult moorland walk. If you aren't blessed with clear weather, then you will have to take a compass bearing towards Linduff and hope that you hit the track at the correct point.

First, you have to get down the rocky edge. There is a significant gash in the cliff-line, and you should be able to locate the rather steep and gritty path that earlier visitors have worn down this way. You will find yourself proceeding downhill beneath ominously leaning towers of gritstone. These look unstable, and have done for years, so you are advised to keep your distance: earlier towers might well have collapsed, judging by the massive boulders you will have to scramble across on the way down to Lough Atona's shores. After that, you are at the mercy of the weather and your own map-reading skills. You will be crossing the headwaters of the Belbarrinagh River and the Owenbrean River, which both drain water from the tussocky moorlands into the Marble Arch Cave system. There is a fence to cross just before you finally land on the end of the track at Linduff.

Simply follow the track roughly northwards off the moor. There are gates and a building to pass, as well as interesting areas of scrub and swallow holes to investigate. One last gate leads on to the Marlbank Scenic Loop, where you turn left and follow the road a short way. The next turning to the right is the access road for the Marble Arch Caves. While following it, you can take a last look back towards distant Cuilcagh before reaching the car park. Even if you have arrived too late to enjoy a tour of the caves, you might still be able to avail yourself of the restaurant on site, and maybe just catch the last audio-visual presentation of the day.

# Alternative routes

Apart from the advice 'don't go' in really nasty weather, your escape options from Cuilcagh are limited. Assuming you are heading for the summit, and run into difficulties, your best option would be to turn around and abandon the walk. However, if you are already on the summit and simply wish to reach the nearest road in an emergency, then you might head southwards to reach the R200. Alternatively, you can follow the waymarked Hiker's Trail downhill towards Legacurragh, and pick up bog roads, which join minor roads that in turn lead down to the A32 between Florence Court and Swanlinbar.

As you will no doubt appreciate, escape routes such as these have little to commend them against continuing with the route as planned, but all the same you should bear them in mind. The descent toward the track-end at Linduff is as good an escape route as any, but the track can only be reached after crossing featureless moorlands, where an error in map-reading can lead you into still further difficulties.

If you start early and are prepared to finish late, you can savour more of the wilderness qualities of Cuilcagh. The whole of the ridge could be followed between Cuilcagh's main summit cairn and the prow of Tiltinbane. A descent from Tiltinbane could be linked with the easy waymarked course of the Cavan Way, which could be followed to the source of the mighty River Shannon at Shannon Pot. If the Cavan Way is followed to the village of Blacklion, the Ulster Way could be followed back to the Marble Arch Caves. If this option is chosen, there will be some road walking to be endured. Do not try to head straight up to the caves by following the Marlbank Scenic Loop, but keep on the lower road until you reach Cladagh Bridge. At this point, the Ulster Way follows a very interesting path up the Cladagh Glen. This path is structured as a nature trail and is equipped with information boards. Protected as a National Nature Reserve, the glen is lavishly wooded and has lively rivers. The path also crosses Marble Arch – a natural arch of limestone spanning the river near the entrance to the caves. Flights of steps and board-walks lead back to the Visitor Centre.

# Route 14: BELMORE MOUNTAIN

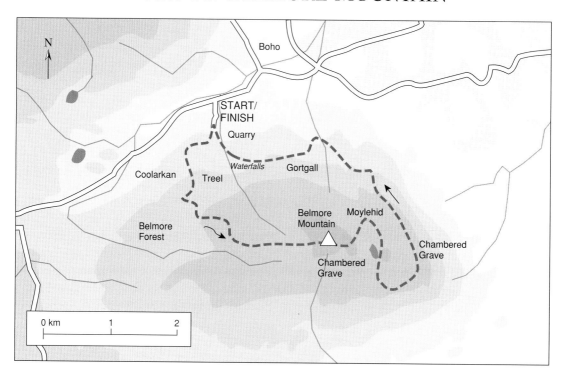

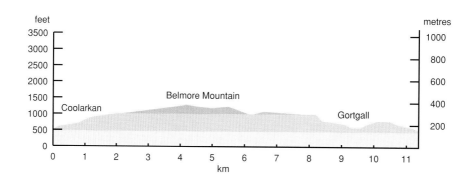

# Route 14: Belmore Mountain

**TIME ALLOWANCE**   4 hours.

**STARTING/FINISHING LOCATION**
Coolarkan, near Boho.
OSNI Discoverer 17: GR 122433.
Small car park in an old quarry.
Ulsterbus 59A is a limited service to Boho.

**OVERVIEW/INTEREST**
Easy forest tracks in Belmore Forest, rugged
    moorland on Belmore Mountain.
Fine cliff walk with good views.
Nearby archaeological remains.
Close to the Ulster Way.

**FOOTPATHS**
Forest tracks are clear and firm.
Upland moorlands have no trodden paths.
Some higher parts are wet and boggy.

**STATISTICS**
**WALKING DISTANCE**   12km (7½ miles)
**TOTAL HEIGHT GAINED**   350m (1,150ft)
**PRINCIPAL HEIGHT**
Belmore Mountain   401m (1,316ft)

## The way to Belmore Mountain

*Allow 1½ hours*

Belmore Mountain is a relatively isolated height, mostly seen by people travelling along the southern side of the mountain using the main road from Enniskillen to Belcoo. The starting point for the walk is on the northern side, and is best reached by following the signposted scenic road from Belcoo to Boho. If you are using the Ulsterbus 59A service to reach Boho, you should be aware that this currently runs only on Thursdays and you therefore need to be quite sure of the timetable to avoid being stranded after completing the walk. Quite close to Boho is a sign for Belmore Forest, and you should turn off the scenic road and drive up the forest access road. After passing a row of white forestry cottages and a barrier gate on the right, proceed through another barrier gate straight ahead. Turn left to park in an old quarry. Horse riders sometimes bring trailers into this quarry, before riding their horses along a way-marked route through the forest.

When you leave the old quarry, turn left and start following a forest track uphill. You will see a small waterfall just to your left, while to your right is a clear-felled area. As you follow the forest track uphill it bends to the right, then swings to the left to continue climbing. When it next bends to the right, it begins to run along at a more level gradient. At this point look out for another forest track on the left, where a small tin hut marks the junction. Turn left along this track and continue into an area of younger trees, where you have some views of the higher moorlands. The track describes sweeping zigzags as it progresses and, despite an early downhill dip, proceeds uphill by degrees. Follow the forest track to its very end, which is a broad turning area for forestry vehicles. A short, rushy, wet and boggy forest ride leads to a ditch and the forest fence. Cross over the ditch and the fence to reach the slopes of Belmore Mountain.

If you walk roughly eastwards you will reach the summit of Belmore Mountain. The ground which needs to be crossed is covered in tussocky grass and heather, liberally sprinkled with boggy patches. If you look ahead you will spot the trig point which marks the summit of this rugged moorland. It stands at 401m (1,316ft), and at that point you might as well pause for breath and admire the surrounding countryside. Despite Belmore Mountain being so well forested, at least the summit area has been spared and the view has been maintained. As the hill is fairly isolated, it is the distant prospects which feature well. Let your eye roam around the skyline to spot some of the following features:

NNE   Bolaght Mountain, Inishowen Peninsula
NE   Mullaghcarn, Sperrin Mountains

| | |
|---|---|
| ENE | Brougher Mountain |
| E | Slieve Beagh |
| ESE | Upper Lough Erne |
| SE | Slieve Rushen |
| S | Cuilcagh |
| WSW | The Playbank |
| SW | Arigna Mountains |
| W | Thur, Dough, Truskmore |
| NW | Ballintempo Forest |
| NNW | Knockmore Cliffs, Blue Stack Mountains |
| N | Lower Lough Erne |

### The way back to Coolarkan    *Allow 2½ hours*

Walk eastwards to descend from the summit of Belmore Mountain. You should look out for the little pool of Lough Nagor and keep to its northern, or left side. The lough is half inside Belmore Forest and half out on the slopes of Belmore Mountain, so it is an easy feature to spot. You will need to cross the forest fence, then climb uphill along an unplanted strip of ground inside the forest. Beware of tussocky grass and heather, holes and ditches full of water, and other ankle-wrenching conditions. As you climb over the rise, you may feel that the trees are going to close in and deny you further access, but in fact you will be led along a forest ride which descends straight towards a clear forest track. Until you land on the firm forest track, take care descending on this steep ground, as it is very uneven all the way down.

Turn right to start following the forest track over a gentle rise. If you are following your map closely you will realize that there is a chambered grave hidden away in the forest to the left. This feature is not easy to find, so if you decide to search for it

*Belmore Forest ends on a cliff edge to allow fine views across country.*

you should allow extra time. The forest track runs downhill and begins to swing to the left. In fact, it swings so much that it eventually ends up almost doubling back on itself. At this point you will be following the track along the edge of a sheer limestone cliff. Find a handy perch on the edge of this cliff, as the view eastwards is quite pleasant.

You should be able to spot the watery levels of Upper and Lower Lough Erne, and find the town of Enniskillen sitting in between them. Some people maintain that Fermanagh is one-third underwater, and a glance at a map of the county tends to confirm it. The Erne system is so extensive that there are only a mere handful of places where you can cross from one side of Fermanagh to the other. It was for this reason that Enniskillen grew at a strategic crossing point – the town is actually situated astride an island in the River Erne in between Upper and Lower Lough Erne. It naturally became a garrison town and features a military museum.

When you have sampled the view from the cliff, continue walking along the track, which eventually passes through a minor gap and begins to run downhill. Keep to the left and don't be drawn down a dead-end track off to the right. The track climbs uphill a short way, then descends again. Keep to the right this time, as another track runs in from the left. After passing through a gate you will briefly leave the confines of the forest and walk close to a few farm buildings as you pass some fields. There is a charming view northwards during this pastoral interlude, as you look towards Ross Lough and Carran Lough.

When the track re-enters Belmore Forest, it bends to the left and climbs uphill, then bends to the right and after a while begins to level out. You pass through a clear-felled area before descending towards a barrier gate. Keep to the right to follow a farm road downhill. You pass above the farm buildings and follow a concrete road back into Belmore Forest. This road runs along the rim of the quarry where you parked at the start of the walk, and if you turn left and left again at the next junction, you will be led back into the quarry.

As this walk is fairly short and shouldn't take too much time, you might like to enjoy a scenic drive through Boho and along the foot of Knockmore Cliffs to reach Derrygonnelly. The area abounds in archaeological remains and the scenery is interesting throughout.

## Alternative routes

ESCAPES

There is little opportunity to come to grief while following the forest tracks through Belmore Forest, but it is possible that the rugged moorland slopes could prove difficult to traverse in poor visibility if you are a dodgy navigator. If you simply want to enjoy a short walk without grappling with tussocky moorland, then consider a circuit along the looped forest track on the eastern side of Belmore Mountain. If you run into any difficulty on Belmore Mountain, it would be safest to retreat using the tracks followed on the ascent, rather than continuing onwards.

EXTENSIONS

As Belmore Mountain is a relatively isolated height, extending the walk over neighbouring ones will result in some very long walks. You are unlikely to be able to create large circular routes without having to walk along roads for considerable distances. The Ulster Way crosses the western slopes of Belmore Mountain, and it is possible to link with this enormous waymarked trail and follow it either northwards or southwards. Going northwards, it runs through Ballintempo and Big Dog Forests, then proceeds through Lough Navar Forest to reach the Cliffs of Magho. Heading southwards, it passes Lough Macnean Lower, then runs up through the Cladagh Glen to reach the Marble Arch Caves. At that point you would be able to head towards the broad and bleak Cuilcagh. Going either north or south, extensions from Belmore Mountain will probably mean you should arrange to be collected at some other place, so planning is required.

*OVERLEAF:*
*Looking towards Ross Lough, lying north of the village of Boho.*

# Route 15:  CLIFFS OF MAGHO

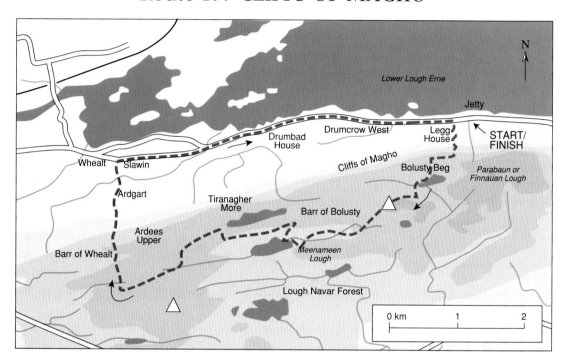

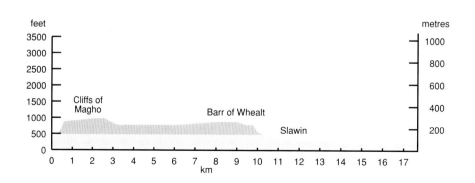

# Route 15: Cliffs of Magho

**TIME ALLOWANCE**   7 hours.

**STARTING/FINISHING LOCATION**
Legg, Lower Lough Erne.
OSNI Discoverer 17, OSNI Lower Lough Erne
  Map: GR 062583.
Small car park.
Ulsterbus 99 is a limited service.

**OVERVIEW/INTEREST**
Routed along a loop of the Ulster Way, following a
  popular pathway on to the Cliffs of Magho.
Splendid views across the Lower Lough Erne and
  towards Donegal.
Interesting little loughs hidden in the forest.

**FOOTPATHS**
Uses a mixture of paths, tracks and roads.
Many paths have been surfaced with gravel; some
  are boggy or only lightly trodden, with the
  descent route largely untrodden.
Waymarks are widely spaced around the circuit.

**STATISTICS**
**WALKING DISTANCE**   18km (11 miles)
**TOTAL HEIGHT GAINED**   290m (950ft)
**PRINCIPAL HEIGHT**
Cliffs of Magho   290m (950ft)

## The way to the Cliffs of Magho *Allow 1 hour*

Park beside the A46 on the southern shore of Lower Lough Erne at Legg, inbetween Belleek and Enniskillen. The car park is surrounded by trees and is furnished with a couple of picnic tables. Across the road is access to the shore of Lower Lough Erne, and another car park if this is required. The whole of this circuit is routed along a loop of the Ulster Way, which originally followed the A46 from Rosscor to Legg, before climbing on to the Cliffs of Magho. However, in an effort to cut out some of the road walking, an alternative ascent was provided from Whealt to the Barr of Whealt.

By ascending from Legg to the Cliffs of Magho and descending from the Barr of Whealt to Whealt, a complete circular walk can be enjoyed which is entirely routed along a short stretch of the immense Ulster Way.

Leading off from the roadside car park at Legg is a small gate, followed by a sign reading 'Steep trail – walking shoes recommended'. A path rises gently uphill through a delightfully mixed woodland. When the gradient increases, short flights of steps appear, and the path zigzags across the steep, wooded slope. The floor of the woodland is lushly vegetated with an array of flowers and ferns. As the slope steepens further there are longer flights of steps, and even occasional benches where you can rest and catch your breath, if you have started too quickly! As you climb, views begin to open out across Lower Lough Erne, stretching northwards into Donegal. On the final uphill pull, you will find yourself briefly walking alongside conifers, before climbing up past a small stone well at the side of the path. Beyond this point you reach the top of the Cliffs of Magho.

You may feel cheated to arrive at a car park on top of the cliffs, but anyone enjoying the view the easy way has had to pay an entrance fee to follow the scenic drive through the Lough Navar Forest. A section of an Ordnance Survey map used to be displayed on a small stone plinth, but this has long since vanished. However, you can lay out your own map and identify distant features in view. Ranks of forest trees block out any view southwards, so you have, in effect, only half a view. Even so, there is plenty to see throughout mountainous Donegal. Look along the skyline for some of these features:

| | |
|---|---|
| WNW | Slieve League, Carrick Peninsula |
| NW | Castle Caldwell, Breesy Hill |
| NNW | Blue Stack Mountains, Errigal, Muckish |
| NNE | Inishowen Peninsula |
| NE | Boa Island, Bolaght Mountain, Sperrin Mountains |

## The way to Glenereawan Lough

*Allow 2 hours*

Walk westwards from the viewpoint car park, and you will find a clear path routed along the top of the Cliffs of Magho. Enjoy the expansive views, because you follow this line for only a short way. There are a couple of benches if you want to sit down for a while and take in everything at leisure. A wooden fence and a waymark post indicate a sudden left turn. You follow a narrow path, which can be wet and squelchy underfoot, through deep heather cover on a broad moorland plateau. The path leads you towards the extensive Lough Navar Forest, where you proceed along a forest ride to reach a small and scenic lough. The map calls this Parabaun or Finnauan Lough. If you keep to the right you will be led around the western end of the lough, before being taken along another forest ride to reach a firm forest track.

Turn right to follow this track, which mostly runs along the level between tall stands of trees. Further on you will pass an expanse of heathery ground on the right, which was left unplanted, at Bolusty Beg. The track later runs downhill and the forest trees are screened by attractive belts of birch. At the bottom of this track is a barrier gate, which you simply walk around to reach a narrow tarmac road. Turn right to follow this road for a while. It rises very gently before a gentle descent. Watch out for a marker post pointing left, where a gravel path leads into the forest. This becomes rather muddy for a while, but you soon turn right to follow a better path along the northern shore of Meenameen Lough. You will cross a small footbridge over the outflowing stream, and then be led towards a small car park which is largely used by fishermen.

At this point, you may notice a sign reading 'Ulster Way' and marker posts indicating that you should continue along the shore of Meenameen Lough. In fact, these indicate the 'main' route through Lough Navar Forest, while your walk follows the 'alternative' route towards the Barr of

*The Cliffs of Magho rise steeply above the levels of Lower Lough Erne.*

84

*Looking across an expanse of Lower Lough Erne towards Donegal.*

Whealt. If you walk up to the small car park and turn right, you will immediately reach a road junction. At this point, a left turn, confirmed by an old marker post, is signposted for Glenereawan Lough. Simply follow this narrow road uphill, then downhill to reach another fishermen's car park. Glenereawan Lough is revealed as a long, narrow and quite scenic lough perched near the edge of the cliffs.

## The way to Whealt        *Allow 2 hours*

Before you reach the small car park at Glenereawan Lough, turn left and follow a clear path towards the foot of the lough. You should notice a narrower path heading off to the left, which climbs uphill only a short way. This path passes small trees and shrubs, and features a lush vegetation cover. For most of the way, you will find that you have a narrow screen of trees between the path you are following and the southern shore of Glenereawan Lough. You will also find that the firm surface of the narrow path eventually runs out and you will be walking along a rather wetter and more overgrown track. In fact, this path may become rather vague as you proceed beyond the marshy head of the lough.

When you come up against a stand of forestry, turn right and walk alongside the edge of the forest. You may notice a forest ride leading almost immediately between the trees, but continue a little further before turning left to enter the forest.

You will be able to pick up the course of a firm forest track, which you follow onwards. The track swings left, and you continue to use it until you reach a junction. At this point, turn right and follow another track straight onwards. Eventually, this track reaches the edge of the forest and swings left. Don't follow it, but turn right to follow a broad firebreak alongside the edge of the forest. This firebreak is a deep and broad peaty channel, excavated from the blanket bog of the moorland at the edge of the forest. In fairly dry conditions it should take your weight. If not, you will have to walk along the rougher heathery ground flanking the break. You will cross the head of Glennalong and may notice that the view includes a portion of hilly country shared between Sligo and Leitrim, the northern slopes of which fall quite steeply. You will climb over the moorland rise of the Barr of Whealt, and turn right around the very edge of the forest.

At this point, on the left, you should spot a step-stile crossing a fence. The two upright posts of the stile have been painted orange. Cross it, and start following a fence down a steep, rugged slope. The lower ground is predominantly rushy, and if you begin to veer off to the right through the lower ground you will find another stile with orange-painted uprights. As you proceed onwards, you will pass through a gate beside a shed, and then further along you will reach a much firmer track. Turn left along this track and go through another gate. Turn right along a narrow road and follow this over a rise of ground. The short descent leads you on to a minor road in between Whealt and Slawin. Turn right to follow this road.

## The way back to Legg *Allow 2 hours*

At first you walk uphill, then descend towards the main A46, which you simply follow straight onwards. As you pass Drumbad and Drumcrow you will be able to see stretches of Lower Lough Erne, but of course the views at this level are nowhere near as extensive as those from above. You will be passing fields for most of the way along the main road, but if you look ahead you will spot the wooded slope plunging down from the Cliffs of Magho to the shore of Lower Lough Erne. The car park where you started is indicated in advance, and when you reach it your walk is over. If you feel the need for a short countryside stroll after the walk along the main road, then you might enjoy the nearby walk along the Loughshore Path, which is also signposted from the roadside.

## Alternative routes

ESCAPES

Once you have climbed up all the steps to reach the viewpoint and car park on the top of the Cliffs of Magho, the only logical escape route is to walk back down again – unless you can persuade a motorist to give you a lift back around! If you continue along the route and need to cut the walk short for any reason, then you can follow the narrow tarmac road of the Lough Navar Scenic Drive back towards the viewpoint and descend the steps to the main road. Once you get as far as Glenereawan Lough you might as well continue with the route, as you would most likely land down on the main road rather more quickly than if you tried to retrace your steps.

EXTENSIONS

You could extend the distance of this walk by forsaking the course taken by the Ulster Way and using any other track in Lough Navar Forest. You could add an extra loop to discover little Lough Achork and Lough Navar, before using the course of the Ulster Way to reach Meenameen Lough and continue with the route. The Ulster Way running through Lough Navar Forest and Big Dog Forest was the first stretch to be declared open, and you might like to follow the entire course from Legg to distant Belcoo. In fact, this was the first long waymarked trail to be declared open anywhere in Ireland. As another alternative, you could follow a walk based entirely on the upland network of forest tracks and paths, structuring your route to and from the viewpoint car park, and thereby omitting the walk along the main road down by Lower Lough Erne.

# Route 16: SLIEVE LEAGUE

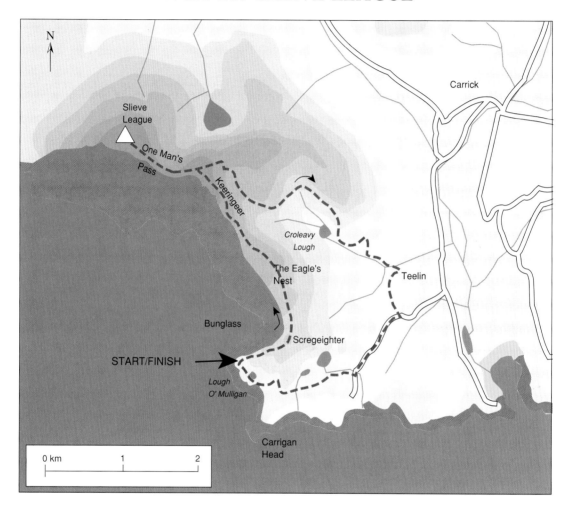

Carrick

Slieve League

One Man's Pass

Keeringeer

Croleavy Lough

The Eagle's Nest

Teelin

Bunglass

Scregeighter

START/FINISH

Lough O' Mulligan

Carrigan Head

0 km    1    2

N

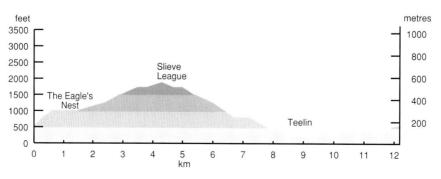

feet
3500
3000
2500
2000 — Slieve League
1500 — The Eagle's Nest
1000
500 — Teelin
0
0  1  2  3  4  5  6  7  8  9  10  11  12
km

metres
1000
800
600
400
200

# 6

# CARRICK PENINSULA

## Route 16: Slieve League

**TIME ALLOWANCE**  6 hours.

**STARTING/FINISHING LOCATION**
Bunglass, near Teelin.
OSI Discovery 10: GR 558757.
Small car park at Bunglass.
Bus Eireann Table Number 296 serves Carrick.

**OVERVIEW/INTEREST**
Full-length view of awe-inspiring cliffs plunging
   into the Atlantic, plus far-reaching views inland.
Optional scramble on a knife-edge ridge.
Includes an old pilgrimage path.

**FOOTPATHS**
Paths are clear for most of the ascent, but largely
   absent on the summit.
Some peaty paths are becoming eroded.
The descent uses a clear pilgrim path and roads.

**STATISTICS**
**WALKING DISTANCE**  15km (9 miles)
**TOTAL HEIGHT GAINED**  660m (2,165ft)
**PRINCIPAL HEIGHT**
Slieve League  595m (1,972ft)

## The way to Slieve League

*Allow 2½ hours*

There is no bus service running closer to this route than Carrick, so you will have to either walk or drive to the start. As you travel from Carrick to Teelin, you will see a sign pointing to the right for Slieve League, but that is the road to the pilgrim path, so don't go that way. When you reach Teelin, where you pass a roadside pub, another sign on the right indicates the road to Bunglass and the cliffs. This narrow and winding road needs to be followed all the way to its end. Along this road you will pass through a gate – please be sure to close and fasten it behind you. When the tarmac ends, park on the gravelly patch close to the cliff edge. They call this place Radharc Mór – the Big View. Here you will see almost 600m (2,000ft) of rugged, broken, rocky slopes plunging into the Atlantic. Bracken and heather-covered patches ensure that the colours vary throughout the seasons, although sometimes the whole place may be shrouded in mist, denying you one of the most amazing coastal views in Ireland.

There should be no problem with route-finding. If you can see the cliffs, then you can see which way you need to go – as well as which way not to! There is a trodden path by a fence near the car park. The fence soons ends, but the path continues uphill over rough and occasionally rocky ground to reach a summit called Scregeighter. Here, the cliff-line changes direction, so that you are following a clifftop path roughly northwards. Stay clear of the edge as you cross the next rise, as the cliffs of The Eagle's Nest actually overhang at the top. The path descends across a gap and crosses a hump ahead. You will notice that some of the blanket bog covering the rock is becoming badly eroded – try not to make it any worse. You will later climb steeply uphill for a while, before either crossing or passing another hump on the crest. You are approaching the ridge of Keeringear, which in recent years has attracted the name of One Man's Pass, although this is properly a feature found later in the route. The ridge steepens and sharpens, so

89

that it becomes a ridge of rock. At this point, you will need to look at your options.

In wet weather or strong winds, the safe option is to omit the ridge and use a bouldery path on the landward side to bypass the difficulty. You then take a path uphill which will lead you on to Slieve League's summit plateau. In good, dry weather, you should be able to manage the rocky ridge if you have a good head for heights. The hardest part involves actually getting on to the ridge, so if you can manage that the rest of the scramble should be easy to accomplish. The ridge slopes upwards, but generally has a good top furnished with plenty of holds for hands and feet. Unless you are used to such exposed situations, it is recommended that you crawl up the ridge on all fours. It may seem ungainly, but while you are down on all fours you should in fact have nowhere to fall! When you reach the end of the rocky ridge, cross a rocky notch and keep to the right-hand side of the next ridge to climb steeply uphill. All that remains is to follow a path further uphill until it levels out on the broad summit plateau of Slieve League.

This wide, stony area is not in fact the true summit of Slieve League: you need to be further north-west to be on the highest point. The two broad summits of the mountain are connected by a narrow ridge, which is the original One Man's Pass. There are actually no real difficulties along this ridge, which is a simple high-level crest bearing an obvious and well-trodden path. A short, steep, rocky climb at the end leads on to the summit plateau, where you simply head for a large cairn. The map marks a trig point at 595m (1,972ft), but if this is actually present it must be buried beneath the cairn! Views across the sea should be fairly constant throughout the ascent in clear weather, but from the top of Slieve League you will be able to see well inland too. Some of the more distant views are far across the sea, including some of the following points:

NNE   Slievetooey, Aran Island
NE    Slieve Snaght, Errigal

*The rugged cliffs of Slieve League as seen from the road-end at Bunglass.*

| ENE | Mulnanaff, Blue Stack Mountains |
| E | Crownarad |
| SE | Cuilcagh |
| SSE | Truskmore, Benbulbin |
| S | Ox Mountains |
| SW | Nephin, Nephin Beg Range |
| WSW | Benwee Head |
| NW | Leahan |

## The way to Teelin

*Allow 2½ hours*

You will need to retrace your steps for a while to continue with this circuit. Walk back along the One Man's Pass connecting the higher of Slieve League's summits with the lower one. As you follow the path across the lower summit, make sure you aren't drawn off towards the rugged cliffs you followed on the ascent. Instead, keep well to the left, aiming to walk roughly north-east down a

*Scrambling along the One Man's Pass – a rocky edge needing care.*

stony slope. Somewhere among these stones are the ruins of an oratory associated with St Assicus, the goldsmith to St Patrick, who is reputed to have spent seven years on the summit of Slieve League. You will be following a clear pilgrim path downhill which was constructed in honour of the saint. Keep an eye out on the descent, looking to the right, or eastwards, to spot the path as it starts to run downhill. If you land on a broad gap then you have gone too far, and will need to come back a short way.

The pilgrim path falls steeply at first, then runs down at a gentler gradient. If you look up the rugged slopes of the valley, you will be able to identify the rocky ridge you scrambled along earlier in the walk. With a bit of luck, you may be entertained by the sight of someone else crawling along the ridge! Continue downhill crossing a stream – you will notice that the path has actually been constructed on the mountainside using a considerable amount of stonework and labour. Further on you will cross a stream featuring a series of waterfalls, and continue downhill at a gentle gradient along a broad track. This passes the little Croleavy Lough before reaching a small car park. From here, follow a narrow road downhill until you reach a junction with another narrow road at a small bridge. You have two options to consider before bringing the circuit to a close: one is to walk straight on towards Teelin, which has a shop and pub, while the other involves turning sharply right and heading more directly back towards the car park at Bunglass.

## The way back to Bunglass      *Allow 1 hour*

Assuming that you want to return as quickly as possible to Bunglass, turn sharp right at the road junction by the bridge and walk uphill a short way before turning left. The narrow road begins to feature a considerable central strip of grass, so it obviously sees very little traffic. Follow this road onwards and upwards, before it begins to fall and joins another tarmac road. Turn right and follow this other road – it is in fact the one you drove along to reach the car park at Bunglass. It twists and turns uphill and passes a few houses; you will go through the gate, which you should again remember to fasten afterwards. The road loops around Carrigan Head, and if you look carefully you will see the word 'EIRE' spelt out in stones on the headland. This was a device used during World War II to dissuade any passing warplanes from landing in neutral Ireland. (There was in fact a 'secret air corridor' to Lower Lough Erne in Fermanagh which Allied warplanes were accustomed to use, but sometimes aircraft strayed off course.) The road passes Lough O'Muilligan before terminating back at the car park on the cliff-top at Bunglass. With luck, the sun may be throwing a golden evening light across the cliff face of Slieve League, which may look even better than when you started the walk.

## Alternative routes

ESCAPES

For the most part, the cliff walk from Bunglass to Slieve League is fairly straightforward, but it is exposed in places and needs care. The rocky scramble now known as the One Man's Pass is technically not too difficult, but its situation would prove too exposed for some cautious walkers. The only real way to avoid this difficulty is to bypass it using a path on the landward side of the ridge. There are no real escape routes on the ascent of Slieve League, although it is possible to drop down steep, stony and heathery slopes to reach the pilgrim path down in the valley. This would, however, seem to be a pointless move, as you could just as well have altered the start of the route and made the easy course of the pilgrim path your line of ascent.

The route can be cut short by turning it around on the first of Slieve League's twin summits. In fact, in misty weather there is little point in proceeding as far as the taller summit, as there will be no views for you to enjoy. There is no escape route available which is easier than the line of the pilgrim path which some walkers refer to as the Old Man's Pass.

EXTENSIONS

It is difficult to extend this circuit in a logical fashion and still return to the starting point. If, however, you can arrange to be dropped off at either Teelin or Bunglass and collected at Malin Beg, you could extend the route quite well. You would cross both of Slieve League's summits, and then drop down to make your way over a wide and boggy gap. The broad-shouldered Leahan could then be crossed before a descent is made towards the strand at Trabane. Rathlin O'Birne Island may be seen very well from here in clear weather, but the end of your walk will be the scattered village of Malin Beg.

An alternative descent from Leahan could take the walk to Malin More, from where a fine hill track can be followed over to Glencolumbkille. At this point, of course, you could also consider linking into the coastal walk beyond.

93

# Route 17: GLENCOLUMBKILLE COASTAL WALK

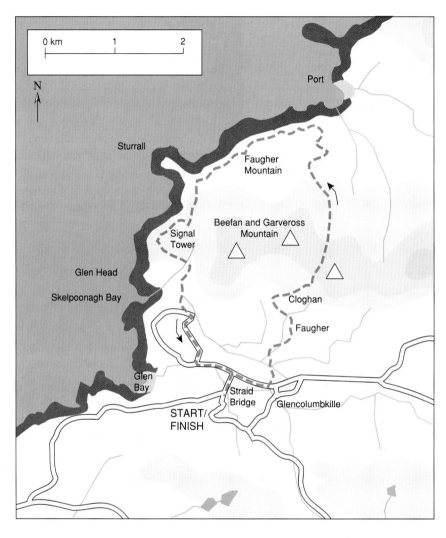

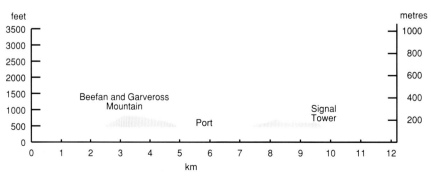

# Route 17: Glencolumbkille Coastal Walk

**TIME ALLOWANCE**   6 hours.

**STARTING/FINISHING LOCATION**
Glencolumbkille Cultural Centre.
OSI Discovery 10: GR 525847.
Car park at the Centre or at the Folk Village.
Bus Eireann Table Number 296 serves
   Glencolumbkille.

**OVERVIEW/INTEREST**
Completely revitalized village, with Cultural
   Centre and Folk Village.
Pleasant moorland walk, and spectacular coastal
   cliffs.
Many interesting features, including a holy well,
   pilgrimage route and ancient cairns, and a
   nineteenth-century signal tower.

**FOOTPATHS**
Starts and finishes on minor roads.
Moorland tracks can be grassy or gravelly; cliff
   paths can be steep in places.
Sections of paths can be muddy.

**STATISTICS**
**WALKING DISTANCE**   13km (8 miles)
**TOTAL HEIGHT GAINED**   480m (1,575ft)
**PRINCIPAL HEIGHT**
Signal Tower, Glen Head   222m (730ft)

## The Way to Port
*Allow 3 hours*

Although there are small car parks in the village of Glencolumbkille, these are often attached to churches or pubs, so if you wish to use them please ask for permission and try to avoid occupying space when they are likely to be needed by local people. If you follow the R263 straight through Glencolumbkille you will reach the Cultural Centre, and beyond that is a car park which almost overlooks Glen Bay. You can park here and follow the road back towards the village. Turn left along a minor road to cross Straid Bridge, which spans the Murlin River. When this road bends to the right, follow it towards the CofI church, which occupies a solitary and prominent position beside the road and away from the village. After passing the church, turn left and follow a narrow, winding road onwards. Further on this begins to climb, and you will pass straight through a crossroads as you climb. Just a short distance further uphill the road bends to the right, but you should go straight through a gate to follow a clear track uphill. This is your access track to the higher moorlands.

Follow the track uphill at Cloghan. It runs north-west at first, then swings roughly north-east to continue climbing. The track crosses the broad crest of the moorland at around 260m (850ft). At this point you will be aware of the purpose of this track – it serves a tall mast perched high on the moorland. The mast is an intrusion in this bleak and boggy wilderness scene, but you walk straight past it and it falls behind in the view. Ahead, however, you will come upon some tantalizing views towards an exceptionally rugged coastline. The track descends at a fairly gentle gradient as it runs roughly northwards, and there are some sweeping zigzags which switch back and forth as you descend the rugged moorland slopes. You may notice a track leading off to the right which descends towards Port, but make sure you don't go that way. Instead, bear left to complete the descent and cross a stream. Seaward views feature the long crest of Toralaydan Island, and a host of amazing shattered stacks of rock.

## The way to the Signal Tower
*Allow 1½ hours*

There is initially a fence guarding the edge of the cliff line as you set off roughly westwards along the cliff path. The fence runs out later, but the path remains fairly clear throughout. There are peaty areas to be crossed, but beyond these the path runs mostly over slopes of short green grass and is therefore fairly dry underfoot. Watch carefully as

95

the path swings inland when it crosses a couple of deeply cut little valleys. You may also notice the jagged crest of Sturrall coming into view. This promontory could be reached by crossing a rugged gap, and its crest features a narrow, rocky scramble. A diversion to sample this is only for those walkers with a good head for heights and previous scrambling experience.

The cliff edge is again protected by a fence for a while, and views down on to the sea feature rocky stacks and an interesting arch carved by constant pounding by the waves. The path has been fairly obvious and foolproof up to now, but as you begin to progress southwards there is a choice of paths which the unwary might miss. The one you are following begins to drift into a valley, but you should look out for another path which runs off to the right. This crosses over the little valley and climbs steeply uphill for a short way. At an earlier

*A series of shattered cliffs and rocky sea stacks around the inlet at Port.*

stage in the walk this slope may have looked like a pyramidal peak, but in fact its summit levels out into a broad top, crowned by the stout, square remains of a signal tower at 222m (730ft). This structure was built during the Napoleonic Wars as a response to perceived threats of invasion. Although coastal views have been good throughout the walk, they have necessarily been limited to the immediate vicinity of Glencolumbkille. In clear weather, however, you might now be able to see as far as the distant Benwee Head on the North Mayo Coast.

## The way back to Glencolumbkille

*Allow 1½ hours*

You will find a fairly clear path running roughly south-east away from the signal tower, saving you an awkward walk across rocky and boggy ground. Follow the path downhill and it will become much clearer, before reaching another track. Turn right to continue downhill on this track, which is broad and clear. It zigzags downhill, and if you turn left you will reach a house situated quite high on the hillside. If you look straight uphill to the left before reaching the house, you may spot a small white sign perched high up the slope. This indicates a huge cairn and a holy well dedicated to St Columbkille. The short, steep climb uphill from a small gate near the house is worth the extra effort. When you return to pass the house, note the ruins situated on a low rise just in front of the house, where further 'stations' on the local pilgrimage route include the ruins of a small church. St Columbkille seems to have been a colourful character and a Donegal man to the heart. Many stories are told about him, and he was responsible for founding the monastic community on the Isle of Iona in Scotland. Follow the nearby rough-surfaced track down to a narrow road, and turn left at the bottom to return towards Glencolumbkille. Keep left to pass an inlet of Glen Bay beside the narrow road, then turn right to cross over Straid Bridge to reach the village. Turn right or left, depending upon where you decided to park your car originally.

Do not leave Glencolumbkille without appreciating some of its background. This remote valley community was particularly down at heel many years ago, but largely through the enthusiastic lobbying of the parish priest, it has become a thriving and industrious community. Be sure to visit the Cultural Centre and Folk Village. Better still, given the charming range of moorland, mountain and coastal walks in the area, aim to spend a while in Glencolumbkille, which has a range of accommodation, shops and pubs.

## Alternative routes

ESCAPES
This circular walk doesn't really offer any escape routes. If you set off uphill from Glencolumbkille to the tall mast on the moorland, you will either have to turn around in adverse weather or simply continue. You could descend to the cliffs and make a decision whether or not to continue, but if you did carry on you might as well complete the circuit. In the event of strong, blustery gales, walking near the cliffs is in advisable, and the optional scramble on to the crest of Sturrall would definitely be dangerous. If weather conditions dictate a rapid retreat towards the end of the walk, you could omit the climb to the signal tower and follow the path through the little valley to link with the clear track zigzagging towards Glencolumbkille.

EXTENSIONS
If you want to enjoy an extended coastal walk, you could start at Glencolumbkille and climb to the signal tower. Follow the coastal path around towards Port, but don't cut inland. Instead, continue over to Glenlough, then climb high on the slopes of Slievetooey. You need to be sure of your stamina and ability on this long and rugged coastal walk, or you could end in darkness. Assuming you keep going along the coast and climb high above Loughros Bay Beg, you will eventually be able to descend to join a road at Maghera. You will either have to be collected on this road or walk along it, beside Maghera Strand, possibly all the way to distant Ardara.

# Route 18:  CROAGHANIRWORE

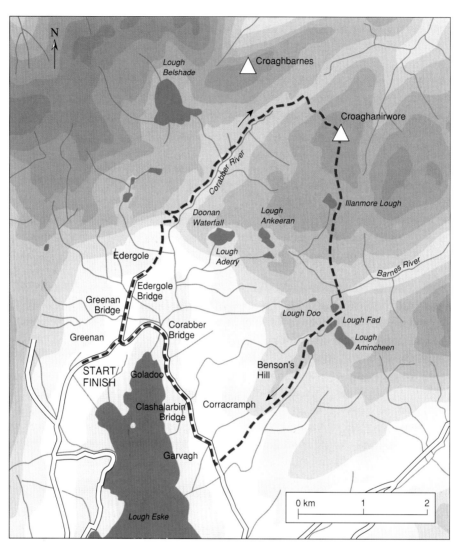

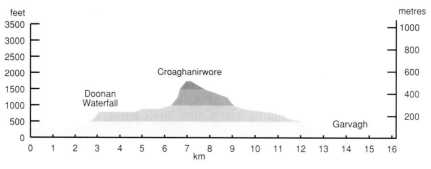

# 7
# BLUE STACK MOUNTAINS

## Route 18: Croaghanirwore

**TIME ALLOWANCE**  7 hours.

**STARTING/FINISHING LOCATION**
Lough Eske.
OSI Discovery 11: GR 965857.
Small car park with picnic tables.
No bus services nearer than the main N15.

**OVERVIEW/INTEREST**
Rugged mountain surroundings and extensive
  views, including across Lough Eske.
Includes a stretch of the Ulster Way, and part of an
  old monastic route.
Optional short diversion to see Doonan Waterfall
  on the Corabber River.

**FOOTPATHS**
Lower parts of the route feature roads and tracks.
Hardly any trodden paths over the mountain, plus
  plenty of wet, rocky and boggy ground.
River crossings may be difficult after heavy rain.

**STATISTICS**
**WALKING DISTANCE**  16km (10 miles)
**TOTAL HEIGHT GAINED**  500m (1,540ft)
**PRINCIPAL HEIGHT**
Croaghanirwore  548m (1,794ft)

### The way to Croaghanirwore   *Allow 3 hours*

Lough Eske is signposted from the main N15 on
the way from Donegal Town towards Letterkenny.
You could drive around either the western or
eastern side of Lough Eske, as the small car park
you are aiming for is on the northern side of the

lough. There is already a fine view across Lough
Eske from this point, and there will be other views
of it to enjoy at intervals throughout the day. An
alternative start could be considered from one of
the bed & breakfasts on the eastern side of Lough
Eske. The Harveys Point Country Hotel on the
western side is less convenient without a car, as
you would need to walk along roads for a while to
reach the start.

Walk north-east along the minor road from the
car park, until the road suddenly starts to zigzag
downhill. Don't go down the zigzags, but follow a
rough and narrow road northwards, off to the left.
This road crosses Greenan Bridge and Edergole
Bridge, both of which feature small waterfalls.
Watch out for a stony track veering off to the left
at Edergole. There is a square board on a post
bearing a 'walking man' picture, denoting that the
track is part of the Ulster Way which traverses the
length of Donegal. Follow this track along the top
side of a forest, noting the clumps of invasive
rhododendron that are growing higher up the
slopes. The track reaches a river flowing down
from Lough Gulladuff. There are a number of very
large stepping stones near an attractive waterfall –
if these are submerged, it is advisable to abandon
the walk at this point. There are further river
crossings ahead, although they are likely to be less
swollen than this one.

The track continues uphill in sweeping zig-zags,
and eventually runs beside the Corabber River. At
this point, a short diversion off to the right is
recommended to see the Doonan Waterfall.
Although it is initially out of sight, you should be
able to hear the water plunging down into a deep

pool even from the track. Return to the track and continue along it. You will pass a water intake point at a deep pool, and the firm track you are following ends at the same place. As you proceed further upstream alongside the Corabber River, you will find that the path is rather worn and squelchy in places. Later it diminishes, and there is little evidence to remind walkers that the path was once used as a through route by monks from Donegal Abbey. You will need to cross the river flowing down from Lough Belshade.

Do not follow the main river up to Lough Belshade, but continue walking north-east alongside a lesser river. The ground is boggy and bouldery, and virtually pathless. If you look ahead, you will be able to spot occasional posts on a few hummocks. These mark the course of the Ulster Way and are simply topped with white paint to confirm that you are still on course, without indicating any specific direction. The posts eventually begin to drift off uphill to the left, but you should actually bear right to reach the head of the valley. The area is broad and boggy, and in mist it can be difficult to determine exactly where the head of the valley really is – somewhere around 300m (1,000ft). From this point, you head roughly south-eastwards and start climbing steeply uphill. The slopes of Croaghanirwore are quite steep and rugged, but are also fairly easy to climb. The rocky parts aren't too difficult, and in fact they can almost be used as flights of steps. Be a bit more careful with the vegetated areas, which could be slippery in places. The slope is fairly consistently uphill at first, although there are a couple of rugged gashes at a higher level. When the slope begins to ease, look ahead to spot the summit cairn at 548m (1,794ft). In fair weather the view can be quite extensive, featuring the following near and distant features:

| | |
|---|---|
| N | Muckish |
| NE | Inishowen Peninsula |
| E | Sperrin Mountains |
| ESE | Croaghnageer |
| SE | Croaghconnellagh |
| SSE | Cuilcagh |
| SSW | Truskmore, Benwhiskin, Benbulbin |
| WSW | Crownarad, Slieve League |
| W | Lough Belshade, Blue Stack Mountains |
| NW | Croaghbarnes |
| NNW | Gaugin Mountain, Slieve Snaght, Errigal |

## The way back to Lough Eske    *Allow 4 hours*

Descending from Croaghanirwore can be fairly simple or rather difficult, depending on the weather. Aim to walk roughly southwards down the rugged slopes of the mountain, towards Illanmore Lough. If you follow the crest of the ridge first you will find plenty of rocky ground, although there are no great difficulties. However, if you keep only just to the west of the crest you may be able to pick up and follow a natural grassy line down towards the lough. In poor visibility, you will need to travel using map and compass, as it would be easy to be drawn off course. You could follow the Barnes River downstream for a while, although it does make a pronounced dog-leg turn which you might prefer to omit. To make a more direct descent, head from Illanmore Lough towards Lough Doo, crossing the Barnes River at the foot of the rugged moorland descent.

Just beside Lough Doo is the end of a bog road, which you follow by turning right. The track runs towards Lough Fad, passing an old abandoned Massey Ferguson tractor, and could be deep underwater after heavy rain, as the lake easily spills over on to the low-lying path. Continue walking roughly south-west along the track, descending with a view across Lough Eske. After passing water-intake tanks and going through a gate, you continue down a narrow tarmac road. When you reach the bottom of this road at Garvagh, turn right (or left if you are returning to any of the nearby bed & breakfasts). The road later drops down to cross Clashalarbin Bridge, and runs close to a small pier on the shore of Lough Eske. As you cross the Corabber Bridge, you have a view back towards the rocky, hummocky slopes of Croaghanirwore. The road climbs uphill from the bridge, zigzagging up towards wooded slopes. Keep left and you will be led straight back to the small car park at the head of Lough Eske.

## Alternative routes

ESCAPES

Croaghanirwore has rocky, boggy and hummocky slopes, so the route chosen offers fairly straight-forward inward and outward routes which follow rivers and firm tracks. The amount of time spent on the broad, rugged, featureless slopes is therefore limited. The logical escape route on the ascent is simply to turn around and retrace your steps. When using the descent, there is no point trying to vary the route, as there is no easier one available. Short-cutting directly towards Lough Eske will quickly lead you into difficulties, especially when you reach the lower slopes.

*A waterfall above the stepping stones near the start of the walk.*

EXTENSIONS

The sparsely waymarked course of the Ulster Way climbs alongside the Corabber River and crosses a gap on Croaghbarnes to descend alongside the Owendoo River. This line offers an alternative descent to Letterkillew. To add more mountains to the walk you could include Croaghnageer and Croaghconnellagh, and maybe descend to the main road on the Barnesmore Gap. If tackling extended walks, be aware that these rugged and largely pathless mountains can prove quite confusing in poor visibility. For a long upland walk, suitable for experienced walkers only, try ascending via the descent route, then continuing over Croaghbarnes, to link with the route over the Blue Stack Mountains. A track can be picked up later that leads back to the road on the west side of Lough Eske.

# Route 19:  BLUE STACK

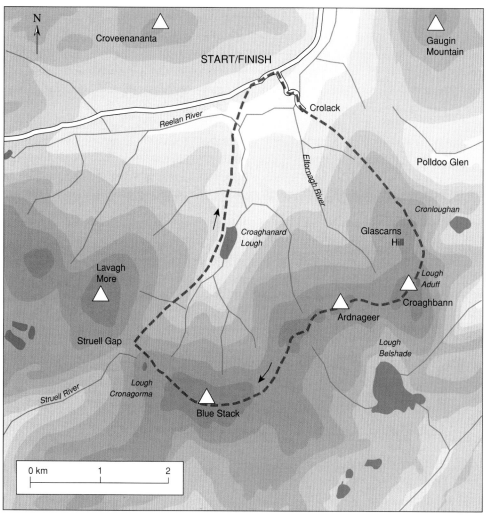

N

Croveenananta

Gaugin Mountain

START/FINISH

Crolack

Reelan River

Polldoo Glen

Ellonagh River

Cronloughan

Croaghanard Lough

Glascarns Hill

Lavagh More

Lough Aduff

Croaghbann

Struell Gap

Ardnageer

Lough Belshade

Struell River

Lough Cronagorma

Blue Stack

0 km      1      2

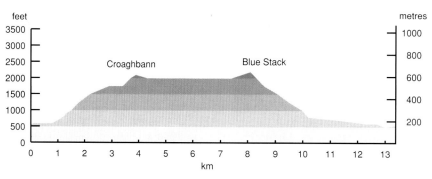

# Route 19: Blue Stack

TIME ALLOWANCE 6 hours.

TIME ALLOWANCE   6 hours.

STARTING/FINISHING LOCATION
The Croaghs, Reelan River.
OSI Discovery 11: GR 959942.
Small parking space beside a former National
  School.
No bus services.

OVERVIEW/INTEREST
Wilderness walk over rugged, bouldery mountains
  with splendid views.
Interesting outcrop of white quartz.
Includes a stretch of the Ulster Way.

FOOTPATHS
Short and firm access roads in the glen.
No paths in the mountains; sparsely waymarked
  Ulster Way is barely trodden.
Plenty of boggy and rocky ground.

STATISTICS
WALKING DISTANCE   14km (9 miles)
TOTAL HEIGHT GAINED   715m (2,345ft)
PRINCIPAL HEIGHTS
Croaghbann   641m (2,100ft)
Ardnageer   642m (2,118ft)
Blue Stack   674m (2,219ft)

## The way to Croaghbann   *Allow 1½ hours*

The R253 runs between Glenties and Ballybofey, while between Lough Ea and the little village of Commeen there is a narrow minor road which runs into the valley of the Reelan River. Follow this narrow and twisting road into the remote glen until you notice a solitary old National School on the right. There is space for a couple of cars to park there. Just a short way back, running downhill from the road, is a farm access lane. It serves the small farm at Crolack, just across the Reelan River. Follow the farm road downhill and cross the bridge over the Reelan River. You will notice an older

bridge crossing the river a little further downstream. When you reach the little farm at Crolack, keep to the left of it to pass through a sheep pen. Beyond the sheep pen are the open slopes of Glascarns Hill. You simply start walking straight uphill to begin this wild and rugged walk through the Blue Stack Mountains.

The slopes of Glascarns Hill are broad and boggy, with more and more boulders becoming apparent as the ground steepens. Due to the way the slope is curved, you will not really be able to see the summit until you are quite close to it. The slope only gradually begins to level out and you will eventually be able to see the summit cairn at 578m (1,900ft). Views are already beginning to open up, and feature most of the Donegal Highlands. Cross a low gap beyond the cairn on Glascarns Hill and continue uphill on a gentler bouldery slope. The broad top of Croaghbann bears a pool of water called Lough Aduff and a cairn at 641m (2,100ft).

## The way to Blue Stack   *Allow 2 hours*

Soon after leaving the summit of Croaghbann, you will find yourself walking down slopes of granite. These take the form of ribs of rock separated by strips of more boggy, grassy ground. The granite ribs are tilted at a reasonable angle and you should have no real problem walking down them: you can always transfer on to adjacent grassy strips if necessary. Clear weather is a distinct advantage hereabouts, and the terrain can be quite confusing in mist. When you later reach the bottom of the slope and look back, you might wonder how you got down the rocky ground so easily.

The gap you land upon is rather a complex area of rock, bog and pools of water, and when you look ahead you should already be thinking about your choice of route, as the next slope is quite steep and rugged. It is covered with heather and features occasional rocky outcrops, but it is possible to outflank any difficulties, so choose a route to suit your particular ability. Even so, you may still need to use your hands occasionally. Above this initial steep slope, there is a gentler slope of bouldery ground, then the summit cairn on Ardnageer is reached at 642m (2,118ft).

An easy descent from the summit of Ardnageer is followed by a slight reascent across bouldery ground. You will pass a cairn on a rather broad and insignificant summit. Away to the right is a feature of note – a prominent peak of white quartz stuck on to the side of the mountain. This is worth a detour, and when it catches the light on a sunny day it can be quite dazzling in this otherwise muted terrain. The granite of the Blue Stack Mountains often contains streaks of quartz, but nowhere else does it display such an abundant mass. Some large crystals might be noticed in little hollows or 'geodes'; otherwise, the outcrop is fairly amorphous.

On a sunny day, the Blue Stack Mountains might appear suddenly dull after inspecting the bright quartz outcrop. Head downhill towards a broad, rocky and hummocky gap. Although you continue by climbing towards the highest part of the range, the ground is noticeably less rocky than the previous slopes. The predominantly grassy

*Fearsome terrain even on a fine day – the aggressively bouldery Blue Stacks.*

ascent leads to a broad and grassy summit. The top of Blue Stack reaches 674m (2,219ft) and is marked by a cairn fashioned into a shelter. The views are quite extensive, taking in much of Donegal and stretching far beyond too. Try to identify some of the following sights from the summit as listed below:

| | |
|---|---|
| N | Croveenananta, Slieve Snaght, Errigal, Muckish |
| NE | Gaugin Mountain, Inishowen Peninsula |
| E | Croaghanirwore, Sperrin Mountains |
| SSE | Lough Eske, Cuilcagh |
| SSW | Truskmore, Benwhiskin, Benbulbin |
| SW | Nephin, Nephin Beg Range |
| WSW | Slieve League |
| W | Slievetooey |
| NW | Lavagh More |

## The way back to The Croaghs

*Allow 2½ hours*

The descent from the summit of Blue Stack to the Struell Gap is quite lengthy, and is accomplished on grass and boggy ground, passing a few boulders and the little pool of Lough Cronagorma before landing on the gap. You will notice a stout wooden marker post on the gap, and if you look carefully off to the right you will spot another one. These posts show you the course of the Ulster Way through the bleak uplands of Donegal. The idea is to follow these markers all the way back to the start of the walk, but you should be aware that they are very sparsely planted through this rugged terrain, and in poor visibility you may lose sight of one marker before spotting the next one in line. There haven't really been enough walkers using the route to define a clearly trodden path from one marker post to the next, so you will need to watch carefully throughout this descent to maintain the correct course.

Broadly speaking, you need to walk roughly parallel to a stream running downhill to the north-east from the Struell Gap, but you also need to drift away from it as you descend. The ground you cross can be bleak, boggy and tussocky in places, and all the inflowing streams need to be crossed. The Ulster Way through Donegal was designed as a wilderness walk and so doesn't feature too many waymarks, footbridges and other pieces of infrastructure. You will have a view of Croaghanard Lough and an area of bog planted with forestry off to the right. By keeping the marker posts in view you will be led across the lower, tussocky, boggy ground towards the Reelan River, where you will find an old footbridge to cross. It is very important that you locate this footbridge in wet weather, or you may find the Reelan River quite impassable and therefore have to detour upstream to a farm bridge to make your crossing. Once across the river, look again for the marker posts on a broad and boggy slope, and walk uphill to join the narrow road which serves the few small farms in this valley. Once you hit the road, turn right to return to your car parked alongside the former National School.

## Alternative routes

ESCAPES
The Blue Stack Mountains are broad, bleak, boggy and rocky; there are no simple escape routes from this particular circuit. If you have reached Croaghbann you could simply turn back, but if you reach Ardnageer then you might as well continue with the full circuit. Descents through the boggy area planted with forestry are definitely not recommended, no matter how rough and boggy other routes may be. The course of the Ulster Way used on the descent at least has the benefit of waymark posts, although these are admittedly quite widely spaced. In foul weather these mountains are best left alone, and anyone visiting them in poor visibility needs to be a very good navigator with map and compass: any route-finding errors in this range tend to be magnified owing to the rocky, hummocky nature of the terrain. Although the route follows the main crest of the Blue Stack Mountains, this is not a clearly defined ridge. If you descend in error on the Lough Eske side of the range, you will be faced with a long walk to correct your mistake.

EXTENSIONS

The circuit described can be extended easily enough by continuing the high-level theme. Lavagh More and Lavagh Beg are two more largely grassy mountains which can be climbed from the Ulster Way on the Struell Gap. If you continue this way, you can make a steep and rugged descent to the track at the head of the Reelan River and simply turn right to follow it back towards the old National School. Separate spurs of the Ulster Way are found at either end of the route described, so there are options to extend the walk onwards. The Ulster Way runs southwards to Lough Eske and northwards to Fintown. If you were to descend south-westwards from the Struell Gap using a spur of the Ulster Way, then you could inspect the fine waterfall called the Grey Mare's Tail. In fact, the crest of the Blue Stack Mountains can also be walked in a circuit from the Lough Eske side. The rugged, rocky recesses of the Blue Stack Mountains are made for wilderness walkers who are able to navigate successfully with map and compass, and there are many isolated rocky peaks and lonely loughs waiting to be discovered by those with the ability to seek them out.

*An Ulster Way marker on the Struell Gap, before a tough moorland descent.*

# Route 20:  GLENVEAGH

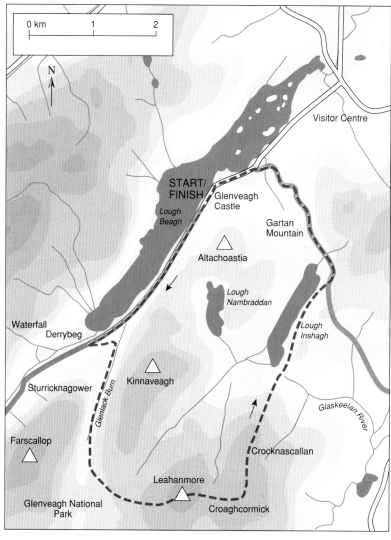

0 km    1    2

N

START/
FINISH
Glenveagh
Castle
*Lough
Beagh*
Gartan
Mountain
△
Altachoastia
*Lough
Nambraddan*
*Lough
Inshagh*
Visitor Centre
Waterfall
Derrybeg
△
Kinnaveagh
Glenlack Burn
Sturricknagower
*Glaskeelan River*
Farscallop
△
Crocknascallan
Leahanmore
△
Glenveagh National
Park
Croaghcormick

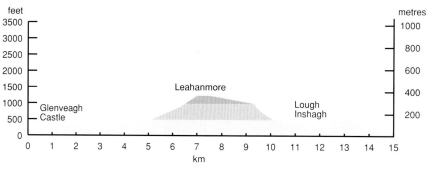

| feet | | metres |
|---|---|---|
| 3500 | | 1000 |
| 3000 | | |
| 2500 | | 800 |
| 2000 | | 600 |
| 1500 | Leahanmore | 400 |
| 1000 | | |
| 500 | Glenveagh Castle | 200 |
| 0 | | |

Lough Inshagh

0  1  2  3  4  5  6  7  8  9  10  11  12  13  14  15
km

# 8
# GLENVEAGH NATIONAL PARK

## Route 20: Glenveagh

**TIME ALLOWANCE**  6 hours.

**STARTING/FINISHING LOCATION**
Glenveagh Castle.
OSI Discovery 6: GR 020210.
Large car park at the entrance to Glenveagh.
Shuttle bus from the Visitor Centre to the castle.
No private vehicle access to Glenveagh Castle.
No bus service passes the park entrance.

**OVERVIEW/INTEREST**
Rough hill and moorland walk over superbly
   rugged glen, lough and woodland terrain, with
   fine views.
Opportunity to visit Glenveagh National Park
   Visitor Centre, plus Glenveagh Castle and
   gardens.
Chance to spot herds of red deer.

**FOOTPATHS**
Low-level tracks in Glenveagh are firm and clear.
No paths over boggy, rocky Leahanmore; those
   beside Lough Inshagh are vague.

**STATISTICS**
**WALKING DISTANCE**  16km (10 miles)
**TOTAL HEIGHT GAINED**  460m (1,510ft)
**PRINCIPAL HEIGHT**
Leahanmore  442m (1,461ft)

## The way to Leahanmore          *Allow 3 hours*

Visitors to Glenveagh National Park are required to pay an entrance fee and park near the Visitor Centre. There is plenty of background information available, as well as an audio-visual presentation and restaurant. Most visitors seem to head straight towards Glenveagh Castle and its gardens – either by walking along the narrow tarmac access road or by using the frequent shuttle-bus service, which is provided free of charge. Entry to Glenveagh Castle does incur a further charge, but the gardens can be inspected for free.

Whether you sample the delights of the Visitor Centre, castle or gardens is entirely up to you, but make sure you have enough time available to complete the walk. It is largely as a result of the infamous Glenveagh Evictions that the area is so wild and underpopulated – many people feel that it has the air of a Scottish glen. Before you start the walk, you need to check the following: time of the last shuttle bus back from the castle to the Visitor Centre; closing time of the park; likelihood of deer culling (using high-velocity rifles) in the winter months; and you might as well advise the park staff of your intended route for safety reasons.

This route description assumes that you will be starting and finishing at Glenveagh Castle. Leave the shuttle bus and walk behind the castle. You will pass some outbuildings, including a teashop, and then a sign indicating a clear path up to a viewpoint above the castle. Do not take the viewpoint path, but keep low on the broad track running parallel to the wooded shores of Lough Beagh. You may notice that the steep slopes falling into the lake are exceptionally bouldery and might well have proven almost impassable without the construction of the track you are following. The woodlands are predominantly ancient oak, with a mossy floor, but the slope seems somewhat devastated after the clearance of invasive rhododendron – in time it should recover and present a more natural outlook. You will follow the track all the way to the very head of Lough Beagh at Derrybeg. In wet weather, the waterfall across the glen on the Astelleen Burn looks really quite impressive.

When you pass the head of Lough Beagh, you will notice a small cottage on the right at Derrybeg. Just beyond this, turn sharply left on to another track which is narrower, and more grassy than gravelly. It climbs gently uphill on the wooded slopes, turning to the right on the ridge of Sturricknagower to enter Glenlack. There is a deer fence to the left of the track, which later runs out of the woods into the open glen and begins to diminish. Keep walking up through Glenlack at a gentle gradient, until you have to cross Glenlack Burn. The track will be rather muddy in wet weather, but you should continue to follow the floor of the glen towards its rather tussocky and boggy head.

When Glenlack Burn peters out at the head of Glenlack, swing left to climb eastwards up a rugged slope. There is plenty of long grass and squelchy bog before you reach a broad gap between the rounded hills of Kinnaveagh and Leahanmore. Now maintain a roughly easterly course to climb up the rugged slopes of Leahanmore. These are boggy in places, and punctuated with boulders. Depending on the line you follow, you could find yourself walking alongside a tall deer fence. If this is the case, then be sure to drift away to the left later and cross more bouldery ground to reach the summit of Leahanmore. There is a cairn at 442m (1,461ft). Views in the westerly quadrant are limited by the height of the Derryveagh Mountains, but in other directions they can be quite distant in clear weather. Look for some of the following features:

| | |
|---|---|
| NE | Loughsalt Mountain, Knockalla Mountain, Urris Hills |
| ENE | Slieve Snaght, Scalp Mountain |
| E | Croaghcormick |
| ESE | Sperrin Mountains |
| SE | Mullaghcarn, Bessy Bell |
| SSW | Blue Stack Mountains |
| SW | Moylenanav, Glendowan Mountains |
| WSW | Slieve Snaght |
| W | Farscollop |
| NW | Dooish |
| N | Muckish |

## The way back to Glenveagh Castle

*Allow 3 hours*

Walk eastwards away from the summit cairn on Leahanmore, heading down a rocky and boggy slope to reach a gap. Ahead is the broad and bouldery summit of Croaghcormick. You can decide whether to climb all the way to the summit before heading northwards, or simply begin to bear gradually northwards while crossing its shoulder. Either way, you will follow a broad and bouldery crest out to Crocknascallan and reach a prominent cairn from which there is a fine view across Lough Inshagh. Spend some time studying this view, because presently you will be walking that way and you might as well cast your eye over any potential difficulties.

Make a descent from Crocknascallan towards the southern end of Lough Inshagh, aiming for the point where the Glaskeelan River flows from the lough. The descent crosses rocky and boggy ground, becoming more level towards the lough, but featuring long, tussocky grass in places which makes walking decidedly difficult. The outflowing river cuts a deep channel from time to time, but there are also areas where large boulders protrude above the level of the water. You may not be able to cross without getting wet feet, and after heavy rainfall you may not be able to cross at all! If you head for the very point at which the river flows from the lough, you will find a good number of large, solid boulders to use as stepping stones. One or two crucial boulders are likely to be submerged, but use them anyway, rather than taking a chance with the watery depths in between.

*Derrybeg, at the head of Lough Beagh, before leaving the broad, clear track.*

After emerging from the river, simply aim to follow the shore of Lough Inshagh onwards. You may find a vaguely trodden path a short distance away from the shore, which seems to owe its existence more to migrating deer than to human traffic. You will cross areas of long grass and heather, and should beware of holes and hollows hidden in the vegetation along the way. The surrounding hills rise pleasantly above the shores of the lough and make good photographic subjects on a clear day. You will notice a small boathouse towards the head of the lough, and might think that you will find a path leading away from it. Unfortunately, this is not the case, but a short walk up a rugged slope leads on to a firm, clear track, where any difficulties you may have been experiencing with the terrain come to an end.

The track runs between Church Hill and Glenveagh Castle. To return to Glenveagh Castle, you need only to turn left and let the track lead you there. The track climbs very gently for a short while before descending towards Lough Beagh. There are clumps of gorse and rhododendron alongside it, but you are spared from having to negotiate the rugged moorland slopes. The track winds downhill to reach the shore of Lough Beagh, where you turn left along the tarmac access road leading to Glenveagh Castle. Check again the times of the last shuttle buses back to the Visitor Centre. Any spare time you have could be used in three ways. For those wanting a little extra walking, proceed behind the castle and take the signposted path up to a viewpoint overlooking Glenveagh Castle and Lough Beagh. For a gentler, low-level stroll, simply explore the amazingly well-stocked gardens beside the castle. These have a distinctly tropical air about them in direct contrast to the surrounding bleak mountains. For those who want to explore the castle itself there are guided tours available, although it would be wise to check the times of these before embarking on the walk.

On your return to the Visitor Centre, you can either wait in a shelter for the next shuttle bus, or walk back along the tarmac road. If you wait in the

*Distant Muckish seen far beyond the lonely Lough Inshagh.*

112

shelter during the summer months, you may find that you are being eaten alive by midges. Your attention is therefore drawn to a series of cartoons on boards which show the life-cycle of the midge – illustrating graphically your unwilling and unfortunate part in it!

## Alternative routes

ESCAPES

For a fairly low-lying hill, Leahanmore is quite tough underfoot. If the nature of the terrain or the weather just aren't to your liking, your only real escape is to retrace your steps down through Glenlack. Once you reach the summit of Leahanmore, you might as well continue with the route and link with the track running back to

Glenveagh Castle. If the weather is really quite bad at the outset and yet you are determined to complete a walk in Glenveagh, your best option is to walk from Glenveagh Castle to the head of the glen, using a broad track and a clear path, and either arrange to be collected there or walk back through the glen to the castle. In very wet weather, at least the waterfalls are worth seeing.

EXTENSIONS

Glenveagh National Park is Ireland's largest national park, following the acquisition of another tract of wilderness which made it larger than the Killarney National Park in the south-west of Ireland. Walks within the area of the park can therefore be quite lengthy. There are a handful of fairly low hills grouped around Leahanmore, which some call the Scallops. They are all quite

rugged underfoot, but if you want to you can complete a walk over all of them. Instead of leaving the castle using the track through the glen, climb to the viewpoint above it, then aim to stay high over as many of the little hills as you like. Just remember that there is plenty of rugged country to traverse, and a circuit might take you rather longer than you would normally expect. A much longer extension would take in Dooish on the opposite side of Glenveagh, but that would really be a whole new day's walk, given the length and difficulty involved. If you do decide to venture into the remoter parts of Glenveagh, the park staff would like you to tell them where you are going. This is especially important in the winter months, not just because of the shorter days and likelihood of bad weather, but because this is the time when deer are culled using high-velocity rifles.

# Route 21:  SLIEVE SNAGHT (DERRYVEAGH)

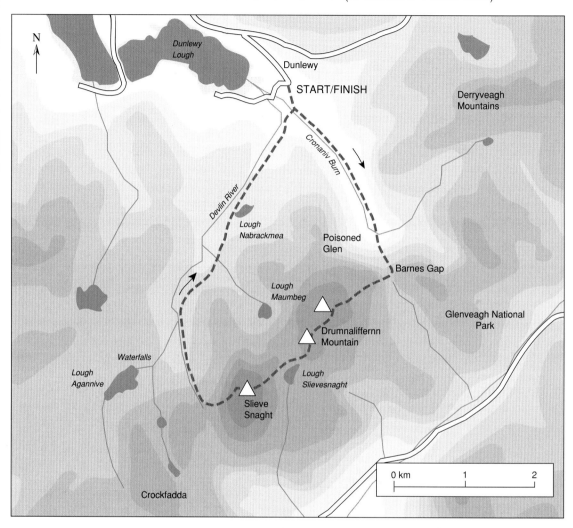

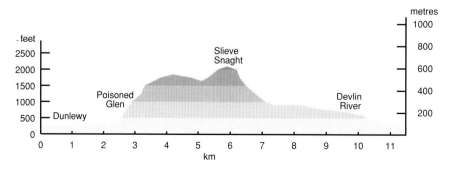

# Route 21: Slieve Snaght (Derryveagh)

**TIME ALLOWANCE**   7 hours.

**STARTING/FINISHING LOCATION**
Ruined church, Dunlewy.
OSI Discovery 1: GR 929191.
Small parking places alongside a minor road.
Small parking places above Dunlewy on the R251.
No bus service.

**OVERVIEW/INTEREST**
Ascent via the rock-walled Poisoned Glen.
Crosses the rugged granitic Derryveagh
     Mountains, with exceptional views of the
     Donegal Highlands.
Includes parts of the Ulster Way and Glenveagh
     National Park.

**FOOTPATHS**
Vague paths in the boggy glens; no paths over the
     rocky mountains.
Plenty of rocky and boggy ground.

**STATISTICS**
**WALKING DISTANCE**   13km (8 miles)
**TOTAL HEIGHT GAINED**   720m (2,360ft)
**PRINCIPAL HEIGHT**
Slieve Snaght   678m (2,240ft)

## The way up the Poisoned Glen

*Allow 2 hours*

The village of Dunlewy comes in two parts. The part you should aim for is at the eastern end of Dunlewy Lough, where a narrow minor road signposted 'Poisoned Glen' leaves the R251 and runs down past a straggly line of houses and farms. The roofless ruin of an old CofI church stands just before a pronounced right turn on the road. You will find only small parking spaces for one or two cars at a time along this road, so use them wisely, and ask for permission if in doubt. If you find nowhere to park along this minor road, you should find a space on the R251 just above this part of Dunlewy. Alternatively, you might be based at the Radharc na Gleann bed & breakfast just a short way back from the ruined church, in which case you will be able to use their parking space.

Head for a pronounced bend in the road just below the roofless church, and you will notice an old track heading out south-eastwards across the bog. Follow this track and you will be led across an old stone-arched bridge over a river. The track peters out all too soon in an extensive area of bog which occupies the floor of the Poisoned Glen. The glen gets its name from the plant known as the Irish spurge, which grew along the banks of the river and made the water undrinkable. It was ruthlessly cleared and now no longer grows in the area. Although completely unwaymarked in these parts, the route of the Ulster Way passes through the Poisoned Glen on its way through Donegal from Pettigo to Falcarragh.

As you cross the bogland, you should notice a vaguely trodden path which is never too far away from the Cronaniv Burn. The grassy bog is in places lavishly covered in bog myrtle, and in very wet weather can be completely awash. You will notice the huge slabs of granite which rise up from the glen to the summits of the surrounding mountains, and if you turn around completely you will see the pyramidal peak of Errigal apparently blocking the mouth of the glen. Looking ahead again, keep your eye fixed on the rocky notch of Barnes Gap at the head of the Poisoned Glen, because you will be climbing up to that point to reach the high mountains. Take the boggy floor of the Poisoned Glen in your stride, and cross the course of the Cronaniv Burn when you suddenly find it flowing in from the left, after its descent from distant Lough Beg.

After crossing the burn, you can start climbing in earnest – some 300m (1,000ft) from the floor of the glen to the notch of Barnes Gap at the head of the glen. The burn you crossed marks the boundary of the Glenveagh National Park for a short way, and you will remain on park lands until you descend from the mountains. The boggy floor of the glen rises and you will pass the first of many large boulders. There are steep slopes of boulders and deep heather ahead, but if you look carefully you will find a vaguely trodden path leading up through it all. Be careful not to step on slippery vegetation or greasy slabs of rock. Your line of ascent is largely restricted by nearby buttresses of granite, riven by gullies and featuring a startling pinnacle. You may notice that this dark, damp north-facing cleft provides a home to ferns, wood sorrel and St Patrick's cabbage. If you pause on the higher parts of this steep climb and turn around, you will find that the view of Errigal is now accompanied by the neighbouring Aghlas. A little further uphill and the gradient in the rocky cleft suddenly begins to ease. The boulders become absent and a slope of grass leads up to the top of a

gap, leaving you facing across the Derryveagh Mountains to the dome of Moylenanav in the Glendowan Mountains.

## The way to Slieve Snaght          *Allow 2 hours*

When you reach Barnes Gap at the head of the Poisoned Glen, turn right and work your way up a rocky slope. The rocks are mainly in the form of boulders, slabs and low outcrops, so they are fairly easy to negotiate. The ground in between them tends to be squelchy, and there may be pools of water. There is no path through this wilderness upland, and in poor visibility you will need to be a competent navigator, using a series of small loughs and rocky summits as guides. Little Lough Maumbeg is flanked by low cliffs falling sheer into its waters. Beyond it is a short climb up on to a

broad and bouldery summit at around 580m (1,900ft). At this point, views should be opening up considerably in clear weather, and you may even be able to determine patterns in the jumble of slabs and boulders which litter the broad, domed summits of the Derryveagh Mountains.

You pass another small lough and cross another broad and bouldery summit before descending towards the head of Lough Slievesnaght. You have a choice on the descent towards the lough of using either predominantly rocky or predominantly grassy ground. Either way, the head of Lough Slievesnaght is a level area of boulder-strewn granite. The final climb up the boggy and bouldery slope to the summit of Slieve Snaght is around 180m (590ft). The steep gradients gradually ease and the top is revealed as a broad area of short grass crowned with a large cairn at 678m (2,240ft). The view is remarkably extensive in fine weather,

taking in almost all of the major heights in Donegal, but also stretching to more distant features. A sample of all the features in view could include:

| | |
|---|---|
| N | Errigal |
| NNE | Aghlas, Muckish |
| NE | Dooish |
| ENE | Scallops, Inishowen Peninsula |
| ESE | Glendowan Mountains, Sperrin Mountains |
| S | Blue Stack Mountains |
| SW | Carrick Peninsula, Slieve League |
| W | Aran Island |
| WNW | Crocknafarragh |
| NNW | Tievealehid, Tory Island |

## The way back to Dunlewy     *Allow 3 hours*

There are reasons to take great care on the descent from Slieve Snaght. First and foremost, the broad, domed summit obscures the steep and rocky flanks which fall away in many directions. Do not even think about a direct descent to Dunlewy – even though the village may be plainly in view to the north. Make your initial descent roughly south-west from the summit, aiming to land on a gap in the mountains. Even so, you will need to be careful with your exact choice of route, as the steep slopes of Slieve Snaght are littered with boulders and slabs, which require short detours in some instances. Also, take care not to slip on steep and wet grass or moss. The slope later curves to allow you a clear view down towards the gap in clear weather, so that you can pick your way down to it more easily. Maps mark a small lough, but this is no more than a shallow pool which may dry up completely in hot and dry weather.

When you land on the gap, you should change direction and continue your descent roughly northwards. Try to avoid being drawn down into a rocky cleft which is used by a small watercourse, as this can be difficult. Instead, keep away from it

*The Poisoned Glen and dome of Slieve Snaght, seen from the slopes of Errigal.*

and stay on the open slopes alongside. Again, you will need to keep your eye on occasional boulders and slabs, as well as on steep, wet grass or moss. On this steep descent you will leave the area of the Glenveagh National Park, although the boundary isn't marked by any particular feature in the landscape. You might also pause and look ahead at the course of the Devlin River. It describes intricate meanders across an upland bog, which you do not need to follow in detail. There are also small pools on the surface of the bog which can prove difficult to negotiate. The best course of action is to keep well away from the Devlin River at first, then gradually drift towards its banks later on. You may also notice the spectacular waterfall descending from Lough Agannive, and might even consider it worthy of a slight detour.

The Devlin River runs roughly north-eastwards across the rugged moorlands, so that you will cross areas of heather and tussocky grass as you follow it downstream. Don't walk too close to the river, but aim to trace a vague path which runs roughly parallel to it. After crossing the stream flowing out of little Lough Nabrackmea, the river runs down a slightly steeper slope. Here it is confined to a rocky cleft which contains quite a variety of trees – no doubt the remnants of the forest which once clothed the Derryveagh Mountains, whose very name is derived from the oak and birch. At the foot of the rocky cleft, the Devlin River emerges in a fine waterfall. Continue down across rugged bogland, aiming roughly towards the roofless church. You will need to ford the Cronaniv Burn to return towards the narrow tarmac road leading back into Dunlewy.

## Alternative routes

### ESCAPES

There are no easy escape routes from the Derryveagh Mountains. The crest of the range is flanked with boilerplate slabs of granite which have the potential to leave descending walkers stranded on immense cliff faces. If you start climbing to the head of the Poisoned Glen in bad weather, the ground could become dangerously slippery and you would be advised to retreat. A safe descent could be considered from Lough Slievesnaght to Lough Maam and on down to the Devlin River, but this omits Slieve Snaght, which is one of the crowning glories of the Derryveagh Mountains. Once you gain the summit of Slieve Snaght, you might as well make your descent by way of the Devlin River, following the route description outlined.

### EXTENSIONS

The Derryveagh Mountains are a wonderfully wild and rugged range. From one end to the other they feature domed summits, lough-strewn gaps, boulders and slabby outcrops of rock. It is marvellous walking country in fine weather, but potentially confusing in mist, or when a long day's walk runs into dusk and darkness. When planning extensions, consider also the rugged nature of the terrain. Peaks along the crest of the Derryveagh Mountains which are also part of the Glenveagh National Park include Dooish, Slieve Snaght and Crocknafarragh. A walk along the length of the range to include all three of these prominent summits would be well worth considering, and it could be achieved in a lengthy circuit from Dunlewy. Instead of entering the Poisoned Glen, however, it would make more sense to start high on the R251 and climb on to Dooish direct. You would have to cross the deer fence as you entered the national park, and later cross it again near the head of the Poisoned Glen. National park staff would like to know if you were within the confines of the deer fence, especially in the winter months when the red deer are culled using high-velocity rifles. It is also recommended that you slip between the strands of wire on the fence, rather than attempting to climb it. After crossing Slieve Snaght and proceeding across barren uplands to reach Crocknafarragh, it is possible to descend towards the causeway between Dunlewy Lough and Lough Nacung to return to Dunlewy village.

*Looking back through the Poisoned Glen towards the peak of Errigal.*

# Route 22: ERRIGAL

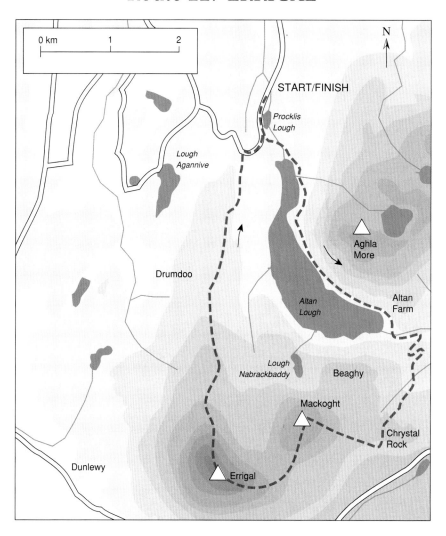

0 km     1     2

N

START/FINISH

Procklis Lough

Lough Agannive

Drumdoo

Altan Lough

Aghla More

Altan Farm

Lough Nabrackbaddy

Beaghy

Mackoght

Chrystal Rock

Dunlewy

Errigal

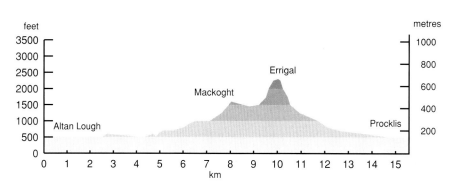

| feet | | metres |
|---|---|---|
| 3500 | | 1000 |
| 3000 | | |
| 2500 | Errigal | 800 |
| 2000 | Mackoght | 600 |
| 1500 | | 400 |
| 1000 | Altan Lough          Procklis | 200 |
| 500 | | |
| 0 | 1 2 3 4 5 6 7 8 9 10 11 12 13 14 15 | |

km

# 9

# DONEGAL HIGHLANDS

## Route 22: Errigal

**TIME ALLOWANCE**   6 hours.

**STARTING/FINISHING LOCATION**
Procklis Lough, Tullaghobegly.
OSI Discovery 1: GR 935256.
Small spaces for cars along the roadside.
No bus service.

**OVERVIEW/INTEREST**
Climbs Errigal – the highest mountain in Donegal,
   with extensive panoramic views.
Features an abandoned tower house at the head
   of Altan Lough.
Includes part of the Ulster Way.

**FOOTPATHS**
Low-level paths and tracks are clear, but can be
   boggy.
Gravelly paths also occur on the ascent of Errigal.
Some parts of the route are not well trodden.
Plenty of boggy ground, steep rock and scree in
   places.

**STATISTICS**
**WALKING DISTANCE**   16km (10 miles)
**TOTAL HEIGHT GAINED**   770m (2,525ft)
**PRINCIPAL HEIGHTS**
Mackoght   555m (1,820ft)
Errigal   751m (2,466ft)

## The way to the head of Altan Lough

*Allow 1½ hours*

Parking near Procklis Lough can be tight. Take
great care when parking not to block farm access
roads, field gates or bog roads. If you can't park
close to Procklis Lough, you will have to park
further back along the road near a fish farm and
walk back towards the lough. There is a metal gate
by the roadside near the head of the lough. It
stands between two posts, but the posts aren't
connected to any walls or fences, so you can walk
straight past the side of the gate. A clear track runs
towards the foot of Altan Lough, with the lough
itself being reached after you have crossed step-
stiles alongside two more gates. Although unwaymarked, this route has long been suggested as
the course of the Ulster Way through Donegal.
There are a couple of small buildings near the foot
of the lough, which are connected with water
abstraction. There is no footbridge across the
outflowing Tullaghobegly River, but there are
plenty of boulders to step on as you make your
way across. After heavy rain you will get wet feet,
and after torrential rain you may not be able to
continue with the walk.

   You will follow the eastern shore of Altan Lough
all the way from the foot of the lough to the head.
This involves first walking across boggy ground
beside the lough, and further on negotiating long
heather and tussocky grass. Later, the slopes of
Aghla More fall more steeply into Altan Lough, so
you will find yourself crossing steeper, rockier
ground. If you look forward towards the head of
the lough you will spot a square tower house, and
it is towards this building you are walking. By the
time you reach it, you will notice a fine sandy
strand along the head of the lake, and could easily
convince yourself that you were at the head of an
inlet from the sea. The tower house, known as

Altan Farm, was built in the mid-nineteenth century by a lawyer from Portadown, reputedly because he wanted to live somewhere with a bit of solitude. One can only hope this remote place suited his needs. No doubt many passing walkers have thought how fine it would be to live in such a wild and remote spot – a pity nothing is being done to arrest its decay, for surely one day it will tumble completely.

## The way to Errigal                    *Allow 2½ hours*

The tower house was served by an access road leading away to distant Dunlewy. To follow it, you first need to cross the nearby river. You will notice a fine waterfall before the river enters the head of Altan Lough. Do not cross at this point, but proceed a little further upstream to locate a series of large stepping stones. These will normally be above water, although torrential rain may submerge them. The track leads up and away to the left, but it has long been disused and the surrounding boggy moorland is gradually encroaching upon it. In effect, it is like a ribbon of bog drawn through a bog! The track runs upstream and passes close to an even larger waterfall, before continuing uphill in a series of broad loops. Avoid the temptation to take a short cut through the loops, as the ground is quite wet and rugged.

Although you could cut away from the track to make an ascent of Beaghy, this little hill has little to commend it except for a view out across Altan Lough. It is perhaps better to stay on the moorland track and bypass Beaghy, crossing a small stream and climbing across a shoulder of rugged moorland. A feature worth a moment of study is shown on the map as Chrystal Rock, and it is found where the track starts to descend towards the R251. The rock lies just up to the right of the track and on close inspection you should be able to find little veins and hollows which are tightly packed with white and clear quartz crystals. By leaving the track, you have also left the line taken by the Ulster Way through this upland region.

Walk roughly westwards away from the Chrystal Rock to begin climbing the slopes of

*The tower house at the head of Altan Lough, below Aghla More.*

Mackoght. The rugged moorland features boggy grass and heather, and becomes rockier as the ground steepens. In mist the summit of Mackoght could be confusing, as it bears all manner of rocky excrescences which could be mistaken for the highest point. In fact, you are aiming for the summit cairn at 555m (1,820ft). In clear weather, it is worth spending a moment studying the ridges leading on to and away from the summit of Errigal, just in case they should later be shrouded in mist. As you view this lofty peak, your ascent route is to the left, and the descent is more or less along the skyline to the right.

First, you will need to descend roughly south south-west from the summit of Mackoght, picking a way down the hummocky slopes of rock, scree and heather. Almost immediately after landing on a gap, you begin climbing up towards the summit of Errigal. The total ascent from the gap to the summit is around 350m (1,150ft). The ground steepens quickly, with heather cover giving way to broken rock and scree. The scree on the higher parts of the ridge has been pulverized into a finer gravel, where paths running straight up from the R251 have delivered walkers and their boots on to the ridge. Simply keep crunching uphill on the ridge path, bypassing any rocky outcrops on the way. The steep part of the ridge suddenly eases at a circular stone shelter on a shoulder. There is also a memorial cairn to Joey Glover of the North West Mountaineering Club – shot in 1976 by the IRA. The path continues up the ridge at a more gentle gradient and soon reaches the summit. The trig point at 751m (2,466ft) toppled off the mountain many years ago and only the crucial brass 'button' set into the rock remains. Another feature of Errigal is that it has twin summit peaks separated by a short, rocky ridge known as the One Man's Pass. More importantly, in clear weather, is the tremendous panorama which can be studied from the summit. Look out for the following features near and distant:

| | |
|---|---|
| NE | Aghlas, Muckish |
| ENE | Urris Hills, Slieve Snaght, Inishowen |
| E | Dooish |
| ESE | Sperrin Mountains |
| SSE | Poisoned Glen, Moylenanav |
| S | Slieve Snaght, Blue Stack Mountains |
| SW | Crocknafarragh, Carrick Peninsula |
| W | Aran Island |
| NW | Tievealehid |
| NNW | Tory Island |

The steep and rocky ground falling away towards Dunlewy is a detached part of the Glenveagh National Park. Crocknafarragh, in view to the south-west, was a property of An Taisce (Irish National Trust), but the area is now managed as part of the Glenveagh National Park too. Maybe in time there will be further land acquisitions to protect and enhance this rugged upland region of Donegal. The national park already has an extensive 'buffer zone' where inappropriate developments are discouraged.

## The way back to Procklis Lough

*Allow 2 hours*

To start the descent from Errigal, first make sure that you have walked along the One Man's Pass, then make sure that you study carefully the ground falling away northwards. Clear weather is most useful on the descent, so that you can see your way down the steep, rocky ridges and slopes of scree. In mist, or while darkness is falling, these could quickly become rather confusing. By walking northwards and outflanking any awkward rocky areas, you will be led down a bouldery slope to reach a broad crest of moorland. Route-finding errors are likely to lead you either towards Dunlewy, or into a barren and bouldery hollow near little Lough Nabrackbaddy.

When the steep northern slopes of Errigal finally run out as an apron of boulders, you should continue across a heathery moorland and keep walking in a northerly direction. The moorland crest is quite rugged in places where the blanket bog is decaying, but you can later make easier progress by walking on patches of stones. The broad crest gradually descends and you will reach a bog road at Drumdoo. Keep to the right and let it lead you along a gentle slope overlooking Altan Lough. The bog road is largely overgrown and can be quite squelchy underfoot; in fact, after heavy rain some sections can convey water in streams. However, it is a clear feature which will lead you directly off the moorland crest. You pass under an electricity transmission line before a slight rise lands you on a minor road. A right turn along this road quickly leads back to Procklis Lough, and if you were to follow the road onwards, the Ulster Way uses its course to end at the village of Falcarragh on the coast.

## Alternative routes

ESCAPES

You will find out quickly enough if the Tullaghobegly River is impassable, and if it is you will have to abandon the walk and choose another route. Once you are following the shore of Altan

Lough you can't actually drop any lower, so the only escape route is back the way you came. However, when you start climbing up towards Mackoght and Errigal the onset of bad weather is no real problem, and it is possible to descend straight downhill to the south-east at almost any point to reach the R251. It is not a very busy road, but there is a possibility that someone will give you a lift down to Dunlewy – although you are of course on entirely the wrong side of Errigal if your car is parked at Procklis. Once you start descending northwards from Errigal the ground is steep and rocky, but you might as well continue that way to return to Procklis, rather than descending westwards to link with farm roads which are rather circuitous. Some people do descend directly from the summit of Errigal to the little village of Dunlewy, but this involves going down steep and highly mobile scree slopes which some walkers simply don't enjoy.

EXTENSIONS

Immediately after crossing the Tullaghobegly River, you could head for the heights by climbing the Aghlas. You could either climb Aghla More direct and descend towards the head of Altan Lough, or head across country towards Aghla Beg before turning towards Aghla More. A more ambitious approach to Errigal is via the high-level course of the Glover Marathon, starting from distant Muckish. Created by the late Joey Glover and continued on an annual basis by the North West Mountaineering Club, the Marathon starts with an ascent of Muckish, crosses Crocknalaragagh and descends to Lough Aluirg. A steep ascent and descent take the route over the Aghlas to reach the head of Altan Lough. After crossing Mackoght and Errigal, the route descends to Dunlewy. It is a tough day's walk which appeals to hardier walkers and is definitely Donegal's classic upland walk.

*Errigal's summit peak and the ridge path known as the One Man's Pass.*

# Route 23: MUCKISH

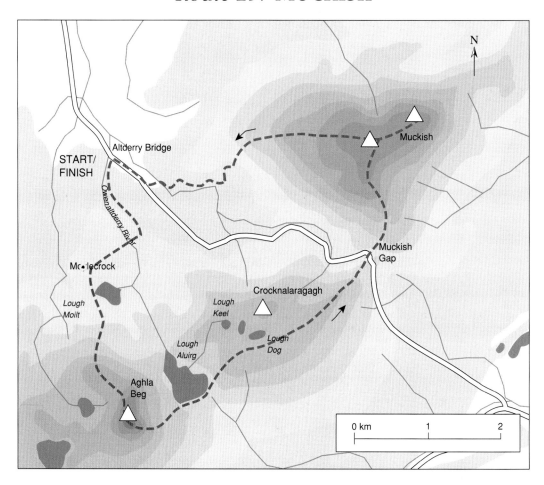

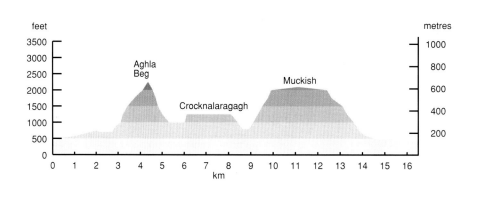

# Route 23: Muckish

**TIME ALLOWANCE**   7 hours.

**STARTING/FINISHING LOCATION**
Altderry Bridge, near Muckish Gap.
OSI Discovery 2: GR 963282.
Small parking space at the roadside by Altderry
    Bridge.
No bus service.

**OVERVIEW/INTEREST**
Rugged mountain walking to a broad, stony
    summit plateau.
Extensive, panoramic views.
Includes part of the Glover Marathon.

**FOOTPATHS**
Clear bog roads at lower levels.
Fences sometimes form useful guides.
Summit of Muckish is a confusing mass of stones.

**STATISTICS**
**WALKING DISTANCE**   17km (10½ miles)
**TOTAL HEIGHT GAINED**   1,130m (3,700ft)
**PRINCIPAL HEIGHTS**
Aghla Beg   603m (1,980ft)
Crocknalaragagh   471m (1,554ft)
Muckish   666m (2,197ft)

## The way to Aghla Beg

*Allow 2 hours*

Altderry Bridge lies on a minor road between Falcarragh and Muckish Gap. There is a bog road on either side of the road near the bridge, with room to park a car or two beside the road. In case of difficulty, you will find other small roadside spaces on the way towards Muckish Gap. In fact, you could restructure the whole route by starting and finishing on Muckish Gap, which also has a small parking space. This route description, however, starts and finishes at Altderry Bridge.

The bog road you need to follow starts running south-west from the minor road just beside Altderry Bridge, following the wooded river of Owenaltderry upstream. The bog road drifts away from the river quite early, and swings along the side of a moorland crest to run roughly south-eastwards. You will be able to see hundreds of ancient tree stumps exposed in the turf cuttings, so you can try to imagine the moorland crest as the forest it must have been in earlier centuries. The bog road crosses over the crest and turns right. It then runs downhill a short way to ford the Owenaltderry. In wet weather you will probably emerge with wet feet. The bog road climbs gently uphill and crosses two other bog roads at right angles, before falling gently and turning left towards Lough Moilt.

You will need to cross a fence and forge through a stretch of cutaway bog to reach a heathery slope beyond. If you look up the slope towards the summit of Aghla Beg, you will spot a fence running steeply uphill. As this fence forms a useful guide, you might as well follow it. First, climb up a steep slope of tough heather to reach a corner of the fence. After that, the slope steepens but the heather becomes shorter. At a higher level there are more stones on the slope, which help your boots to get a grip. Further on the fence leads on to a less steep stony shoulder, then finally conveys you to a large summit cairn at 564m (1,860ft). In fact, this is one of two twin summits, and you continue along the line of the fence to cross a broad gap of short grass and stones. The fence runs uphill, but doesn't actually reach the second summit. You will have to continue carefully up the last part of the blunt ridge without the aid of the fence, to reach a small cairn at 603m (1,980ft). Views of the Donegal Highlands are greatly enhanced by panoramas of coastline and even more distant ranges of mountains.

*OVERLEAF:*
*Lough Nabrackbaddy, Lough Feeane and the Donegal Highlands.*

127

## The way to Muckish
*Allow 3 hours*

Head roughly eastwards to descend towards Lough Aluirg. The ground falls away quite steeply and is mostly clothed in short heather, but there are some stony patches. The slope begins to level out as you approach the head of Lough Aluirg. Cross a fence, then walk along a low ridge in between the head of Lough Aluirg and the edge of a forest. As you walk along this low ridge, look towards the outflow of the lough, where in clear weather you will be able to see a small section of the Atlantic Ocean. More than that, in clear weather you will also be able to see the whole length of Tory Island apparently sailing serenely past the gap!

As you leave Lough Aluirg, a fence can be followed on to the broad, boggy and hummocky hill of Crocknalaragagh. The fence runs uphill, and then branches right and left. Take the left-hand fence to continue up to little Lough Keel. Bear right for a short way across unmarked ground to reach another small pool called Lough Dog. Another fence leads away from Lough Dog, running roughly eastwards and crossing over a hump before following a fairly well-defined crest towards the Muckish Gap. The true summit of Crocknalaragagh is away over to the left, standing at 471m (1,554ft) – if you feel like visiting it. On the way towards Muckish Gap, you may spot a line of white quartz boulders just to the left of the fence. When it begins its final descent towards the gap, the fence runs alongside a forest. You may find it easier to walk down to the gap if you keep well away from the fence. You will reach the road on Muckish Gap close to a small roadside shrine.

Keep well to the left of the little shrine before starting to climb uphill on to Muckish. You will have to cross a fairly gently sloping area of boggy ground first, and then start climbing uphill alongside a small stream. When you reach the top of this stream, bear left to keep climbing steeply uphill. You will find yourself on a slope which is only thinly vegetated with heather, or even creeping juniper and mosses among the stony ground. A final steep and rounded ridge of stony ground leads to the edge of the summit plateau, where there is a cairn. In clear weather you should have no problem reaching the summit of Muckish, but in poor visibility the broad and stony summit plateau could be a very confusing place for walkers who are visiting it for the first time.

In clear weather, it is well worth making a thorough exploration of the summit plateau. First, you should head across the gently sloping stony ground to reach the huge, bouldery summit burial cairn. From there, walk roughly north-eastwards across stony ground to reach the trig point at 666m (2,197ft). Just a bit further along is another prominent cairn, usually sporting a cross or at least a tall wooden post. This point is worth a visit simply for the fine views it offers over the northern coast of Donegal. Also recommended is a view into the steep-sided northern hollow falling from the summit of Muckish, where a disused sand quarry can be studied. With more time to spare, this can be inspected more closely by carefully following a path down into it. Although such broad summits do not normally offer the best views, the view from Muckish is remarkably extensive, including the following features:

| N | Horn Head |
| NE | Malin Head |
| ENE | Slieve Snaght, Inishowen |
| E | Scalp Mountain |
| ESE | Sperrin Mountains |
| SE | Mullaghcarn |
| S | Dooish, Blue Stack Mountains |
| SSW | Slieve Snaght |
| SW | Aghlas, Errigal, Carrick Peninsula |
| WSW | Tievealehid |
| WNW | Bloody Foreland |
| NW | Tory Island |

## The way back to Altderry Bridge
*Allow 2 hours*

Again, you will need to remember that the broad and stony summit of Muckish can be a confusing place in poor visibility. In clear weather there should be no real problem, and you can simply head westwards from the huge, bouldery summit cairn. The stony ground gradually steepens, and as it does so it is more likely to become covered in heather. You will need to swing slightly to the left later when you see a bog road looping around turf cuttings in low-lying ground near the road. The ground is very steep on the final run down towards the bog, and you will need to be careful if you are drawn on to any slopes of large boulders. When you land on the bog road, turn right to follow it. This road can be awash with water after heavy rain, and as you follow it you will reach a junction. Keep to the left and follow the track until it suddenly appears to end. In fact, it is simply overgrown and can still be traced down towards the Ray River. Turn right to follow the river downstream a short way, then ford it – wet feet at this late stage are not a problem. The bog road runs up to a minor road, where a right turn quickly leads back to the Altderry Bridge.

*The broad, bleak and bouldery summit of Muckish needs care in poor visibility.*

## Alternative routes

### ESCAPES

Assuming that you have climbed on to Aghla Beg, there are really only two escape routes to consider. Either retrace your steps downhill and back along the bog roads, or descend to Lough Aluirg and follow the outflowing river until you can link back into the bog road network. Once you cross the hummocky Crocknalaragagh and reach the Muckish Gap, the minor road offers the most obvious escape route back to Altderry Bridge. If you have climbed Muckish, again there are only really two routes back down. The simplest escape is to retrace your steps to Muckish Gap and the road, while the only other route worth considering is to complete the whole circuit as described.

### EXTENSIONS

Muckish, Crocknalaragagh and the Aghlas are crossed on the annual Glover Marathon, which runs all the way from Muckish to Errigal. The whole of this high-level walk can be observed from the Aghlas or from Muckish, so that you will have some idea of the nature of the route. It is Donegal's classic upland walk and is organized in mid-September each year by the North West Mountaineering Club, of which Joey Glover was a founder member. The ascent of Muckish at the start of the Glover Marathon uses a steep and stony scramble on the northern slopes. This zigzag line was trodden out by miners employed at a now disused sand quarry, and is known as the Miner's Path. The quarry was a source of pure sand for use in optical glass manufacture. Quarry workers used to have a rapid method of descent at the end of each day, when they slid down a wooden sand-chute at high speed! The ascent is worth the effort, even if the novelty of the miner's descent is no longer available. To complete the Glover Marathon route, you climb first on to the summit of Muckish, then cross Muckish Gap to climb over boggy Crocknalaragagh, passing Lough Aluirg before climbing over the Aghlas. A steep descent leads to the ruined tower house at the head of Altan Lough. After crossing Beaghy and Mackoght, the route scales lofty Errigal, before a final descent to the village of Dunlewy. If you have parked a car on the northern side of Muckish, you are going to have problems recovering it!

# Route 24: SLIEVE SNAGHT (INISHOWEN)

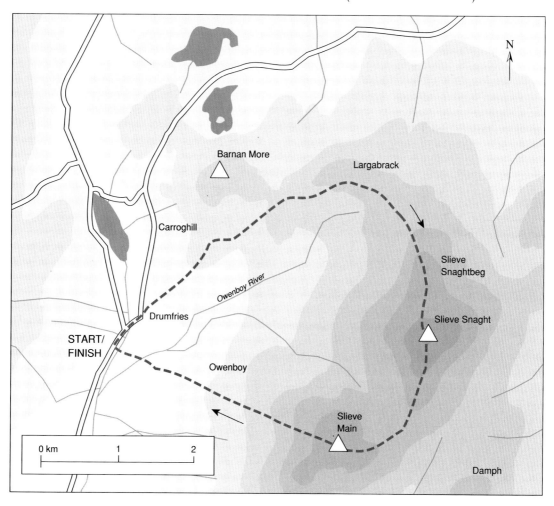

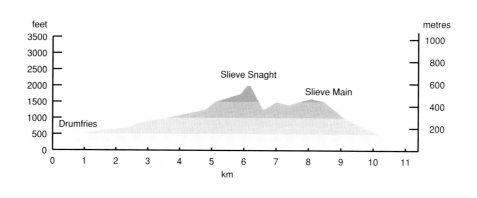

# 10

# INISHOWEN PENINSULA

## Route 24: Slieve Snaght (Inishowen)

**TIME ALLOWANCE**   5 hours.

**STARTING/FINISHING LOCATION**
The North Pole, Drumfries.
OSI Discovery 3: GR 385390.
Small pub car park – ask permission.
Lough Swilly buses serve Drumfries.

**OVERVIEW/INTEREST**
Climbs to the highest point on Inishowen, with
  panoramic views from the summit.
The mountain is surrounded by extensive blanket
  bogs.

**FOOTPATHS**
Low-level bog roads.
No paths over the high ground.
Plenty of bog and heather, becoming stony on top.

**STATISTICS**
**WALKING DISTANCE**   12km (7½ miles)
**TOTAL HEIGHT GAINED**   665m (2,180ft)
**PRINCIPAL HEIGHTS**
Slieve Snaght   615m (2,019ft)
Slieve Main   514m (1,557ft)

### The way to Slieve Snaght          *Allow 3 hours*

It's not every day that you can claim to have
started a walk at the North Pole – but you can do
it at Drumfries. The North Pole in this case is a pub
situated at the point where the R238 and R244
branch apart. Drumfries is little more than the pub,
a post office and a school, with a handful of farms
and houses. On maps it tends to be written as
Drumfree. The pub has a small car park, so you
might ask permission to leave your car there, or
you could use small roadside spaces elsewhere
in the village. Alternatively, there are quite a few
Lough Swilly buses passing through Drumfries
each day from places such as Buncrana, Carndonagh and Clonmany.

Leave the North Pole pub by following the R244
as if heading for Carndonagh. However, as soon as
this road bears to the left, you should keep right,
walking straight up a narrow minor road. This road
climbs uphill past a couple of houses, then you
continue through a gate beyond the last house to
follow a grassy, gravelly track. You will have a
fence on your right at first, but after passing
through another gate you will have a fence on
your left instead. You will be walking through a
sort of crossroads of tracks, where you keep
heading straight onwards towards the rocky
summit of Barnan More. However, you should
turn right along the next bog road; this is easily
recognized, if only because of the rubbish dumped
alongside it at the start. The road expires on the
high moorlands at about 250m (820ft).

It is largely up to you how you proceed towards
Slieve Snaght. There are three options you could
consider. The first is a direct ascent, forging across
a broad and heathery hollow before tackling the
steep slopes of heather and rock. The second is
similar, but you aim straight towards Slieve
Snaghtbeg and use it as a sort of 'stepping stone'
towards the main summit. The third option is
slightly more circuitous, but offers the most gently

133

graded ascent, and this is recommended above the other two. It is simply a matter of keeping as high as possible along the ill-defined moorland crest of Larganbrack. There are small rocky outcrops, which are easily outflanked, and no trace of paths worth following. The broad and hummocky crest can be followed uphill in stages, and it is worth taking the deep heather and boggy patches steadily to conserve your energy. Looking ahead, you will see that the ground steepens before Slieve Snaghtbeg, and on the last gently graded part of the moorland crest you will find the end of a bog road and some turf cuttings.

The steep and stony climb on to Slieve Snaghtbeg is also quite short. The heather cover is short too, and the stony patches are easily outflanked. The little dome of heather is crowned with a cairn which will have been visible from afar. A pleasant heathery ridge runs roughly southwards into the more rugged flank of Slieve Snaght. The slope isn't too steep and stony patches are easily avoided. You will notice what appears to be the summit cairn in clear weather, but it is actually a circular stone enclosure which surrounds the trig point at 615m (2,019ft). The bouldery dome of Slieve Snaght is covered in small cairns and upended spikes of rock. Every visitor likes to leave their little monument, but in mist it makes the top of the mountain a bewildering place

*Looking back to Slieve Snaght from a farm access road near Drumfries.*

for the first-time visitor. In clear weather, however, the views across country and towards Scotland are far-reaching and include the following:

| | |
|---|---|
| NE | Islay, Jura, Scotland |
| E | Knocklayd, Antrim Mountains, Scotland |
| ESE | Binevenagh |
| SE | Benbradagh |
| SSE | Sawel, Dart |
| S | Scalp Mountain, Mullaghcarn |
| SW | Inch Island, Lough Swilly, Blue Stack Mountains |
| WSW | Muckish, Errigal |
| W | Aghaweel Hill, Horn Head |
| WNW | Urris Hills |
| NW | Raghtin More |
| N | Malin Head |

## The way back to Drumfries          *Allow 2 hours*

It is possible to return directly from the summit of Slieve Snaght to Drumfries, but it is more satisfying to stay high for a while longer and include the neighbouring summit of Slieve Main. Leave the summit of Slieve Snaght by walking roughly southwards, then begin to swing more to the south-west. You should make a careful study of the broad gap between the two mountains as you descend towards it, as there is plenty of rugged bog there which is chopped into hags and groughs. Aim to steer an easy course through the gap, then start climbing straight up the slopes of Slieve Main. The heathery ground may feature some squelchy spots, while the summit bears a few rashes of stones. There is a small cairn on top, but it does not seem to sit exactly on the 514m (1,557ft) summit.

If you descend fairly directly from the top of Slieve Main towards Drumfries, you will be walking roughly west north-west. The heathery ground falls away in both steep and gentle slopes, with occasional rocky outcrops posing no real problem. When the slope runs out into more gently graded boggy ground, you will have to cross a fence. Continue down towards a couple of farms – you can choose between them according to the state of the Owenboy River. If the day has been dry and

the river is likely to be low, head for the farm on the right, ford the river and use the access road to return to Drumfries. If there has been plenty of rain and the river is running high, head for the farm on the left, whose access road features a narrow bridge over the river. In this case you land on the R238 just outside Drumfries, but a right turn leads you back to the North Pole in only a few minutes. If you are relying on the Lough Swilly buses, be sure that you have a copy of the timetables.

## Alternative routes

ESCAPES

There aren't really any escape routes worth considering. Slieve Snaght is so broad, bleak and boggy that you either climb it or you don't. The ascent and descent on the Drumfries side uses bog roads and farm roads, and these are fairly straightforward. If you make any other descents, then beware of the course of the Owenboy River during wet weather. Descents in other directions will leave you a long way from Drumfries, and so should be avoided. If you want to make a short there-and-back ascent with the minimum amount of effort, then you might be better starting higher on the R244 and using bog roads at the start.

EXTENSIONS

This route covers the highest parts of Slieve Snaght, and the only hill in the range left to cover is little Crocknamaddy. An alternative extension away from Slieve Snaght would be towards Bulbin. Minor roads and bog roads would need to be linked to bring this solitary height into the route, and its inclusion would easily double the distance. In some views Bulbin appears almost as a peak, but in others it is quite shapeless. A tall concrete monument crowns its 494m (1,620ft) summit, making it instantly recognizable in the immediate surroundings. To stay on Slieve Snaght, perhaps the longest walk you could undertake would be an end-to-end crossing from the Buncrana side to the Carndonagh side, but expect this to be mostly a rugged moorland walk.

# Route 25: THE URRIS HILLS

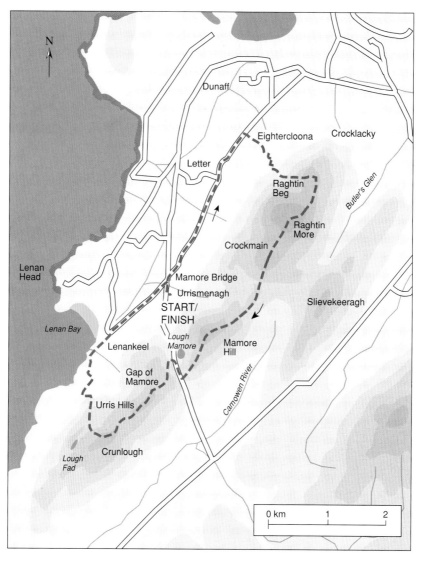

- Dunaff
- Eightercloona
- Crocklacky
- Letter
- Raghtin Beg
- Butler's Glen
- Raghtin More
- Crockmain
- Lenan Head
- Slievekeeragh
- Mamore Bridge
- Urrismenagh
- START/ FINISH
- Lenan Bay
- Lough Mamore
- Mamore Hill
- Lenankeel
- Gap of Mamore
- Carrowen River
- Urris Hills
- Crunlough
- Lough Fad

N

0 km    1    2

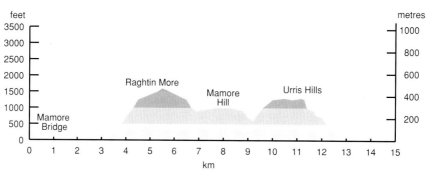

feet
3500
3000
2500
2000
1500
1000
500
0

metres
1000
800
600
400
200

Raghtin More

Mamore Hill

Urris Hills

Mamore Bridge

0  1  2  3  4  5  6  7  8  9  10  11  12  13  14  15
km

# Route 25: The Urris Hills

**TIME ALLOWANCE** 7 hours.

**STARTING/FINISHING LOCATION**
Mamore Bridge, Gap of Mamore.
OSI Discovery 2 or 3: GR 317442.
Small car park on the Gap of Mamore road.
No bus service.

**OVERVIEW/INTEREST**
Heathery and rocky ridge walk over a splendidly
    rugged range of hills.
Superb coastal and hill views.
Features a holy well near Lough Mamore.
Not far from Dunree Fort on Dunree Head.

**FOOTPATHS**
Clear tracks on the lower slopes.
Vague paths only over some of the hills.
Fairly dry heathery or rocky ground throughout.

**STATISTICS**
**WALKING DISTANCE** 18km (11 miles)
**TOTAL HEIGHT GAINED** 930m (3,050ft)
**PRINCIPAL HEIGHTS**
Raghtin More 502m (1,657ft)
Mamore Hill 423m (1,381ft)
Urris Hills 417m (1,379ft)

## The way to Raghtin More

*Allow 3 hours*

Park beside the Gap of Mamore road, in between
the actual Gap of Mamore and Mamore Bridge.
Walk downhill on the last part of the zigzag road
and turn right at a crossroads. Follow signposts for
Clonmany, Four Arches bed & breakfast and
Mamore Cottages – a group of charming thatched
cottages with their roofs well tied down against
Atlantic gales, and their backs against the slopes of
Raghtin More. When you have passed these,
continue along the road until you reach a little
Roman Catholic chapel on the right-hand side of
the road. Turn right to pass through its car park,
and continue straight onwards along a gravel

track. This track appears to head straight towards
the steep slopes of Raghtin More, and you pass
through a gate before using a series of zigzags to
start climbing up the hillside. There is about 450m
(1,475ft) of ascent and as you climb some fine
views open up behind, over the scattered
settlement of Dunaff and the rugged excrescence
of Dunaff Head.

When the zigzag track ends on a steep, heathery
slope, you have two options to consider. Ahead is
a large heathery hollow in the hills, and you can
either keep to the right to make a steep and direct
ascent of Raghtin More, or keep to the left to climb
Raghtin Beg first. The latter option makes easier
work of the steep slopes, as you climb a slightly
gentler one to reach the minor summit of Raghtin
Beg, then cross a stony and heathery gap before a
short and steep pull up on to Raghtin More. The
broad, domed summit is covered in heather and
boulders, and bears a huge and ancient bouldery
cairn which has been fashioned into a wind
shelter. There is also a trig point at 502m (1,657ft).
For some strange reason, the Ordnance Survey
maps show the cairn and trig point occupying
opposite positions, but they are fairly close
together in any case and this error shouldn't cause
you any inconvenience. Views around Inishowen
and Donegal are first class, as well as those views
stretching much further afield, and you should
be able to spot the following features in clear
weather:

| | |
|---|---|
| NNE | Malin Head |
| NE | Binnion |
| E | Causeway Coast, Scotland |
| SE | Slieve Snaght |
| SSE | Bulbin, Sperrin Mountains |
| S | Inch Island, Lough Swilly |
| SSW | Blue Stack Mountains |
| SW | Mamore Hill, Urris Hills |
| WSW | Muckish, Dooish, Errigal |
| W | Fanad, Horn Head, Tory Island |
| NW | Dunaff Head |

## The way to the Gap of Mamore

*Allow 2 hours*

Walk roughly south-westwards to leave the summit of Raghtin More. You will be able to see Mamore Hill and the Urris Hills arranged before you in a rugged line, but first you must pick a way down from Raghtin More. There is a steep slope of heather and boulders, but it quickly runs out on to a gap. A short walk uphill leads across the subsidiary summit of Crockmain. A longer and more rugged descent leads down to another gap, where you should notice the course of an old bog road on the gap. This old track actually climbs up to the gap from the car park where you started walking, so it makes a good escape route if required. You should spot a vague path running alongside the rugged crest of rock and heather, which then climbs steeply up the slopes of Mamore Hill. After the initial steep pull, the crest of the hill is set at a gentler gradient and the summit is easily reached. There is a cairn at 423m (1,381ft).

Walk roughly south south-west to descend from Mamore Hill. Again, you should notice a vague trodden path running down a quite clearly defined ridge. Take care as you walk down this, as there are a few rock-steps to negotiate before you reach the tarmac road below. You could of course simply cross the tarmac road and continue straight up the next hill in line, but you might like to turn right and walk across the gap first, descending a short way to a holy well by the roadside above the tiny pool of Lough Mamore. If you were to follow the road any further downhill, you would within minutes reach the roadside car park where you started the walk – again, an obvious escape route.

## The way back to Mamore Bridge

*Allow 2 hours*

If you continue down the road a short way past the holy well, you can turn left on to an old bog road which zigzags uphill. Although overgrown with heather in its upper parts, the road is set at a fairly easy gradient and is generally easy to trace, as it has built-up stonework along its sides which makes it stand out from the rugged slopes. The bog road leads up into a heathery hollow where turf-cutting has long since ceased and you may not be immediately aware of the terraced cuttings rising ahead. If you bear to the right and climb straight up the steep slope of rock and heather, you can reach a cairned summit which indicates that you are back on the high-level ridge again.

Walk roughly southwards a short way to descend from the cairned summit to a little gap. Climb uphill again and you will be able to walk along a delightful ridge at around 400m (1,300ft). You will pass a cairn as you continue roughly south-westwards. It is hard to say how many summits and gaps there are along the crest of the Urris Hills – it all rather depends on your point of view. However, keep your eye trained a couple of humps ahead, as you are aiming for the highest summit on this part of the ridge at 417m (1,379ft). This summit, like others, bears a cairn and offers views stretching back to Raghtin More, as well as ahead towards the old coastal fort at Dunree Head, and downhill to the two pools of Crunlough and Lough Fad.

You will need to identify these two little loughs before starting your descent from the Urris Hills. There is a steep slope of heather and rock below, so perhaps it is best to aim more towards Lough Fad, then when you can see more clearly what the ground is like, swing more towards Crunlough. You should aim for the outflowing stream from Crunlough and follow this down through a narrow valley. When the valley begins to broaden, head away to the left and pick up an old bog road which starts to zigzag downhill. When you are faced with alternative tracks, always head for the lower route, and keep to the right towards the golden strand at the head of Lenan Bay. The track runs along the clifftops to reach the small settlement of Lenankeel, where you keep to the right along a narrow tarmac road. The road runs between near-level fields and steep hill slopes to pass a handful of cottages. There are small waterfalls to admire from the roadside before you return to the crossroads passed early in the day's walk. At this point, turn right and walk uphill a short way to return to your car.

## Alternative routes

*The Urris Hills as seen from near the Roman Catholic chapel, before climbing Raghtin More.*

ESCAPES

There are two fairly obvious escape routes, assuming that you have already crossed Raghtin More before having any need of them. One is an old bog road on the gap in between Crockmain and Mamore Hill, which zigzags downhill roughly westwards to lead back towards the car park. Once you are committed to climbing Mamore Hill, you should wait until you reach the road on the Gap of Mamore before considering any further escapes. In this case, the road itself runs straight back down to the car park. Once you climb into the Urris Hills, you might as well complete the entire walk and descend towards Lenan Bay using the series of old bog roads.

EXTENSIONS

Raghtin More and the Urris Hills are arranged in a line, so that any extensions simply increase the length of time you will be out and make it more difficult to complete a circular walk which returns to your car. If you can arrange to be dropped off and collected, you could walk the full length of the range using an old track in Butler's Glen to climb Raghtin More, and then continue along the Urris Hills to descend towards the old fort on Dunree Head. You might notice an apparent geological continuation of the range on the far side of Lough Swilly, leading the eye onwards towards Knockalfa Mountain, Loughsalt Mountain and even further beyond. In fact, despite Donegal's apparently chaotic arrangement of hills, headlands, rivers, loughs and bays, there is a pronounced north-east to south-west alignment in the landscape. Unfortunately there is no easy way, short of commandeering a boat, to continue the walk through the Urris Hills across Lough Swilly and over Knockalfa Mountain. Remaining on Inishowen and in the Dunaff area, it is possible to extend the walk to include the rugged Dunaff Head, which has some spectacular cliffs.

139

# Route 26: MULLAGHCARN

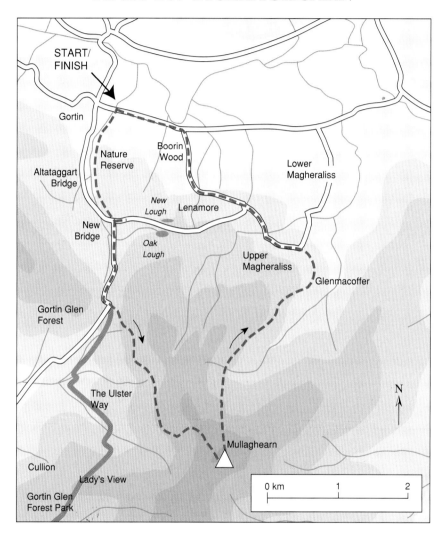

START/
FINISH

Gortin

Nature
Reserve

Boorin
Wood

Lower
Magheraliss

Altataggart
Bridge

*New
Lough*

Lenamore

New
Bridge

*Oak
Lough*

Upper
Magheraliss

Glenmacoffer

Gortin Glen
Forest

The Ulster
Way

N

Cullion

Lady's View

Mullaghearn

Gortin Glen
Forest Park

0 km          1          2

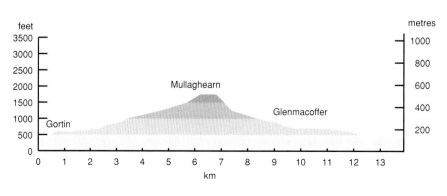

feet                                                                    metres
3500 ──                                                              ── 1000
3000 ──
2500 ──                                                              ── 800
2000 ──                      Mullaghearn                             ── 600
1500 ──                                                              ── 400
1000 ── Gortin                                Glenmacoffer           ── 200
 500 ──
   0 ──
      └──┬──┬──┬──┬──┬──┬──┬──┬──┬──┬──┬──┬──┬──┬──
         0  1  2  3  4  5  6  7  8  9  10 11 12 13
                              km

# 11

# SPERRIN MOUNTAINS

## Route 26: Mullaghcarn

**TIME ALLOWANCE**  5 hours.

**STARTING/FINISHING LOCATION**
Gortin Burn, Gortin.
OSNI Discoverer 13: GR 494857.
Car parking in the village.
Ulsterbus 92 serves Gortin.

**OVERVIEW/INTEREST**
Pleasant riverside walk, including part of the
  Ulster Way.
Passes close to Gortin Glen Forest Park and the
  National Nature Reserve at Boorin.
Extensive viewpoint at Mullaghcarn.
Ulster History Park close by.

**FOOTPATHS**
Clear paths and tracks from Gortin to the summit;
  vague path down from the summit.
Clear track and roads back to Gortin.
Mostly firm and dry underfoot.

**STATISTICS**
**WALKING DISTANCE**  15km (9 miles)
**TOTAL HEIGHT GAINED**  480m (1,575ft)
**PRINCIPAL HEIGHT**
Mullaghearn  542m (1,778ft)

### The way to Mullaghcarn          *Allow 2½ hours*

Mullaghcarn rises above the Gortin Glen Forest
Park, so there is an immediate contrast between
the forested western slopes and the open, heathery
eastern slopes of the hill. Mullaghcarn is crowned
with an array of masts, which makes it something
of a landmark despite its otherwise rather undis-
tinguished profile. The Ulster Way passes through
Gortin Glen and visits Lady's View on the slopes of
Mullaghcarn. However, a diversion from the
course of the Ulster Way can bring the summit of
Mullaghcarn underfoot, and a route on the open
hillside can be used to return to Gortin.

Start on the main road in the village of Gortin,
where the road crosses Gortin Burn. There is a
large sign indicating the start of a walk up
alongside the burn. The Burn Walk is also the
course taken by the Ulster Way. Although a broad
track initially runs upstream, you soon cross a
step-stile by a gate and continue upstream using a
narrower path. You will find that the path is largely
surfaced as a narrow strip of concrete, and it
crosses and recrosses Gortin Burn several times
using a series of footbridges. When you climb
higher, the path drifts up to the left above the
stream, and you cross a ladder-stile to reach a
narrow access road. Turn right to follow this road
alongside the heathery National Nature Reserve at
Boorin. A slight detour along the scenic road to the
left is worth considering to see a couple of
interesting kettle-hole lakes. Oak Lough and New
Lough are easily seen from the side of the road, but
there are a handful of others which you could see
by crossing the heathery moorland. You will need
to retrace your steps back towards the B48 if you
divert to see any of these features.

As you continue along the B48 a short way
towards the Gortin Glen Forest Park, you will find
an Ulster Way marker post pointing off to the right
into the forest, next to a disused firing range.
Follow the track only a short way, then turn left
along another track. This track runs up the floor of

a forested glen, and you may be aware of the main road above you to the left. Later, however, you will actually be walking above the level of the road, before a step-stile on the left leads down on to the B48. Cross over the road to reach another step-stile by a gateway. This leads on to a narrow tarmac road which climbs uphill above the Gortin Glen Forest Park. As you start climbing, you will find that there is a reasonable prospect down through Gortin Glen, as the trees aren't tall enough to obscure the view. This view is lost later, however, when you climb up into a more mature part of the plantation. The road eventually climbs out of the forest and proceeds up on to the final heathery shoulder of Mullaghcarn. The summit bears a

*The Ulster History Park off-route at Cullion, with Mullaghcarn rising beyond.*

cluster of tall masts, but there is also a trig point just beyond at 542m (1,778ft). The view in clear weather is tremendous and seems to embrace the whole of Ulster, encompassing the following near and distant features:

| NNE | Dart, Sawel |
| NE | Trostan, Slieveanorra, Antrim Mountains |
| ENE | Slieve Gallion, Slemish |
| E | Belfast Hills |
| SE | Mountains of Mourne |
| S | Slieve Beagh |
| WSW | Slieve Rushen |
| SW | Cuilcagh |
| WSW | Truskmore |
| W | Bessy Bell, Carrick Peninsula |
| NW | Errigal, Muckish |
| N | Slieve Snaght, Inishowen Peninsula |

## The way back to Gortin     *Allow 2½ hours*

Leaving the summit trig point on Mullaghcarn, cross the wire fence and head roughly northwards. You will notice a line of concrete posts which you can follow downhill. They will lead you down to a small lough tucked away in a steep-sided hollow – a feature which simply isn't apparent until you almost walk into it. The posts lead onwards to another small lough in another steep-sided hollow. If you continue walking roughly northwards across the heathery glen-head, you can pick up the end of an overgrown track. It is useful if you can identify the line of this track while you are still on the summit of Mullaghcarn, as it can be difficult to spot at closer quarters. One small feature to look for is a solitary little tree which stands quite close to the end of the old track and looks as if it has escaped from Gortin Glen Forest.

The track can be wet and squelchy underfoot, and is generally distinguished from the heathery moorland by its line of rushy vegetation. Follow the course of the track, which becomes easier to walk on further downhill. You will pass a sheep pen, as well as the ruins of an old farmstead, before you go through a gate. You might notice a few more ruined buildings around Glenmacoffer, and it's worth remembering that the area was once quite well populated. As in other parts of Ireland, starvation and emigration led to the decline of many small rural settlements. The track is much clearer as it proceeds further down into Glenmacoffer, and another gate is passed before the track runs down on to a narrow tarmac road. Turn left to follow this narrow road uphill, still enjoying fine views over the glens towards the rounded bulk of the higher Sperrin Mountains. The next road you join is the 'scenic route' which you encountered beside the National Nature Reserve at Boorin. This time, however, you should turn right and follow the road downhill. You can see Boorin Wood off to the left before you turn left along the B46 to walk back into Gortin. The village offers shops, pubs and accommodation if these are needed, as well as a bus service.

## Alternative routes

ESCAPES

Basically, the climb uphill from Gortin follows the floor of a valley, and once the ascent of Mullaghcarn commences you are simply following a narrow tarmac road. There should be no difficulty reaching the summit in all but the most appalling weather. If foul weather makes it inadvisable to descend across the open slopes of the hill, either retrace your steps to Gortin or descend into the Forest Park to sample some of the shorter waymarked nature trails. You would only be on the open slopes of Mullaghcarn for a short while in any case, although you would need to be quite sure of reaching the track leading off the moorland slopes otherwise you could run into the lower enclosed pastures and have difficulty hurdling fences.

EXTENSIONS

Although Mullaghcarn has broad and sprawling moorland shoulders, any extensions to this route have the unfortunate result of leaving you with a lot of road walking to return to Gortin. The Ulster Way runs through Gortin Glen and its course might tempt walkers away from Mullaghcarn in either direction. If you were to head northwards towards the higher Sperrins, the route would take you along a mixture of minor roads and gravel tracks, offering fine views across the glens and passing through the narrow Barnes Gap to reach Glenelly. In the other direction, the Ulster Way leaves Gortin Glen and heads towards the Ulster American Folk Park near Omagh. This is all accomplished on roads, but beyond the Folk Park there is a climb to the summit of Bessy Bell above the Baronscourt Estate. If you find you have time to spare after the short walk over Mullaghcarn, then a visit to the nearby Ulster History Park at Cullion is recommended. Mullaghcarn forms a backdrop to the many reconstructed historic dwellings which have been created on site, and it is a good place to appreciate the history behind some of the features you see in the countryside.

# Route 27: SAWEL AND DART

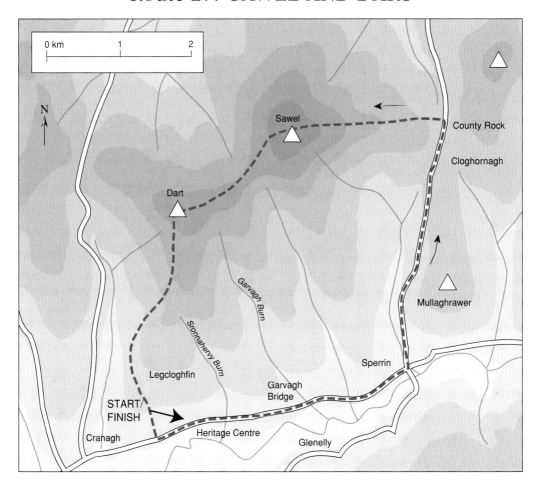

0 km        1        2

N

Sawel

Dart

County Rock

Cloghornagh

Garvagh Burn

Sronnahervy Burn

Mullaghrawer

Legcloghfin

Sperrin

Garvagh Bridge

START/FINISH

Cranagh

Heritage Centre

Glenelly

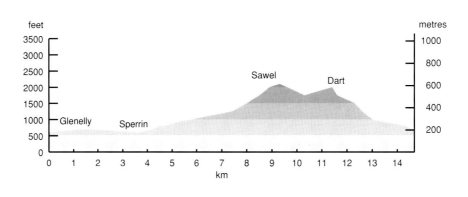

feet        metres
3500        1000
3000
2500        800
2000        600
1500
             400
1000    Glenelly    Sperrin
 500                               200
   0

Sawel        Dart

0   1   2   3   4   5   6   7   8   9   10   11   12   13   14
km

# Route 27: Sawel and Dart

**TIME ALLOWANCE**  5½ hours.

**STARTING/FINISHING LOCATION**
Sperrin Heritage Centre, near Cranagh.
OSNI Discoverer 13: GR 603935.
Car park at the Heritage Centre.
Ulsterbus 213 is a very limited summer service.

**OVERVIEW/INTEREST**
Starts and finishes at the Sperrin Heritage Centre.
Wilderness moorland walking to the summit of
   Sawel – the highest in the Sperrins – with
   extensive views.
Close to the Ulster Way.

**FOOTPATHS**
Low-level road and tracks.
One fence forms a useful guide.
No trodden paths over the hills.
Some parts can be quite boggy.

**STATISTICS**
**WALKING DISTANCE**   15km (9 miles)
**TOTAL HEIGHT GAINED**   610m (2,000ft)
**PRINCIPAL HEIGHTS**
Sawel   678m (2,240ft)
Dart   619m (2,040ft)

## The way to Sawel

*Allow 3 hours*

There is very little in the way of parking in Glenelly. The only real car park is the one at the Sperrin Heritage Centre. You could ask for permission to park there while you take a walk, but this may not be possible if the Centre is busy. It is worth having a look through the Heritage Centre, which features an interesting audio-visual presentation in 3D and has its own resident ghost. By the time gold is mentioned, you may well find yourself frantically panning for it in a nearby stream, and you can abandon all hope of attempting this walk until your 'gold fever' has subsided! If you park anywhere else in Glenelly,

please ask for permission first and do not block any farm access tracks or gates.

To start the walk from the Heritage Centre, you might as well get all the necessary road walking completed first. Turn left as you leave the car park and follow the B47 towards the top end of Glenelly. This road rises and falls as you cross Sronnahervy Bridge and Garvagh Bridge on the way to the crossroads hamlet of Sperrin. There are numerous little farmsteads scattered along the length of Glenelly, with broad, bleak and boggy moorland slopes rising high above them. There is a small pub on the staggered crossroads in Sperrin, and you should turn left along a minor road which climbs over the Sperrin Mountains towards Park. As you follow this road uphill, the fields gradually fall behind and you reach the higher moorlands above. You then cross the slopes of Mullaghrawer, the summit of which is on your right, while the vast bulk of Sawel rises ahead of you. You will cross a couple of cattle grids as you follow the road uphill towards the low-slung gap in between Sawel and Meenard Mountain.

When you reach the top of the gap and cross the cattle grid, turn left and cross a roadside fence close to a gateway made of pallets, then follow another fence steeply uphill. The gradient eases a little as you climb, but then the slope begins to rear up and you climb more steeply again. The fence doesn't in fact convey you all the way to the summit, but heads off to the left at a higher level. However, if you keep climbing straight uphill you will eventually reach the broad, domed, grassy summit of Sawel, which is marked by a trig point on a bouldery cairn at 678m (2,240ft). After the long haul up the mountain, clear weather is greatly appreciated because the view is especially far-reaching, stretching all the way from Donegal to

*OVERLEAF:*
*Dart and Sawel raise their sprawling summits above Cranagh in Glenelly.*

the Mournes. Look out for some of the following features as you allow your eye to track around the horizon:

| | |
|---|---|
| NNE | Mullaghash, Binevenagh |
| NE | Benbradagh, Scotland |
| ENE | Meenard Mountain, Mullaghaneany |
| E | Agnew's Hill, Antrim Mountains |
| ESE | Slieve Gallion |
| SE | Carnanelly, Mountains of Mourne |
| SW | Dart, Mullaghcarn, Cuilcagh |
| WSW | Mullaghclogha |
| WNW | Learmount Mountain, Donegal Highlands |
| NNW | Inishowen Peninsula |

## The way to Dart
*Allow 1 hour*

Clear weather is also a distinct advantage when you leave Sawel in the direction of Dart, allowing you to look ahead and work out how you are going to cross a broad and boggy gap. When you leave the summit of Sawel, you immediately cross a post-and-wire fence, using one of two small step-stiles. There is no path and nothing to guide you down the steep, grassy slope leading roughly south-westwards down to the broad gap. You will pass a few boulders poking out of the grass. As you cross the gap, you may decide to walk on areas where the soft peat has entirely washed away, leaving a firm surface of stones; at other times, you will have no option but to forge straight across the boggier parts of the gap. Looking ahead, you can see that the slopes of Dart are quite rocky, and in fact this hill is the only really rocky one in this part of the Sperrin Mountains. You should pick whichever way suits you on the short, steep, rocky ascent to the summit cairn at 619m (2,040ft). In poor visibility, the corner of a post-and-wire fence will help to confirm that you are in fact on top of Dart. Do not, however, cross the fence.

*Looking from Dart to Sawel, where the broad gap needs care in mist.*

## The way back to the Heritage Centre

*Allow 1½ hours*

Although it might be tempting to follow the fence down to the top of the minor road in between Dart and Mullaghclogha, many walkers have been challenged for following this fence to and from the summit of Dart. While it is always possible that this conflict might be resolved, it would be inadvisable for walkers to descend that way unless they are quite sure that it is not going to cause annoyance. Instead, leave the summit cairn on Dart by walking roughly southwards along a broad spur of the mountain, before drifting to the right, or south-westwards, to descend even further. When you have a clear view down the slope, you should be able to pick out the line of a track which roughly contours across the hillside. You should aim to join this track, turn left, and follow it all the way down into Glenelly. The track eventually leaves the open hillside and runs down through enclosed fields finally to land on the B47 in between the little village of Cranagh and the Sperrin Heritage Centre. You need to turn left to return directly to the Heritage Centre.

If you plan your return carefully, the restaurant on site may still be open and you can end your day's walk with something to eat and drink. If you are relying exclusively on the summer only Ulsterbus 213 service – the Sperrin Sprinter – you should be aware that this currently operates only on Tuesdays and leaves you with only around four hours to complete the walk. Obviously, you would need to keep moving! At present, there is no accommodation in this part of Glenelly. In fact, services and facilities of all kinds seem to be at an all-time low.

## Alternative routes

ESCAPES

Although the high crest of the Sperrin Mountains is divided only by occasional fences, the lower slopes of the mountains have been divided into numerous fields. In effect, there are no easy escapes from this walk. If the weather, time, or your fitness is are against you, walk somewhere else. If you are a poor navigator in bad weather, you might come adrift on the exposed higher parts of the mountains and discover just how bleak this terrain can be. There are extensive bogs to negotiate in some places before you reach a network of fences on lower ground. Even if you make it to Dart, remember that you could get into trouble following the fence straight down to the high gap crossed by a minor road. It is better, and shorter, to descend towards Glenelly by the course outlined in the route description.

EXTENSIONS

Perhaps the most ambitious route ever suggested in the Sperrin Mountains came from the late Joey Glover. He suggested a 'Sperrin Skyway' – crossing all the main summits along this broad, high-level crest all the way from Craigagh Hill to the Butterlope Glen. This is undoubtedly a fine challenge, but again it involves crossing the gap in between Dart and Mullaghclogha, where walkers have often been challenged while going to or from the mountains. Extensions to this circuit are therefore limited. The waymarked Ulster Way passes through Glenelly, but unfortunately it is entirely routed along roads from Leaghs Bridge at the head of Glenelly to the Barnes Gap, where it leaves Glenelly to head for Gortin.

# Route 28: BENBRADAGH AND CARNTOGHER

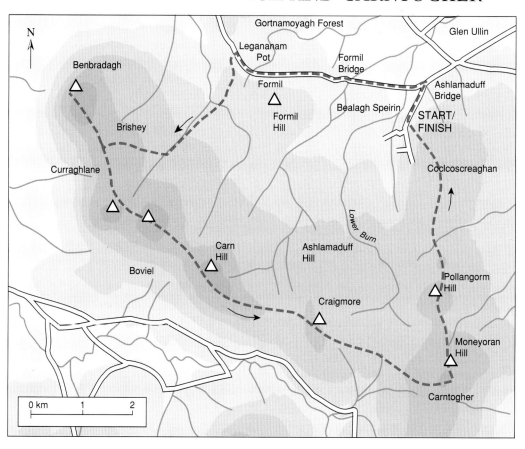

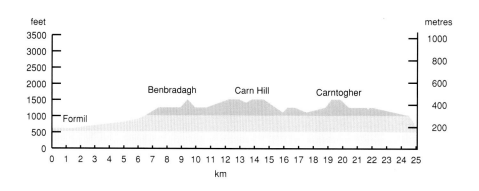

# Route 28: Benbradagh and Carntogher

**TIME ALLOWANCE**   9 hours.

**STARTING/FINISHING LOCATION**
Bealach Speirin, Glenullin.
OSNI Discoverer 8: GR 787112.
Small parking spaces by the roadsides.
No bus service.

**OVERVIEW/INTEREST**
High-level access road to Benbradagh, followed by
    exposed walking on extensive heather
    moorlands.
Good views from the summits.
Includes part of the Ulster Way.
Close to Ulster's highest pub!

**FOOTPATHS**
One high-level access road; the uplands are
    virtually pathless.
Fences occasionally serve as guides.
Some parts can be wet and boggy.

**STATISTICS**
**WALKING DISTANCE**   26km (16 miles)
**TOTAL HEIGHT GAINED**   630m (2,065ft)
**PRINCIPAL HEIGHTS**
Benbradagh   465m (1,525ft)
Carntogher   464m (1,522ft)

*A prominent upright stone on the broad gap between
Carn Hill and Craigmore.*

## The way to Benbradagh                *Allow 3 hours*

The starting location assumes that you will be staying at the Bealach Speirin bed & breakfast in a remote corner of Glenullin, and that is the only accommodation handy for this walk. If you are driving in and out of the area, you will need to get your car off the road using any handy parking space you can find. Take great care not to block any farm access tracks or gateways, and if in doubt ask for permission before parking. There is a car park available in Glenullin village, but using that will add a bit of extra road walking to what is already quite a long walk.

Leaving the Bealach Speirin bed & breakfast, turn left to walk along a minor road, then turn left again at the next road junction. This next minor road does actually carry more traffic, and it crosses Ashlamaduff Bridge and Formil Bridge before running through a forest. The forest is a detached part of Gortnamoyagh Forest, which consists of a handful of large blocks of forestry in this part of the Sperrin Mountains. When you emerge from the forest, look out for a minor road heading off to the left before you reach the scrubby hollow of Legananam Pot. When you turn left to follow this road, you are also following a stretch of the Ulster Way uphill. The road was originally constructed to

151

serve a US military communications station, but the entire installation has been dismantled, leaving only the anchor points of the former masts scattered across the higher parts of the hill. As you climb up the road you will reach a barrier gate, which you simply pass to continue your ascent.

The road climbs straight up the moorland slope at first, then suddenly bends to the right and cuts across the slope for a while. When you reach the crest of the hill, turn right to follow a spur off the road which runs roughly north-westwards. When this narrow road in turn suddenly bends to the right, abandon the road and strike out for the summit of Benbradagh. You will need to cross a small fenced enclosure where a handful of withered trees are trying to grow. Follow a fence straight onwards up the hill until you reach a step-stile close to a gate. When you have crossed it, you might as well climb straight up the last remaining part of the slope to reach the summit of Benbradagh. There is nothing but a few boulders to mark the 465m (1,525ft) summit, and nothing but a trampled fence crosses it. However, the views outwards across the Roe Valley are splendid and you should be able to identify many near and distant sights, such as:

| | |
|---|---|
| NE | Scotland |
| ENE | Slieveanorra, Trostan, Antrim Mountains |
| E | Slemish |
| SW | Carntogher, Glenshane Pass |
| SSE | Mullaghmore |
| SW | Sawel |
| WSW | Blue Stack Mountains |
| W | Donegal Highlands |
| NW | Slieve Snaght, Inishowen Peninsula |
| NNW | Binevenagh |

## The way to Carntogher    *Allow 3½ hours*

After enjoying the view from the summit of Benbradagh, you will have to retrace your steps for a while. Walk back down to the corner on the minor road and follow a stretch of the road back along the crest of the moorland. When you reach the point where you can either turn left or right by road, simply walk straight ahead across the grassy moorland instead. You will be walking

*Benbradagh, as seen from the slopes falling down towards Dungiven.*

almost due southwards, and in clear weather you will see that you have two moorland humps ahead of you. Aim for the one on the left, so that you eventually need to be walking roughly south-eastwards to cross it. There are fences to cross on the way, and the moorland becomes rather boggy in places, as well as featuring heather and tussocky grass. After crossing this first hump of moorland, you can continue walking roughly south-eastwards towards Carn Hill. You will eventually find a fence which is running in your direction, but avoid being drawn off-course by any old bog roads which run off the moorland crest towards the end of a tarmac road above Boviel.

After you have crossed a broad and boggy moorland gap, the fence you are following up the slopes of Carn Hill heads off to the right and ceases to be a useful guide. Climb up the gentle, heathery slope, aiming for any point which seems like the top of the hill. The summit of Carn Hill reaches

448m (1,470ft) and, despite its name, there are only a few rocks on the moorland slopes. You can maintain the same south-eastwards direction as you attempt to stay high on the broad moorland crest, but you should eventually let the crest lead you more eastwards as you head across another broad gap.

A feature to look out for as you cross this gap is a prominent boulder with the appearance of a standing stone. It may well be natural, but other large stones on this broad and bleak crest are lying down in the heather. Whatever the reason for the stone being the way it is, it is a feature you will encounter as you cross the gap on your way towards Craigmore. The slope running south-eastwards up towards the top of Craigmore is quite gentle, but the nature of the vegetation underfoot makes it more difficult to cross. The summit stands at 395m (1,295ft), and you should head roughly westwards when you continue.

You will have to cross a fence on the way down from Craigmore, not far from a low outcrop of rock where the ground is grassier. Ahead of you is another broad and bleak moorland gap, with the bulk of Carntogher rising beyond it. You should be able to discern a couple of tracks scored across this broad gap, where there are also a series of turf cuttings. One of the tracks runs across the gap, as if linking the Glenshane Pass with Glenullin, while the other one seems to be heading towards Carntogher. At least, this is what they appear to be doing, although in actual fact they don't! However, you should aim to cross a fence and pick up and follow the track which seems to be heading towards Carntogher, because it is going in the direction you are travelling for part of the way.

When you eventually leave the track and head more directly up the heathery slopes of Carntogher, there is another fence which needs to be crossed, and then you can continue directly to the top of the hill. The summit stands at 464m (1,522ft), and the view is somewhat different than that sampled from Benbradagh earlier. Because there is a virtually uninterrupted prospect towards the east, you can see practically the whole length of the Antrim Mountains, the Belfast Hills, Slieve Croob and, across the expanse of Lough Neagh, the Mountains of Mourne. Anything you see on a clear day beyond the Antrim Mountains is part of Scotland.

## The way back to Bealach Speirin

*Allow 2½ hours*

Leave Carntogher by walking roughly northwards, although you may be pulled a little off-course when you descend a short, steep, rugged slope and have to cross another fence at the foot of it. You should aim to stay on the wide moorland crest and head towards the broad hump of Moneyoran Hill. As you cross a broad gap, you will pass a small quarry cut into the ground and now lying abandoned. Pollangorm Hill lies further along the moorland crest, and you will hardly be aware that you are crossing over it because its slopes are so gentle. There is some tussocky vegetation to contend with as you cross the next shallow gap, and yet another fence to be crossed. Some of the fencing hereabouts is apparently to stop sheep wandering towards the course of the Inver Burn. You should be able to see that it drains a broad, flat area of blanket bog, but you may also notice that it is almost entirely hemmed in by bright green areas of treacherously soft sphagnum moss. Sheep – and for that matter stray walkers – who venture out towards the Inver Burn are asking for trouble.

With that warning ringing in your ears, you may feel better able to cope with the tough and tussocky grass and heather which you have to cross to keep following the high crest of the moors. As you approach Coolcoscreaghan, you should be looking ahead to spot a line of trees planted at a high level on the moorland slopes. Walk towards the nearest part of this line of trees, then climb over a fence and make your descent towards the valley. The slope running downhill is quite rugged and you will continue through a farmyard to reach the minor road just beyond. Turn right along the minor road and you will soon be back at the Bealach Speirin bed & breakfast. If your car is parked at some other place along the road, or even away in Glenullin village, simply continue along the road until you reach it.

## Alternative routes

*Crossing empty heather moorlands near Pollangorm Hill and Coolcoscreaghan.*

ESCAPES

This is a long and difficult moorland walk – difficult mainly because of the nature of the terrain, which requires plenty of high stepping over tussocky vegetation. The boggy parts aren't too bad, although you have been warned to keep away from the course of the Inver Burn to avoid the worst bogs in the area. With this in mind, escapes are rather limited – you might otherwise think you could short cut across the Inver Burn. In fact, if you are looking for an escape route, the easiest way to abandon the walk at the start is to head back down the former military road from Benbradagh. The only other high-level road available is the Boviel Road, which unfortunately leads down to the main Glenshane Road near Dungiven, leaving you on completely the wrong side of the mountain! The same applies if you try to bail out of the walk by heading down to the main road before Carntogher, although at least you could make your way towards the Ponderosa – the highest pub in Ulster and not too much of a walk up the Glenshane Road. You would ostensibly be going there to phone for a long-distance taxi ride back to Glenullin, but who knows what else you might find to do while you were waiting?

EXTENSIONS

If you are a glutton for punishment, you could start this walk and follow it as far as Carntogher, then head across the main Glenshane Road and follow the Ulster Way through Glenshane Forest, before making an ascent of Mullaghmore. Alternatively, you could climb Carntogher first from Glenullin, then cross the Glenshane Pass to climb Mullaghmore, before following the course of the Ulster Way back over Benbradagh. These sorts of extensions are for hardy bog-trotters only – these boggy moorlands would be ideal for that sort of walker. Lesser mortals will have had enough after the basic circular route described above.

155

# Route 29: CAUSEWAY COAST PATH

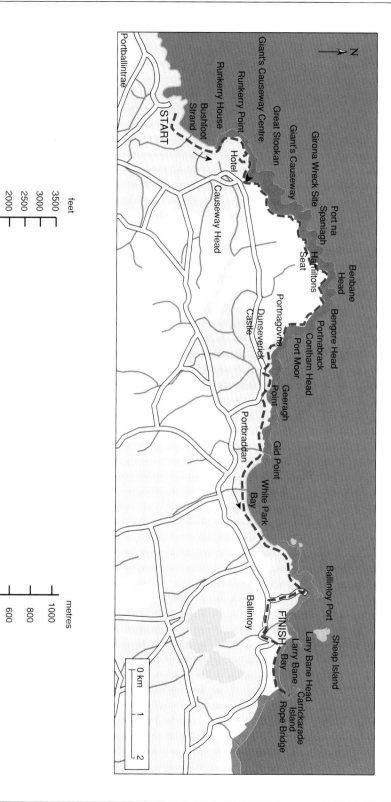

# 12

# ANTRIM COAST AND GLENS

## Route 29: Causeway Coast Path

**TIME ALLOWANCE**   10 hours.

**STARTING LOCATION**
Bushfoot Strand, Portballintrae.
OSNI Discoverer 4 or 5:GR 929424.
Large car park overlooking Bushfoot Strand.
Ulsterbus 132, 138 and 172 serve Portballintrae.
Ulsterbus 177 and 252 operate in the summer.

**FINISHING LOCATION**
Ballintoy.
OSNI Discoverer 5: GR 045445.
Car park at Larrybane, near Ballintoy.
Ulsterbus 172, plus 252 in the summer only.

**OVERVIEW/INTEREST**
The best coastal walk in Ireland – bar none!
Varied geology, and views across to Scotland.
Cliff and beach walks, suitable for children.
The Giant's Causeway and interesting Visitor
    Centre.
40,000 intriguing hexagonal basalt columns.
Ireland's smallest church.
Carrick-a-Rede Rope Bridge (seasonal).

**FOOTPATHS**
Paths are clear for most of the route.
There are some parts which are badly eroded: take
    special care near cliff edges.
Some parts of the route are along the beach.
High tides can make a couple of points impassable.

**STATISTICS**
**WALKING DISTANCE**   22km (13½ miles)
**TOTAL HEIGHT GAINED**   350m (1,150ft)
**PRINCIPAL HEIGHT**   Benbane Head   100m (300ft)

### The way to the Giant's Causeway

*Allow 2 hours*

Portballintrae is a fairly unpretentious little seaside resort. Park at the large car park overlooking Bushfoot Strand. You could, of course, start from the Giant's Causeway Centre, but by starting from Portballintrae you can experience the scenery gradually building up to a climax at the Causeway. Walk away from the car park, following a path which runs down to the mouth of the River Bush. Cross a footbridge and continue walking beside a dune belt alongside a golf course. You will soon find yourself following a broad and firm track – the trackbed of an old electric tramway which once conveyed tourists to the Giant's Causeway. When this track crosses a narrow tarmac road, you could continue straight towards the Giant's Causeway Centre, but it is better if you turn left along the road and reach the Centre by way of Runkerry House. The house itself is quickly passed, and you then continue along a short cliff path which turns around Runkerry Point to reach the Giant's Causeway Centre.

The Centre is a joint venture between the National Trust and Moyle District Council. A large car park is available alongside, and there is a restaurant on site. National Trust wardens are usually on hand to lead parties around the cliff paths and down to the Giant's Causeway. At busy times of the year, there is a minibus shuttle running between the Centre and the Causeway. If you want to absorb plenty of background information about the area, plan to spend a couple of hours in the Centre, which houses a range of

157

informative displays and an audio-visual presentation. Supporting literature is also on sale. If your feet are itching to be on the way to the Causeway, however, there are two approaches. The simple and direct route is to walk down the narrow road from the Centre to the Causeway. A slightly longer route for keen walkers uses the cliff path leaving the Centre, but you will then need to double back to see the Giant's Causeway. This latter route is the one that walkers should feel obliged to take.

A large sign at the start of the cliff path details a number of points that can be reached via the path and offers safety advice, which is basically a matter of applying a bit of common sense – keep clear of the edge, keep children under supervision, and take care in high winds. The path climbs uphill, and you will soon be able to look out across the Great Stookan – a rocky point with a prominent hump on its end. The next point, believe it or not, is the Giant's Causeway. Seen from above, it is a great disappointment, and you may wonder why so many people are milling around it. However, you should continue along the cliff path until you reach a prominent flight of steps descending across the rugged cliff-line.

This is the Shepherd's Path, and when you reach the bottom you will find that you can turn either right or left. Turning right now leads to a dead end, as a rock-fall has closed the most spectacular path in the area, which proceeded across the middle of the cliff-line to reach Hamilton's Seat. Despite this closure, it is still worth going as far as the barrier, simply to peep round into the rugged cove of Port na Spaniagh. The *Girona* – a ship of the Spanish Armada – came to grief on the jagged rocks here in 1588. Turn around and walk back along the path, passing a curiously fluted line of basalt columns for the second time. These are the Organ Pipes, and it is a feature of the Causeway Coast that almost every curiosity has been given a name, if not several names, accompanied by assorted and intriguing myths, legends and tall tales. The pinnacles of rock, formed of isolated basalt columns on a ridge of rock, are known as the Chimney Tops. Some people say that you can even see an old woman cooking beneath them.

Keep low on the path to approach the Giant's Causeway, but look out for a large boulder on the raised beach which is known as the Giant's Boot. When you reach the Giant's Causeway, you should spend plenty of time crawling all over its crazy columns. It is strange to remember how dull it all looked from the clifftop path, because it really is a special place once you reach it. Not for nothing is this a designated World Heritage Site!

## The way to Portbraddan    *Allow 4 hours*

Retrace your steps back up the Shepherd's Path to reach the clifftop path again, and turn left to continue following it. You will pass above the Chimney Tops and Port na Spaniagh, and you will often be able to see the lower cliff path, which sadly has had to be closed. There are numerous rocky headlands and bays to view, and an amazing range of birds have made their nests along the cliff-line. Kittiwakes, fulmars and ravens soar on the updraught, and you may spot red-legged choughs or birds of prey such as merlins and sparrowhawks. You will eventually reach Hamilton's Seat, which is recognizable because of the flight of steps (now barred) leading on to the lower cliff path.

Continue to follow the path around Benbane Head. In clear weather, a wonderful view of the coastline features not only the Antrim coast, but also the rugged Donegal peninsula of Inishowen and a spread of Scottish islands. The view is, in effect, only half a view, as there is nothing really notable to be seen inland. It could all be summarized as follows:

| | |
|---|---|
| wsw | Portrush, Portstewart, Downhill, Slieve Snaght |
| w | Magilligan Point, Inishowen Head |
| wnw | Malin Head, Inishtrahull |
| nne | Islay, Paps of Jura |
| ne | Kintyre |
| e | Rathlin Island, Fair Head, Mull of Kintyre |
| se | Knocklayd |

*The Giant's Causeway and a crazy paving of hexagonal basalt columns.*

Strange that you should be able to see more of Scotland than Ireland, but that's the way the view is arranged. You may find a map of both Scotland and Ireland useful for identifying finer detail on exceptionally clear days, when even the changing hues of Scotland's bracken and heather might be noticed. The path continues from Benbane Head to pass Bengore Head and Contham Head, before turning around Port Moon and Portnagovna. You will finally be led on to the B146 quite close to Dunseverick Castle on its prominent little headland. An information board by a small car park explains how there was a promontory fort here, which was connected by an ancient and long-vanished road to the Hill of Tara in Royal Meath – the political power-house of Ireland. You can walk across the grassy gap and climb on to the headland to inspect the current castle ruin, which has the appearance of a rotten molar tooth.

A less well-defined coastal path turns around Geeragh Point beyond Dunseverick Castle, before climbing on to a minor road. Turn left to follow this road a short way to its end, where a cottage stands next to a car park. Again, you can pick up the line of the coastal path, which turns around a rocky point as a much more well-defined track. Gid Point is unusual, because the coastal path doesn't run around the point, but actually passes through it. A hole in the headland allows the path through to the little fishing cove of Portbraddan. Here, if you look carefully, you will find what some claim is the smallest church in Ireland. It could easily be mistaken for a garden summerhouse, but a sign proclaims it to be St Gobban's – who is, of course, the patron saint of fishermen. Unfortunately, it is not a regular place of worship, so its claim is suspect. A high tide at Portbraddan could prevent you from continuing along the coast, as the waves might be breaking straight into the foot of a sheer chalk cliff.

*The Causeway Coast Path passes above the strange Chimney Tops.*

## The way to Ballintoy Port     *Allow 2 hours*

Assuming that the tides permit, walk around the foot of the chalk cliff to leave Portbraddan. Take care if walking over boulders or inclined slabs of rock, as they can be slippery either with seaweeds or simply because they are wet. You may notice springs of water issuing from the rock, or little niches in the rock holding tiny communities of plants. Beyond the cliff is the great sweep of White Park Bay. There is no actual coastal path: you simply walk along the bright sandy beach with your eyes fixed on the far side of the bay. You may be increasingly surprised to notice what appears to be a flock of sheep grazing on the sands, but these turn out to be rounded, wrinkled boulders of chalk in a group!

An amazing spectacle lies just around the next point. A series of shattered chalk stacks fills the sea with weird and wonderful shapes. In fact, because this is a raised coastline, some of the former sea-stacks are now permanently marooned on dry land. Not only does this chaotic scene look interesting, but with care you can enjoy all sorts of fascinating explorations. Some of the stacks, although towering above the beach, turn out to have a relatively easy line of ascent. Others have been pierced with holes big enough to walk through. Depending on the state of the tide, you could even wander some distance from the shore by scrambling from one stack to another, but only do this with extreme caution, as a lifeboat might not be able to get in easily to bail you out of any difficulties.

The coastal path leads you away from the larger seastacks, past smaller stacks, and finally to Ballintoy Port. This lovely little rocky harbour is backed by a cliff-line featuring caves which were originally cut by the sea, but which are now

*Portbraddan – a little fishing cove where high tides could be a problem.*

entirely on dry land. There is also a large lime kiln to study. A small restaurant on the harbourside might be open and offering food and drink, as well as the edible seaweed known as 'dulse', which is a local delicacy.

## The way to Carrick-a-Rede          *Allow 2 hours*

A corkscrew road climbs steeply uphill from Ballintoy Port, passing a most curious building that is often snapped by photographers. The road climbs further and reaches a fine whitewashed church, which is something of a landmark both on land as well as at sea. There may be new access developments here, as the National Trust are hoping to create a path running more directly towards Larrybane Head and Carrick-a-Rede. This would avoid one having to walk through the village of Ballintoy on the B15. If you find no evidence of a signposted path, continue along the road through the village until you see a narrow road signposted for Carrick-a-Rede.

There is a Visitor Centre on the clifftop near Larrybane Head, if you want to enquire still further into the geology and natural history of this impressive stretch of coast. If you simply want to get straight to Carrick-a-Rede, follow the broad track away from the car park, heading westwards before descending a flight of steps. The Carrick-a-Rede Rope Bridge is a seasonal structure, which is strung between the mainland and the rocky islet of Carrick-a-Rede each summer. When you see it strung across a rocky chasm with the Atlantic swell surging beneath, you may well wish you'd come in the winter months, when it is dismantled! With your heart in your mouth, you are expected to step on to the wobbly planking, grip the shaky ropes and walk across the Atlantic Ocean to reach the rock. Spare a thought for the salmon fishermen, who have to do this in all weathers carrying fish crates. The fishermen use a little cottage by a tiny harbour, and they net the salmon 'road' each year.

The island is the end of the road as far as the Causeway Coast Path is concerned, but of course you will have to come back on to the mainland and find a more practical point at which to end the walk. If you have someone driving a car as a back-up, they can meet you at the car park beside the Larrybane Visitor Centre. You can also walk a little further to end in Ballintoy, which offers food, drink and accommodation. There is an Ulsterbus service which will return you to Portballintrae, although you should be aware of the times of the last couple of buses running that way.

## Alternative routes

### ESCAPES

Foul weather is the only thing which is likely to make you want to abandon this splendid walk: gales could prove particularly unnerving on such an exposed cliff coastline. You can, of course, turn back if you have had enough, or simply continue to the next road and bail out at that point. There is an Ulsterbus service which reaches many points along the Causeway Coast Path, including Portballintrae, the Giant's Causeway Centre, Dunseverick Castle, White Park Bay and Ballintoy. If you are armed with the appropriate timetables, and are aware of the seasonal variations in services, you will know at which points and at what times you can pick up a passing bus. There is no point rushing a coast path such as this one. If you prefer to stop and stare at frequent intervals, this walk is best split at White Park Bay and completed over a full weekend.

### EXTENSIONS

The route described is almost all off the roads and features some of the best coastal scenery in Ireland. If you proceed inland at any point, you will almost certainly be restricted to walking along roads. If you carry on beyond Ballintoy, apart from heading to Carrick-a-Rede, you will have to follow roads all the way to Ballycastle before you have the option of walking on Fair Head. In the other direction, most of the walking beyond Portballintrae would be along roads, but Dunluce Castle is certainly worth viewing from all possible angles. The Causeway Coast Path is one of many highlights of the long-distance Ulster Way, but it is unfortunately flanked by long road walks.

# Route 30: TROSTAN

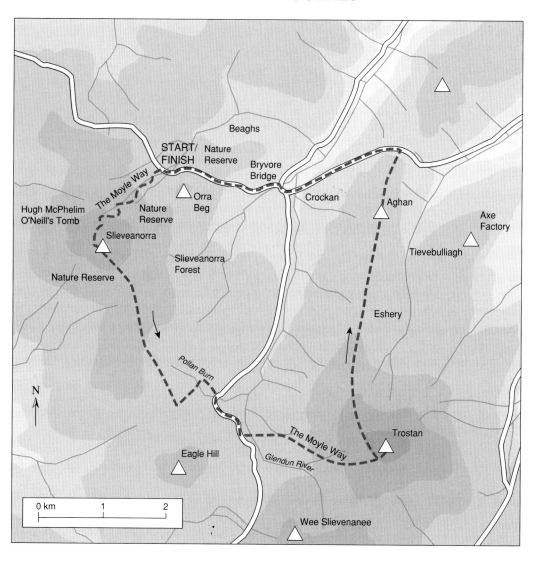

Beaghs

START/
FINISH

Nature
Reserve

Bryvore
Bridge

The Moyle Way

Crockan

Hugh McPhelim
O'Neill's Tomb

Nature
Reserve

Orra
Beg

Aghan

Axe
Factory

Slieveanorra

Slieveanorra
Forest

Tievebulliagh

Nature Reserve

Eshery

N

Pollan Burn

The Moyle Way

Trostan

Eagle Hill

Glendun River

0 km        1        2

Wee Slievenanee

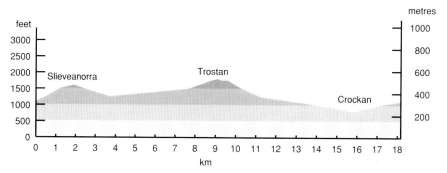

| feet | | | metres |
|---|---|---|---|
| | | | 1000 |
| 3000 | | | 800 |
| 2500 | | | |
| 2000 | Trostan | | 600 |
| 1500 | Slieveanorra | | 400 |
| 1000 | | Crockan | |
| 500 | | | 200 |
| 0 | | | |

0  1  2  3  4  5  6  7  8  9  10  11  12  13  14  15  16  17  18

km

# Route 30: Trostan

TIME ALLOWANCE   6½ hours.

STARTING/FINISHING LOCATION
Orra Beg, Slieveanorra.
OSNI Discoverers 5 and 9: GR 144277.
Small parking space by the roadside.
No bus services.

OVERVIEW/INTEREST
Climbs through forest and across open moorlands,
    to reach the highest point in Antrim.
Passes sections of the Slieveanorra National
    Nature Reserve.
Includes part of the Moyle Way.
Views from the Glens of Antrim to Scotland.
Reminders of the Battle of Orra Beg.

FOOTPATHS
Includes some clear forest tracks.
The Moyle Way is adequately waymarked.
Some paths are wet and boggy; paths alongside
    fences can be vague or absent.
Minor roads complete the circuit.

STATISTICS
WALKING DISTANCE   20km (12 miles)
TOTAL HEIGHT GAINED   520m (1,705ft)
PRINCIPAL HEIGHTS
Slieveanorra   508m (1,676ft)
Trostan   550m (1,817ft)

## The way to Pollan Burn          *Allow 2½ hours*

This walk starts on a high-level minor road
between Cushendall and Ballymoney, or between
the head of Glenaan and Altarichard. It is signposted as a scenic drive. Follow this minor road
through the Slieveanorra Forest on the northern
slopes of Slieveanorra, then look out for Moyle
Way signposts and park at the point where a space
has been provided for cars on the forested slopes of
Orra Beg. There is a stout stone plinth where a map
of part of the Moyle Way can be studied. The plinth

is even equipped with stone seating, where you
can comfortably sit and don your boots for a wet
and boggy walk.

Cross a step-stile beside a gate and start
following a gravel track up through Slieveanorra
Forest. The track twists and turns, then leaves the
forest and starts climbing up a rugged slope of
grass and heather. You do not need to grapple with
the moorland vegetation just yet, as the gravel
track continues all the way to the summit of
Slieveanorra. At one bend in the track, away to the
right, is a feature marked on the map as Hugh
McPhelim O'Neill's Tomb. If you are lucky, you
may find a few stones lurking in the grass and
heather, but you would be better simply considering the story behind the Battle of Orra Beg as
you climb uphill.

It all happened in 1559, when the O'Neills and
McQuillans decided to attack the MacDonnells,
with the action starting on Orra Beg. The
MacDonnells had seen their rivals gathering, and
tempted them on to boggy ground which they had
cunningly covered with rushes. The ruse worked,
and the O'Neills and McQuillans were attacked
while they floundered. However, there were
enough survivors to ensure that the battle raged all
the way down Glenshesk, before the MacDonnells
finally won the day and consolidated their hold
on this corner of Antrim. Hugh McPhelim O'Neill
was buried on the slopes of Slieveanorra, while
McQuillan's Grave can be inspected further down
Glenshesk. Sorley Boy MacDonnell celebrated the
victory by raising a large cairn on top of Trostan,
which you will visit later in this walk.

The gravel track makes light work of climbing
Slieveanorra, and you will soon be standing on
the 508m (1,676ft) summit alongside two tall
transmitter masts. Pass between the two masts and

*OVERLEAF:*
*The summit of Tievebulliagh – site of a neolithic stone
axe factory.*

165

you will see a sign reading 'Slieveanorra National Nature Reserve'. The reserve at this height consists of two areas of upland blanket bog on either side of the summit. There is a third patch on Orra Beg, which you won't be seeing, and a fourth and more extensive area of bog which you will see at the end of the walk. Despite the intrusion of the transmitter masts, you should sample the views around the Antrim Mountains, and far across the sea to Scotland in clear weather.

You start to descend from Slieveanorra using a narrow tarmac road, but only for a short while. Look out for a waymark post bearing a green arrow, just to the left of the road. You will be following a well-trodden path roughly south-eastwards down the slopes of Slieveanorra. A wide strip of rugged grass and heather is kept partially dry by parallel drainage ditches, so the line you follow is quite plain on the ground. You will descend at a fairly gentle gradient, then the ground levels out for a short way before you descend again. Keep to the right of a small stand of trees on the open moorland slopes, then continue downhill and let the boggy path lead you into a broad forest ride. At the end of this, turn left along a firm forest track, and follow this gently downhill a short way. The track crosses Pollan Burn, then you turn right to follow another firm track to a minor road. This is very much like the start of the walk: there are Moyle Way signposts, a small parking space, and a stone plinth bearing a plaque about a stretch of the waymarked trail.

## The way to Trostan                    *Allow 1 hour*

Turn right to start following the minor road. You will cross Pollan Burn again, then the road bends left as it leaves Slieveanorra Forest. A right bend leads the road across open moorland, quickly reaching another Moyle Way signpost and stone plinth. Turn left to leave the road at this point, following another series of waymark posts bearing green arrows. These lead you across the Glendun River; later, you will find yourself following a small stream uphill on the grass and heather slopes. You are climbing on the slopes of Trostan, but the

waymarked course of the Moyle Way only crosses the shoulder of the hill. If you watch carefully to the left, however, you will eventually spot another trodden path leading away from the waymarked route. Follow this other path uphill and you will reach a fence, where you cross a step-stile. Continue uphill and you will reach another step-stile crossing another fence. Just a short walk further uphill is the summit of Trostan. A large cairn of boulders and earth is crowned with a trig point at 550m (1,817ft) – this is the cairn raised by Sorley Boy MacDonnell after the Battle of Orra Beg. All around is a desolate scene, as the top of Trostan is a broad and bleak area of crumbling basalt boulders and poor soil. The former covering of blanket bog has largely been washed away, leaving only a few traces of its former cover, and hardly a blade of grass.

Trostan is the highest point in Antrim, and on a clear day you can enjoy fairly extensive views. However, the broad shoulders of the hill mean that to observe the best views you should walk around the edge of the hill away from the summit cairn. Some of the following features may be in view:

| | |
|---|---|
| N | Isle of Jura, Scotland |
| NNE | Tievebulliagh, Carnanmore, Mull of Kintyre |
| NE | Isle of Arran, Scotland |
| ENE | Lurigethan |
| E | Crockalough, Garron Plateau |
| SSE | Colin Top, Agnews Hill |
| S | Carncormick, Mountains of Mourne |
| SSW | Slievenanee |
| W | Slievenahanaghan, Sperrin Mountains |
| WNW | Binevenagh, Inishowen Peninsula |
| NW | Slieveanorra |
| NNW | Knocklayd |

## The way back to Orra Beg          *Allow 3 hours*

To leave the summit of Trostan, you will need to retrace your steps for a while. Walk back down the slope you climbed on your arrival, and cross the two step-stiles over the two fences, then turn right to follow the course of the second fence. Put simply, this fence will lead you off Trostan and take you down to a distant minor road. In reality, you will have to cross a lot of rugged grass and heather moorland, covered with patches of bog and occasionally featuring peat hags. Persevere: the gradient is gentle enough, and you can feel free to outflank any particularly wet patches of ground in the certainty that the line of the fence will lead you straight back on to your desired course.

You will descend at first along a fairly broad moorland crest, but between Eshery and Aghan the moorland broadens considerably and even rises slightly for a while. The hill off to the right, with a fairly prominent summit, is Tievebulliagh. Its far face is out of sight, but it bore a Stone Age industry turning out polished axes which were hacked from a band of hard porcellanite. The line of the fence passes a couple of places where the underlying rock pokes up through the blanket bog, but not really for long enough to provide a firm footing. Eventually, you will see the minor road which marks terra firma, and a large gate gives access to it. There is a small notice reading 'No Trespassing With Gun or Gundog', but this route down from Trostan is available as an access route for walkers who aren't out for a day's shooting.

Turn left along the minor road and follow it gently downhill. At one point you should be able to discern four roads converging on a stone-arched bridge. This is Bryvore Bridge, at the head of Glendun, with Slieveanorra Forest beyond. The hill rising above the forest, crowned with two masts, is of course Slieveanorra. As you approach the bridge, first turn right to cross it, then turn left as signposted for Altarichard and Ballymoney. The road climbs gently uphill between Slieveanorra Forest and an open moorland. You may notice a grove of mixed trees on the left, and later some cutaway bog on the right. Another area of bogland occurs at a higher level; this is fenced against grazing and has not been cut for turf. It is the largest area of the four patches of blanket bog which make up the Slieveanorra National Nature Reserve. Access is available from a roadside step-stile, but the going underfoot is decidedly tough. You may wish to give it a miss and simply follow the road onwards into Slieveanorra Forest. The

unplanted moorland slope rising to the left leads up to Orra Beg, site of the famous battle. You will quickly reach the small roadside parking space where you started the walk. With all its Moyle Way markers, it is an unmistakable point.

## Alternative routes

### ESCAPES

If you climb on to Slieveanorra in foul weather and decide not to proceed, then simply walk back down the gravel track and flee the place. If, having crossed Slieveanorra, you decide against climbing Trostan, you can abandon the circuit by using one of two low-level options. The simplest is to take the road which virtually bisects the route. Alternatively, if you want to keep fairly low but wish to avoid the road, there is a forest track running roughly parallel to the road which you could use. In fact, you don't even need to cross Bryvore Bridge, as you can use forest tracks to cross Bryvore Water at a higher level before rejoining the road.

### EXTENSIONS

The Moyle Way offers a tough day's walk with Slieveanorra and Trostan included in its course. This is perhaps the most logical way to extend the walk. The Moyle Way is essentially a linear route from Ballycastle to the Glenariff Forest Park, or vice versa. There is no accommodation or any other facilities along its 32km (20 mile) route, so if you are to attempt it as a day walk you will need to be completely self-sufficient.

It is because the route is so bleak and wild that small parking spaces have been provided at the roadsides. These allow for back-up vehicles to park, or enable walkers to be collected or dropped at various points if they wish to complete the route over two or three days. If you are aiming to complete the walk without any back-up, you will probably wish to end at Ballycastle. If you choose to end at Glenariff Forest Park, note that facilities there are very limited, and you should equip yourself with the Ulsterbus timetables for the Ballymena to Cushendall service.

# Route 31: SHANE'S HILL TO GLENARM

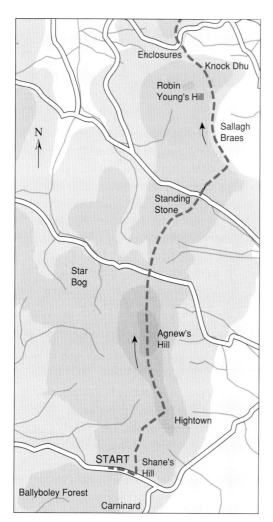

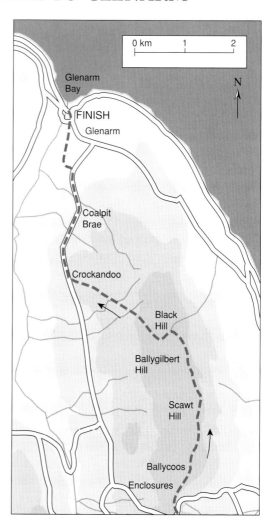

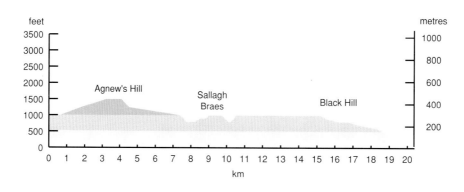

# Route 31: Shane's Hill to Glenarm

**TIME ALLOWANCE**   7 hours.

**STARTING LOCATION**
Shane's Hill, Ballyboley Forest.
OSNI Discovery 9: GR 318989.
Small car park beside the main road.
Ulsterbus 130 serves Larne and Shane's Hill.

**FINISHING LOCATION**
Glenarm Harbour.
OSNI Discoverer 9: GR 312153.
Car park at Glenarm.
Ulsterbus 162 serves Larne and Glenarm.
Ulsterbus 252 also runs in the summer months.

**OVERVIEW/INTEREST**
High-level walk over the Antrim Mountains,
   routed entirely along part of the Ulster Way.
Fine moorland and coastal views.
Includes standing stones and ancient historic sites.

**FOOTPATHS**
The course of the Ulster Way is waymarked.
Upland paths can be rather vague.
Mostly dry underfoot, but there are some small
   bogs.

**STATISTICS**
**WALKING DISTANCE**   20km (12½ miles)
**TOTAL HEIGHT GAINED**   405m (1,330ft)
**PRINCIPAL HEIGHTS**
Agnew's Hill   474m (1,563ft)
Robin Young's Hill   384m (1,268ft)
Scawt Hill   378m (1,249)
Black Hill   381m (1,239ft)

## The way to Agnew's Hill          *Allow 1 hour*

This high-level stretch of the Ulster Way provides a fine day's walking between Shane's Hill and Glenarm. Many parts of the Antrim Mountains can seem broad and bleak, but on this day's walk there is more of a feeling of being on a high-level moorland crest. Views are often quite extensive, stretching well into Scotland on a clear day. This is a fine walk to tackle if you have arrived in Ireland via the port of Larne, and while engaged on the walk you should be able to spot many ferries arriving and departing.

Although there are small parking spaces at either end of this walk, the linear nature of the route means that you will have to return and retrieve your car afterwards, unless you can arrange to be met by another vehicle at the end. Better still, as there are buses serving the terminal points, you could base yourself at Larne and take a bus to the starting point on Shane's Hill. Provided you can reach Glenarm in time to catch the last bus back to Larne, you then have no worries about leaving a car anywhere, or wondering how you will return to it afterwards.

If you do take a car to the start of the walk, there is a small roadside parking space at Shane's Hill, just inside Ballyboley Forest. There is a sign flanking the road reading 'Shane's Hill 1,025ft' as well as a sign for Ballyboley Forest and another sign marked 'P' for the parking space. Walk away from the forest in the direction of Larne using the main A36, until you find a gateway on the left giving access to a clear gravel track. Go through the gate and follow the track across a broad moorland. You will soon pass a point where another track runs in from the left. Stay on the main gravel track, running roughly northwards, but aim to leave it before you reach a small, square plantation of trees.

You should turn right to leave the track, following the course of the Ulster Way. The only clue you will have to the course of the route is if you spot a solitary waymark post on the uphill slope. If you miss this, walk uphill anyway until you reach a cairn on a hump at 412m (1,089ft). There is another waymark post beside the cairn, indicating a left turn. It is tempting to follow the course of a tumbledown wall and post-and-wire fence, as there is a narrow, trodden path alongside. Unfortunately, this will also draw you off-course,

171

ANTRIM COAST AND GLENS

and so must be used with caution. The true course of the Ulster Way is marked by a line of wooden posts, tipped with white paint and bearing yellow arrows. These have been planted along the broad, grassy, heathery crest of Agnew's Hill, but there is no real path trodden out beside them. In mist, you could lose sight of one post before spotting the next one in line. There is nothing to mark the 474m (1,563ft) summit of Agnew's Hill either, except for another waymark post amid the broad and boggy grassland on top of the hill. In clear weather, the view is quite extensive, and you could see some of the following features:

| | |
|---|---|
| N | Black Hill |
| NNE | Sallagh Braes, Knock Dhu, Mull of Kintyre |
| NE | Isle of Arran, Scotland |
| E | Larne Harbour, Island Magee, Galloway, Scotland |
| S | Belfast Hills, Slieve Croob, Mountains of Mourne |
| SSE | Slieve Gullion |
| SE | Lough Neagh |
| W | Douglas Top, Sperrin Mountains |
| WNW | Slemish |
| NW | Carncormick |
| NNW | Trostan |

## The Way to Linford Ancient Site

*Allow 2½ hours*

Walk northwards to leave the summit of Agnew's Hill, crossing boggy ground before climbing a ladder-stile over a fence. Later you will notice a prominent cairn on the way downhill, and if you keep to the left of it a waymark post keeps you on course. Further on, turn left to cross another ladder-stile and follow a fence downhill to reach the Star Bog Road. There are two more ladder-stiles enabling you to cross roadside fences. There are also signs reminding walkers not to take dogs along the Ulster Way. The Way crosses a broad, almost level area of bog, with a fence forming a useful aid to navigation. Simply follow the fence straight across the bog until you have to cross another ladder-stile. Beyond this point, a series of Ulster Way marker posts and a faint path lead towards a prominent standing stone. This makes a good photographic subject, despite nearby electricity transmission lines. Again, there are ladder-stiles crossing the fences flanking a nearby minor road. After crossing them, there is yet another ladder-stile to cross before a thin path leads through deep heather and more waymarks direct you towards the Sallagh Braes.

Turn left to follow a fence which runs along the top of a cliff edge. The Sallagh Braes form a perfect semi-circular cliff-line enclosing low-level fields at Sallagh, before the eye is led towards the rugged Ballygalley Head and the little seaside village of Ballygalley. Ulster Way marker posts are aligned near the clifftop fence, and a small signs asks walkers not to climb over the fence or try to approach the cliffs. There are ladder-stiles provided across any walls you need to cross. In fact, you will have crossed four more ladder-stiles over four stone walls before you find yourself pulling well away from the Sallagh Braes. Another ladder-stile over yet another wall is crossed on the broad, grassy dip in between Robin Young's Hill and Knock Dhu. Although out of sight from the course of the Ulster Way, Knock Dhu bears traces of a

*The moorland course of the Ulster Way as it crosses over Scawt Hill.*

promontory fort – an easily defended, cliff-girt prow backed by an artificial ditch and embankment.

The Ulster Way follows a narrow grassy path downhill, crossing a fence using a simple step-stile before running towards a car park on a gap in the hills. The short green grass all around is in stark contrast to the brown heather and sour grasses of the higher moorlands. You will cross a step-stile to reach the small car park, where an information plaque deals briefly with the course of the Ulster Way and the presence of the Linford Ancient Site. You may have noticed the muddled earthworks of the site on your descent. No one seems quite sure what they represent, but the area seems to have been an important meeting point for people from the Bronze Age to the Norman Conquest. The remains are simply marked as 'Enclosures' on the map, and you might try to puzzle out the whole arrangement in passing.

## The way to Glenarm

*Allow 3½ hours*

There is a ladder-stile on the roadside opposite the car park, then the Ulster Way needs care for a moment, as it is easy to get mixed up in the ditches and embankments of the Linford Ancient Site. Look out for another ladder-stile off to the right, and cross it. After that, the line of a post-and-wire fence can be followed uphill, with fine views over a steep brow towards Ballygalley Head and Larne. You will be walking up a slope of short green grass, and although there is no clear path, the fence keeps you on course until you cross a ladder-stile near a wide gate. You then continue uphill to cross the hump of Ballycoos.

You should now follow Ulster Way marker posts onwards, taking special care to spot them in mist. As you head downhill, you will cross a ladder-stile over a stone wall and continue across a grassy gap. A fine line of waymark posts is accompanied by a grassy path leading over the 378m (1,249ft) summit of Scawt Hill. After crossing another ladder-stile over a stone wall, watch carefully for waymark posts as you cross a broad and undulating gap. There are old tracks climbing across this gap at right-angles to the course you need to maintain, so be sure not to follow the wrong path. After crossing another stone wall using a ladder-stile, a path leads gently uphill. You should spot a rather knobbly standing stone, and the path passes alongside it, still clearly marked with waymark posts.

After crossing another ladder-stile over another stone wall, you might spot the trig point on Black Hill away to the left. You will be walking all the way to the trig point, but at first you may feel that you are walking away from it. In fact, the waymark posts are leading you around the perimeter of a boggy area which has a confusing amount of fencing through it. Simply let the waymarks lead you in a sweeping arc to the left and you will be taken all the way to the 381m (1,239ft) summit of Black Hill. If you reach the trig point on a clear day, you will suddenly be treated to a view of Slemish's distinctive profile of a hump with steep sides directly ahead. Slemish actually owes its distinctive shape to a geological formation known as a lacolith.

Head roughly north-westwards to descend from Black Hill. You will need to cross yet another ladder-stile over a stone wall before following a sparse line of Ulster Way marker posts towards the rugged hump of Crockandoo. In fact, this last stretch of rugged moorland is quite poorly way-marked and features no real path. After passing patches of rock and bracken, you will land on a minor road and should turn right. Simply follow the road onwards, descending across Coalpit Brae. Later, on the left, another minor road called Town Brae Road runs more steeply downhill. It passes alongside a stand of forestry and enters Glenarm village to pass close to a couple of gateways leading into the estate of Glenarm Castle. If you follow the road straight through the village, you will be led on to the main A2 Antrim Coast Road quite close to Glenarm Harbour.

There are a few shops and pubs, with limited accommodation, as well as a bus service running back towards Larne. If you are intending to catch a bus back to Larne, you should of course have referred to the necessary bus timetables before starting the walk.

## Alternative Routes

ESCAPES

This is basically a walk along a high-level moorland crest, so you might assume that any downhill course will serve as an escape route. In fact, you need to take care. Descents westwards from the crest of Agnew's Hill and Sallagh Braes lead on to broad and rugged moorland slopes; descents eastwards can be dangerous at points where steep cliff faces suddenly fall away. Further northwards on Black Hill, descents east and west lead quickly into areas of fencing and are best

avoided. That leaves only the roads as escape routes. There are three minor roads crossing the range of hills between Shane's Hill and Glenarm, and these offer the safest and easiest descents. Follow eastwards to link with Ulsterbus services.

EXTENSIONS

As a high-level linear route, this walk cannot really be extended any further. The Ulster Way at the southern end of the walk wanders through Ballyboley Forest, before using a series of roads to pass through Ballynure. Going northwards, the Ulster Way leaves Glenarm by road to reach Carnlough, before a bleak and boggy crossing of the Garron Plateau, passing between Big Trosk and Little Trosk. Perhaps a more strenuous option would be to walk westwards instead of northwards from Agnew's Hill, to reach the distant and distinctive hump of Slemish. There are some useful bog roads which can be followed in that direction, but most of the time you would be on rough moorland, and there are a number of fences which would need to be climbed.

*Looking from Black Hill's summit towards the distinctive summit of Slemish.*

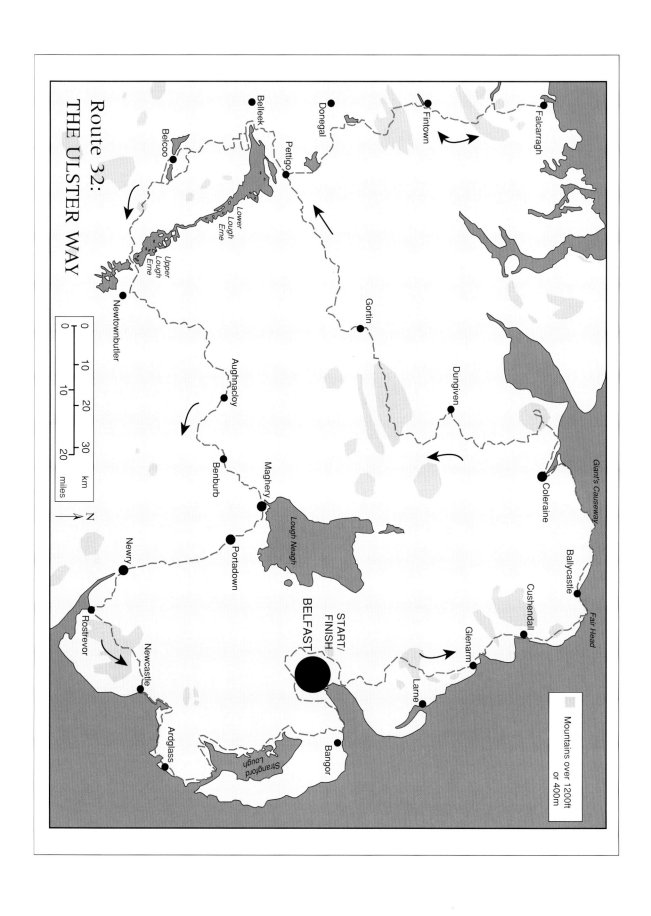

Route 32:
THE ULSTER WAY

Mountains over 1200ft
or 400m

Falcarragh
Fintown
Donegal
Belleek
Belcoo
Pettigo
Lower Lough Erne
Upper Lough Erne
Newtownbutler
Gortin
Aughnacloy
Dungiven
Coleraine
Giant's Causeway
Benburb
Maghery
Lough Neagh
Ballycastle
Fair Head
Newry
Portadown
Cushendall
Rostrevor
Newcastle
Glenarm
Larne
BELFAST
START/FINISH
Ardglass
Strangford Lough
Bangor

0   10   20   30   km
0   10   20        miles

N

# 13

# ULSTER

## Route 32: The Ulster Way

**TIME ALLOWANCE**   5 weeks (no rest days).

**STARTING/FINISHING LOCATION**
Dunmurry, Belfast, although as the Ulster Way is
   an enormous circular, waymarked trail it could
   be started at any other point along the route.
   The starting location would also be the finishing
   location after the completion of the walk.
OSNI Discoverer 4, 5, 7, 8, 9, 12, 13, 15, 17, 18,
   19, 20, 21, 26, 27 and 29.
OSNI Mourne Country, Lower Lough Erne and
   Upper Lough Erne Outdoor Pursuits Maps.
OSI Discovery 1, 6 and 11.

**OVERVIEW/INTEREST**
Longest and most ambitious waymarked trail in
   Ireland.
Main circuit completely encircles Northern
   Ireland, and there is a separate spur running the
   length of Donegal.
Attempts to link all the best walking areas in
   Ulster, and most stretches have been
   waymarked.
Includes both high-level and low-level walking,
   visiting many scenic areas and heritage
   attractions.
Covers mountains, hills, moorlands, coastlines,
   forests, riversides and roads as it visits eight of
   Ulster's nine counties.
Includes numerous heritage features.

**FOOTPATHS**
Features both well-trodden and barely used paths.
   Some sections are particularly well walked,
   others only rarely.

In the few areas experiencing high numbers of
   walkers, there may be erosion and repair
   schemes, but for most of the way the route is
   fairly quiet.
Large numbers of forest tracks and minor roads
   are used to effect links between the main scenic
   areas.
Most of the Way involves walking on fairly firm
   surfaces, and there are only a few boggy areas.
Waymarking varies from area to area, but
   generally there is a system featuring metal
   signposts where the route uses roads, and
   wooden marker posts when the route leaves the
   roads and heads across country.

**STATISTICS**
**WALKING DISTANCE**
Main circuit   929km (577 miles)
Through Donegal   111km (69 miles)
Total walking distance of 1,040km (646 miles),
   plus any off-route detours
**TOTAL HEIGHT GAINED**
15,250m (50,000ft) approx.
**PRINCIPAL HEIGHTS**
Belfast Hills
Antrim Mountains
Sperrin Mountains
Donegal Highlands
parts of Fermanagh
Mountains of Mourne

*OVERLEAF:*
*Ireland and Scotland – Fair Head's cliffs at dawn,*
*seen from Ballycastle.*

## North-eastern Section    *Allow 6 days*

Leaving Dunmurry, the Ulster Way wanders through West Belfast and through the Colin Glen Forest Park to reach the Belfast Hills. The broad, bleak and sometimes boggy crest of the hills is in stark contrast to the urban sprawl of Belfast far below. The route crosses Black Hill, Black Mountain, Divis, Squires Hill and Cave Hill, before descending towards Belfast Zoo. The route stays low for a while, wandering through the city suburbs and along the riverside path at Glas na Bradan to reach the shore of Belfast Lough at Macedon Point. This is far enough for one day, and you can either avail yourself of accommodation around Whiteabbey, or catch a bus back into the city for the night.

The city suburbs are left behind as the Ulster Way follows Three Mile Water into the country-side. Minor roads and farm tracks run uphill and pass close to the County Antrim War Memorial on the rocky brow of Knockagh. You can visit this point for a fine view across Belfast Lough. Staying on the Ulster Way, you head through Woodburn Forest and walk alongside South Woodburn Reservoir for a short way. After passing through the neighbouring North Carn Forest, the route runs down through fields to reach a minor road network. You then walk along roads to reach Ballynure, on the busy A57. There is accommodation, food and drink, and you are still only a short bus ride from the facilities in Belfast.

Leaving Ballynure, you follow minor roads uphill and enter Ballyboley Forest. When you emerge at the top end, you then walk across a broad moorland towards Agnew's Hill. The walk along the crest of Agnew's Hill is excellent in fine weather, but can be a treadmill in mist and rain. Beyond Agnew's Hill are the cliffs of Sallagh Braes, and the promontory fort on Knock Dhu, before you cross a pass where the Linford Ancient Site is located. Continuing the high-level theme, the Ulster Way climbs over Scawt Hill and Black Hill, before gradually descending from the moorland crest and following a road down into the lovely little village of Glenarm. Lodgings are available, as well as food and drink.

A minor road runs above the main coastal road beyond Glenarm, passing a wooded nature reserve at Straidkilly. The main road should be followed onwards to Carnlough, and you might break for food and drink in the village before climbing back on to the exposed Antrim Mountains. You take the Waterfall Road, but don't really see Cranny Falls before a zigzag farm track leads you up to the higher ground. The Ulster Way passes Big Trosk and Little Trosk to get on to the broad and bleak Garron Plateau. Waymarking is sparse, and you need to steer a course passing little moorland loughs before making a steep descent into Glenariff. A road walk leads you through the glen and back on to the main coastal road at Waterfoot. However, you can follow a minor road above the main road to reach the town of Cushendall – also known as the Capital of the Glens. There are many places to stay, as well as to eat and drink.

The Ulster Way follows a minor road over the slopes of Cross Slieve to reach Cushendun, an attractive little village largely preserved by the National Trust. Climbing above the village, an old moorland road is used to gain height, before the Ulster Way crosses the high moorland of Carnanmore. There is a burial cairn on the top of the hill, and a splendid view across the waters of the Moyle towards Scotland. The route descends, and gradually heads towards the sheer cliffs of Fair Head. Turning around this spectacular headland, it continues via Colliery Bay to reach the seaside town of Ballycastle, which has a full range of facilities and a daily ferry service to Rathlin Island.

Although you have to leave Ballycastle by road and don't have a great deal of access to the cliff coast, things get much better by the time you reach Ballintoy. The Causeway Coast Path stretches ahead and you follow it closely. Ballintoy Port, White Park Bay, Portbraddan and Dunseverick are all enjoyed in turn before the route wanders around Benbane Head and allows you to visit the Giant's Causeway itself. Soon after this amazing sight, the coast path heads around the lower cliffs of Runkerry, then crosses a dune belt to reach the little seaside resort of Portballintrae. There is accommodation and sustenance available at this particular point.

## North-western Section      *Allow 7 days*

Beyond Portballintrae, the Ulster Way passes the shattered ruins of Dunluce Castle and proceeds along a road until a low-level shore walk leads towards Portrush. This seaside resort stands on a rocky headland, where you will also find a Countryside Centre among the other attractions. A promenade path and an indented coastline run towards neighbouring Portstewart, where you leave town beneath the crenellated walls of a clifftop school. Although you are heading across to Castlerock, which is not too far ahead, there is unfortunately no ferry service across the mouth of the River Bann. You must therefore turn inland and follow the main road to Coleraine in search of a bridge. Once across the Bann, you can mostly use minor roads to reach Castlerock, another of the seaside resorts on the northern coast. There is one last full range of accommodation options before the route turns inland.

A splendid little clifftop walk leads you into a charming wooded glen at Downhill, where you might detour to inspect the Mussenden Temple and the ruins of the palace built by the Earl Bishop of Bristol and Derry. You then follow the Bishop's Road uphill from Downhill, and reach an airy viewpoint overlooking Lough Foyle and Inishowen. A plaque mounted on a plinth nearby tells how the Ordnance Survey started mapping the whole of Ireland from a baseline measured out alongside Lough Foyle. There is a side-spur to the Ulster Way, enabling you to visit the cliff-girt Binevenagh. After that, you start wandering along forest tracks and roads as you get to grips with the northern Sperrins. The only accommodation hereabouts is a solitary bed & breakfast off-route at Ballinrees, below Formoyle and Sconce Hill.

*Mussenden Temple – a creation of the Earl Bishop of Bristol and Derry at Downhill.*

The Ulster Way now runs through Springwell Forest and crosses the A37, before climbing up on to the slopes of Keady Mountain. Two separate parts of Cam Forest are passed through before the route climbs high on to Tibaran Mountain and crosses the tussocky upper parts of Temain Hill. Roads are followed for a while, taking the route down to Coolnasillagh Bridge before climbing up through Gortnamoyagh Forest. After passing around Legavannon Pot, you will suddenly find the Pot Bar available for food and drinks on a sharp bend. Continuing onwards, you pass through another part of Gortnamoyagh Forest, before following a minor road high on the slopes of Benbradagh. A rapid descent by road leads to Dungiven, which has limited accommodation but plenty of places offering food and drink.

You leave Dungiven via the busy Glenshane Road, but later branch off along much quieter minor roads. Eventually, you are led along an

*The Ulster Way in Donegal passes through bleak country beyond Fintown.*

abandoned road which runs into the Glenshane Forest. Climbing above the forest, you cross a broad and boggy gap in the hills, then descend steeply towards Moydamlaght Forest. A short road walk away from the forest will lead you into the village of Moneyneany, but there is no accommodation available. There are a couple of places to stay near Draperstown, which also has a larger range of shops and pubs. Accommodation becomes a problem as you continue along the Ulster Way, and you need to think about arranging for some back-up or transport off-route.

Leaving Moneyneany, there is a minor road and then a track which zigzags uphill and allows walkers to reach the summits of Crockmore and Crockbrack. After enjoying the views from these high points, the route suddenly descends quite steeply to the head of Glenelly. You follow the B47 gradually downhill into Glenelly, and when you reach the crossroads village of Sperrin there is a pub available. At this point you also switch to a minor road and follow this across the southern side of Glenelly. The road eventually leads you through

the Barnes Gap, and a series of roads and high-level tracks convey you onwards before a descent towards Gortin. There is limited accommodation at Gortin, as well as shops and pubs.

Gortin Burn provides a pleasant riverside stroll on the way to Gortin Glen Forest Park. You follow a mixture of tracks and paths through the Forest Park and eventually climb up to Lady's View. Descending from that point, you follow roads away from the forest through Rosnamuck and Knockmoyle, towards the main A5 near Mountjoy. Although Mountjoy is a little off-route, it has a small shop. There is limited accommodation in the surrounding countryside, as well as the Ulster American Folk Park to visit. If you need a greater range of facilities, you will need to detour into Omagh.

When you leave the vicinity of Mountjoy, you follow minor roads before climbing over the summit of Bessy Bell. After passing a windfarm and a small church on the Baronscourt Estate, you will be led along minor roads and reach a well-stocked shop, where you might want to stock up with a few things for the next couple of days. The Ulster Way crosses Fairy Water and later climbs up on to the moorland slopes of Bolaght Mountain. Beyond these heathery moors is Lough Bradan Forest, and when you emerge from the forest there is a solitary bed & breakfast off-route at Gortnagullion, close to the complex of stone circles at Drumskinney.

## South-western Section

*Allow 7 days*

The south-western section of the Ulster Way is routed entirely around Fermanagh and is also known as the Fermanagh Lakeland Way. Leaving Lough Bradan Forest, the route negotiates some of the blocks comprising Kesh Forest. Beyond the forest, the route overlooks the Termon River and rugged parts of Donegal. You need to watch carefully for waymarks and steer a course through Tullynaloob, over Greaghmore and then round by Aghavore, before descending to a farm near Lurganboy Bridge. The Ulster Way crosses briefly into Donegal to avail of the range of accommo-

dation, shops and pubs in the Border village of Pettigo. There is a spur route off the main circular Ulster Way at Pettigo, running the length of Donegal to reach Falcarragh on the northern coast. This route is outlined on page 186.

Staying on the enormous circular route, leave Pettigo and follow roads to Letter Bridge. A minor road is followed to Tullyvocady and Tullymeenagrean, before the boggy Black Hill is crossed. The route roughly follows a river towards Lough Scolban, and this section needs care. Roads lead above Lough Scolban to a ruined church, from where a woodland path leads downhill towards Castle Caldwell. You link with an old railway trackbed to leave Castle Caldwell, and follow this towards the Rosscor Viaduct. Accommodation is sparse in this area and you may have to detour off-route into Belleek to secure a bed. This Border village also has shops, pubs, and the famous Belleek Pottery.

Beyond Rosscor you have a choice of routes leading up to Lough Navar Forest. You can either climb straight up to the Barr of Whealt and enter the forest, or follow the main A46 alongside Lower Lough Erne before climbing up on to the Cliffs of Magho. Forest tracks and paths alternate with short stretches in open country as you pass from one part of the forest to another. Unless you feel you could cover the distance to Belcoo in a day's walk, you will probably need to detour off-route in search of accommodation. Perhaps you could arrange for someone from Derrygonnelly to collect you at a set time and place, such as Doagh Glebe.

The Ulster Way then then runs into the Big Dog Forest and climbs over the little hills of the Little Dog and the Big Dog. Apart from these viewpoints, you will be largely confined to the forest, apart from short stretches of open country, such as when you visit the Shaking Stone on an unplanted moorland. You will reach a point in the middle of Ballintempo Forest where you have a choice of two routes. One route leaves the forest near Holywell Church before following a minor road down to Belcoo, while the other route crosses over the forested slopes of Belmore Mountain and descends close to a bed & breakfast near the outflow of Lough Macnean Lower. If you go to

Belcoo, this Border village has accommodation, food and drink.

Whether you leave one end of Lough Macnean Lower or the other, you will now be heading for the Cladagh Bridge, where the two alternative routes are reunited. Walk up the wooded Cladagh Glen to reach the Marble Arch Caves, then follow the Ulster Way as it cuts across rugged slopes to Florence Court Forest. When you leave the forest you will cross the slopes of Benaughlin, and you might like to climb up to the summit for the view. Descending from Benaughlin, you follow a mix- ture of roads and tracks, bypassing the village of Kinawley by crossing a cutaway bog. A minor road climbs over a gap between Molly Mountain and Slieve Rushen, before descending to the village of Derrylin. There is limited accommodation, as well as food and drink, available at this point.

Accommodation becomes sparser over the next long stretch of the Ulster Way, and you will need to plan ahead. The route leaves Derrylin by road and uses bridges on Trasna Island to cross over the exceedingly complex Upper Lough Erne. After passing the Share Centre, a network of minor roads has to be negotiated on the way towards Newtownbutler.

The Ulster Way doesn't actually go into Newtown- butler, but you may wish to head there in search of lodgings and sustenance. If there is nothing avail- able, you will have to catch a bus to Lisnaskea to reach a greater range of facilities.

The Ulster Way continues beyond Newtown- butler into a remote area of forested uplands. You will need to take care over selecting which forest tracks to follow as you pass through Tully Forest and Lisnaskea Forest. The route crosses the boggy moorland slopes of Doocarn before descending across a valley. Climbing back into forest, you pass Lough Nadarra and Lough Jenkin before crossing Jenkin Hill. Forest tracks are used to descend on to minor roads, and you gradually make your way past a forestry office to reach Alderwood Bridge. By this time you may have had enough, but the nearest accommodation and other services are found off-route at Fivemiletown. It is best to arrange to be collected from the route if this is possible.

## Southern Section                    *Allow 4 days*

The Ulster Way now follows forest tracks and roads around the northern slopes of the sprawling moorland of Slieve Beagh. The only one of Ulster's nine counties not entered by the Ulster Way is Monaghan, although you might like to cross a Border road to reach a teashop just inside that county. The Ulster Way visits St Patrick's Chair and Well in the lovely Altadaven Wood, and then continues past Favour Royal Forest to reach the town of Aughnacloy. Limited lodgings, but abundant food and drink, are on offer. The main street is particularly wide and is marked out in blocks to accommodate market traders.

There is plenty of road walking to be endured in the days ahead. The main road has to be followed out of Aughnacloy before you can switch on to minor roads for a spell. The estate village of Caledon is passed and you cross the restored Dredge Bridge, which is a suspension footbridge spanning the River Blackwater. The course of the Blackwater is followed using roads, and at times you may also spot traces of a former canal running roughly parallel. At Benburb you will find a short riverside path, and it is also worth climbing up into the town, which still features a fortified bawn. Roads run onwards to Blackwatertown and Charlemont. Cross the bridge from Charlemont to Moy to get lodgings for the night, and a meal.

There is more road walking as you continue to walk parallel to the River Blackwater. The Ulster Way runs past The Argory, where a little wooded access to the banks of the Blackwater is available. Peatlands Country Park is just off-route, based on a wooded bogland. Roads are followed close to the shore of Lough Neagh at Maghery and Milltown, but you will hardly be able to appreciate the true scale of this enormous lough. The route continues to follow minor roads, but this time you are tracing the River Bann upstream towards Portadown. A range of accommodation options, shops and pubs are available at this point.

Between Portadown and Newry, there is a good break from road walking. The Ulster Way is routed either alongside the River Bann or along the line of the derelict Newry Canal. The canal features a good towpath, and this is followed in preference to roads wherever possible. There are interesting little villages along the way, such as Scarva, and you are never too far from the main road or railway. After passing Poyntzpass and Jerretspass, the canal towpath becomes quite well trodden and runs straight towards Newry. This large town has a fine range of facilities, and because of the range of nearby walks it actually supports an annual Walking Festival.

## South-eastern Section            *Allow 8 days*

Minor roads are followed away from Newry. These climb up and down as they cross an area of low hills and are waymarked, but some of the markers are actually painted on the road, so you have to watch your feet! The only break you get from the roads is when you follow a short track near the reedy Milltown Lough. When you climb high on a road at Craignamona you have a fine view across Carlingfrod Lough, and the same applies from the road through Knockbarragh Park. When you descend to Rostrevor you should make the most of the lodgings, food and drink offered, because if you proceed further it will be a long time before you reach anything else.

When you leave Rostrevor you pass through the length of Rostrevor Forest, then proceed across a bouldery hillside to pass a large Mass Rock. Follow a stony track up into a high valley, then cross a rugged gap to reach Rocky Water. A stream leads uphill from Rocky Water to reach the Windy Gap. Batts Wall runs across the Windy Gap, and its course can be followed confidently over Slieve-moughanmore – the highest point reached on the Ulster Way. The wall continues across Pigeon Rock Mountain before descending towards Deers Meadow. The route follows roads from Spelga Dam to Fofanny Dam, then contours around the slopes of the Mountains of Mourne before passing through Tollymore Forest Park. Generally, the Ulster Way stays high in the forest, then runs downhill and heads for Newcastle. This seaside resort has one of the greatest ranges of facilities along the Ulster Way.

The route now wanders along the sandy shore from Newcastle to Murlough, where it passes through the Murlough National Nature Reserve. Roads and a railway path lead through Dundrum and around to Ballykinler. Most of the route onwards uses the main A2 coastal road, but there are many places where you could make your own way down to the beach and pick your way along either a sandy or rocky shoreline at low tide. You can follow a minor road down to St John's Point, then follow a coastal path along a low cliff-line towards the harbour at Killough. Accommodation is rather limited, but there are places offering food and drink.

Follow the main road around the harbour from Killough to Ardglass. There are some fine fortifications that are worth studying. When you leave Ardglass you head for St Patrick's Well above the rocky shore. There is a coastal path from this feature towards the village of Ballyhornan, where Guns Island lies just offshore. As you pass Killard, you should note that there is a nature reserve on Killard Point. After passing Kilclief Castle there is also the Cloghy Rocks National Nature Reserve, where you might observe seals hauled out of the turbulent narrows of Strangford Lough. When you reach the village of Strangford, you may need to cross via the ferry to reach accommodation at Portaferry, where there is also food, drink and an interesting aquarium.

Resuming the walk at Strangford, there are headlands and bays to explore all around the Castle Ward Estate, before you follow a series of roads through St Patrick's Country. The villages of Raholp and Saul are passed, and you will note the statue of St Patrick overlooking this countryside of rolling fields and hedges. Later, you run close to Downpatrick and follow a path around Quoile Pondage, where an arm of Strangford Lough has been dammed and converted to fresh water. This is an area with a particularly profuse bird life. The Ulster Way follows the main road for a while and passes Delamont Country Park; minor roads later reach the shore of Strangford Lough on the way through to Killyleagh. Accommodation may be quite limited, but there are also useful shops and pubs available.

185

oldest inn in Ireland is located. A charming path leads down through Crawfordsburn Glen, before the Ulster Way lands on the shore of Belfast Lough. The route heads for Helen's Bay and turns around the wooded Grey Point. Staying close to the shore of the lough and using an assortment of paths and tracks, the coastal path can be followed all the way to Holywood, where lodgings, food and drink can be obtained.

The last day on this great circular walk starts with a climb on to a wooded brow just outside Holywood. The route passes through the Redburn Country Park, then descends to pass through the suburbs of East Belfast. The Ulster Way passes close to Stormont, and later climbs into fields high above Belfast. After a descent through Cregagh Glen, the route heads for Belvoir Park Forest and sets off along a lovely stretch of the Lagan Canal Towpath. After cutting away from the river through the Sir Thomas and Lady Dixon Park, the Ulster Way ends back where it started – in Dunmurry.

## Donegal Section                    *Allow 4 days*

As mentioned earlier, there is a spur from the main Ulster Way circuit which passes through Donegal. This route runs from Pettigo to Falcarragh and crosses some very bleak country. You leave Pettigo by following a road towards Lough Derg, but branch off before that point to follow a road and track into Crocknacunny Forest. The route mostly follows forest tracks, but some boggy forest rides are also included. One particularly rugged forest ride is used to leave the forest and emerge on to a broad bogland. There are views ahead of the Blue Stack Mountains, and a bog road runs downhill before tarmac roads are joined. Roads are followed along the eastern side of Lough Eske, where a couple of bed & breakfasts are located.

The Ulster Way leaves Lough Eske by following the Monks Path alongside the Corrober River. This route is sparsely waymarked beyond the Doonan Waterfall and you will need to take care when you are required to cross from one bleak gap in the mountains to another. A long and rugged descent leads to the farms at Letterkillew, before you

*Castle Ward – a National Trust property on the shores of Strangford Lough.*

When you leave Killyleagh you pass close to Killyleagh Castle, before the Ulster Way follows roads through rolling drumlin country. Most of the route is on roads, with occasional views across the Strangford Lough. The shore of the lough is followed for a while at Quarterland Bay and beyond, before the route heads more directly for Comber. The town is bypassed using an old railway trackbed, then the Ulster Way makes a beeline for the huge tower crowning the summit of Scrabo Hill. When you descend from the hill, Newtownards has a full range of facilities available – including Bridgedale, who make walking socks!

The Ulster Way leaves Newtownards and climbs up roads and tracks to reach Whitespots, a wooded slope to the north of town. The route wanders past old mines and through woods for a while, then follows roads towards Crawfordsburn, where the follow the river upstream to cross another gap. Descending towards The Croaghs and the Reelan River, you cross over the side of Croveenananta to reach a boggy valley. Once you are across this, you can follow roads towards Lough Finn and the straggly village of Fintown. There is limited accommodation here, with only a couple of shops and pubs.

Leaving Fintown, the Ulster Way passes through a forest and continues through a newly forested valley before climbing on to the higher moorlands near Lough Muck. You again need to look well ahead to spot waymarks, and follow them around the rugged slopes of Crockastoller to reach a remote valley. After following markers around the slopes of Moylenanav, you descend to a road at the head of the Glenveagh National Park. There are no markers beyond this point, but the Ulster Way climbs uphill and descends steeply into the Poisoned Glen before running towards Dunlewy. Again, there is only limited accommodation, a shop and a pub.

The final day on the Ulster Way is easier, although still without markers. You have to climb above Dunlewy by road and follow a boggy old track to a ruined tower house at the head of Altan Lough, in between Errigal and the Aghlas. A vague shoreline path leads alongside Altan Lough, and you cross the outflowing river before it reaches Procklis Lough. Follow a minor road through Tullaghobegly to reach Falcarragh and the end of the route. If you want to end by the Atlantic Ocean, follow a short road down to the strand and finish there. Falcarragh has a fair range of accommodation options, as well as food and drink.

## Alternative routes

### ESCAPES

Even in outline, you will realize that the successful completion of a mammoth route such as the Ulster Way depends on careful advance planning. There are many places where accommodation is particularly sparse – mostly the remoter inland stretches. You may find that you occasionally have to cover almost 40km (25 miles) to get from one bed & breakfast to another. Obviously, you can get around this problem by backpacking and being completely self-sufficient, but if you want a few creature comforts then you will have to plan well ahead. Some bed & breakfast proprietors will be willing to collect you at a prearranged time and place, if their accommodation is off-route, but you must be sure to stick to your plans to avoid causing any inconvenience.

When you are crossing bleak and remote countryside, you will occasionally be crossing roads. Some of these may have bus services, and again it is useful to know about these in advance. Maps often mark the location of telephones in rural areas, and this allows you to call for help when you have had enough after a really wet and miserable day. Provided that you set out each day knowing your own limitations, having checked the weather, and understanding what facilities are ahead, then you should realize what your options are as you progress around the Ulster Way. Alternatively, complete the route in easier stages of a weekend or a week at a time, maybe with helpful vehicular back-up, and let the sense of satisfaction stretch over a longer period of time.

### EXTENSIONS

There may well be times when you want to extend the course of the Ulster Way. You may want to stay higher in places, such as the Antrim Mountains or the Mourne Mountains. If this is the case, there are a number of high-level walks in this book which link in with lower stretches of the Ulster Way, so you can refer to them and construct your own extensions. You may want to climb Cuilcagh in Fermanagh instead of creeping around its lower slopes, or cross over the summit of Slieve Beagh instead of following roads. The Ulster Way also links in with other trails, such as the Moyle Way, which offers a higher and more remote route from Glenariff to Ballycastle. There is a short spur called the Cavan Way, which allows you to leave the Ulster Way at Belcoo and Blacklion and walk towards Dowra. If you went that way, you could branch off the Cavan Way to climb either Cuilcagh or The Playbank, and chart a more exacting course to continue.

# APPENDIX: USEFUL ADDRESSES AND INFORMATION

## General Tourist Information

NORTHERN IRELAND TOURIST BOARD,    (01232) 246609
59 North Street,
Belfast,
Northern Ireland.

## Local Tourist Information

TOURIST INFORMATION CENTRE,    (01247) 270069
34 Quay Street,
Bangor,
Co Down,
Northern Ireland.

TOURIST INFORMATION CENTRE,    (013967) 22222
10–14 Central Promenade,
Newcastle,
Co Down,
Northern Ireland.

TOURIST INFORMATION CENTRE,    (01693) 68877
Town Hall,
Newry,
Co Down,
Northern Ireland.

TOURIST INFORMATION OFFICE,    (047) 81122
Market House,
Monaghan,
Co Monaghan,
Ireland.

TOURIST INFORMATION OFFICE    (049) 31942
Farnham Street,
Cavan,
Co Cavan,
Ireland.

TOURIST INFORMATION CENTRE,    (01365) 323110
Wellington Road,
Enniskillen,
Co Fermanagh,
Northern Ireland.

TOURIST INFORMATION OFFICE,    (073) 21148
Donegal Town,
Co Donegal,
Ireland.

TOURIST INFORMATION OFFICE,    (074) 21160
Derry Road,
Letterkenny,
Co Donegal,
Ireland.

TOURIST INFORMATION CENTRE,    (01504) 267284
8 Bishop Street,
Londonderry,
Northern Ireland.

TOURIST INFORMATION CENTRE,    (01662) 247831
1 Market Street,
Omagh,
Co Tyrone,
Northern Ireland.

SPERRIN HERITAGE CENTRE,    (016626) 48142
274 Glenelly Road,
Cranagh,
Co Tyrone,
Northern Ireland.

GIANT'S CAUSEWAY CENTRE,    (01265) 731855
44 Causeway Road,
Bushmills,
Co Antrim,
Northern Ireland.

TOURIST INFORMATION CENTRE,    (01265) 762024
Sheskburn House,
7 Mary Street,
Ballycastle,
Co Antrim,
Northern Ireland.

TOURIST INFORMATION CENTRE,    (01574) 260088
Narrow Gauge Road,
Larne,
Co Antrim,
Northern Ireland.

## Accommodation

The tourist information centres listed above can usually book your accommodation for you. However, there is also a central accommodation reservation service which operates on an all-Ireland basis, for which you need a credit card and access to a telephone. The number is Freefone (0800) 317153.

## Getting to Ireland and Ulster

Ferries, flights and car hire are all easily arranged. It is possible to catch ferries and even flights as simply as you would catch a bus or train, but obviously if you can plan ahead you can take advantage of special fares – and if you deal with a travel agent you can let them handle everything for you.

You can reach Ulster direct by flying into one of the two Belfast airports, choosing between Belfast City and Belfast International. Alternatively, you could fly to Derry City Airport, or even Enniskillen Airport or Carrickfinn Airport in Donegal, but there will obviously be fewer flights to the minor airports. Fast and frequent ferries are available between Stranraer and either Larne or Belfast, with a longer ferry running from Liverpool to Belfast. You could of course arrive in Ireland via Dublin using ferries or flights, then drive north-wards, or catch frequent trains or buses. Cars can generally be hired from the major airports and ferryports, but it is as well to enquire in advance and of course make sure you carry all the appropriate documentation.

Travel between Britain and Ireland, as well as across the Border, has always been a passport-free affair, and this is now becoming the case for travellers from all around Europe. If you are travelling from further afield, you might like to check in advance to see if you will require a passport and/or visa to gain entry.

## Public Transport

ULSTERBUS INFORMATION HOTLINE, Belfast.
(01232) 333000
CITYBUS INFORMATION, Belfast.    (01232) 246485
LOUGH SWILLY BUSES, Derry.    (01504) 262017
BUS EIREANN, Letterkenny.    (074) 21309

## Mountain Rescue

No matter which side of the Border you are on, get to the nearest telephone, dial 999, and ask for the Mountain Rescue. This may well be co-ordinated through the RUC in Northern Ireland and the Gardai in the Republic of Ireland. Do not waste time trying to contact Mountain Rescue teams direct. Carefully follow any instructions you are given.

# INDEX

Page references in *italics* refer to illustrations